Telling Tales about Jesus

Telling Tales about Jesus

An Introduction to the New Testament Gospels

Warren Carter

Fortress Press
Minneapolis

TELLING TALES ABOUT JESUS

An Introduction to the New Testament Gospels

Cover image: Christ in Majesty between the four evangelists / Supermat – Wikimedia Commons

Cover design: Tory Herman

Library of Congress Cataloging-in-Publication Data

Print ISBN: 978-1-4514-6545-7

eBook ISBN: 978-1-5064-0811-8

This book was produced using Pressbooks.com, and PDF rendering was done by PrinceXML.

Contents

Maps and Illustrations

Sidebars

Preface

This book is an introduction to the Gospels in the New Testament and to some of the diverse critical methods by which they have been studied. Chapter 1 considers the genre of the Gospels. Chapter 2 looks at two ways scholars have described how traditions about Jesus were transmitted in the time between Jesus' crucifixion and the writing of the first Gospel, namely, through activities in particular community life settings that shaped individual units of tradition—a process described by form criticism—and through the oral performance of more extended speeches.

Then in chapters 3–10, I discuss each of the four Gospels, devoting two chapters to each Gospel: Mark (chapters 3–4), Matthew (chapters 5–6), Luke (chapters 7–8), and John (chapters 9–10). The first chapter of each pair adopts a narrative approach to outline the tale of Jesus that each Gospel narrates. The second chapter of each pair uses a critical method to discuss an aspect of how that particular Gospel makes meaning of the tale of Jesus in relation to a particular context. Utilizing sociohistorical approaches, I think about how folks living in difficult circumstances such as those experienced in imperial Rome might have engaged the Gospel of Mark (chapter 4). Using redaction criticism, I show how Matthew's Gospel edited traditions about Jesus to address folks defining their identity and way of life in competition with synagogue communities in the troubled and challenging post-70 circumstances (chapter 6). Taking a literary-thematic approach, I argue that Luke's Gospel addresses a context of uncertainty to offer assurance and security to followers of Jesus concerning God's workings or "kingdom" that embrace Jews and Gentiles, women and men, Roman power and the non-human world (chapter 8). Employing an intertextual approach, I propose that John's Gospel employed wisdom traditions to present Jesus as the definitive revealer of God's presence and purposes, and that he did so to provide a way ahead in the quest for divine knowledge in the post-70 world (chapter 10).

In the concluding chapter 11, I briefly take up two matters, one concerning how these four Gospels came into the New Testament canon, and the second concerning the relationships between the Gospels and the historical Jesus.

I am aware that any book on the Gospels could be many times longer than this volume given the complexity of the Gospels themselves and the fecundity of critical study on the Gospels by various methods. I have made choices that I hope will be helpful to students in experiencing some of the richness of the Gospels themselves as well as something of the valuable contributions various approaches make to their reading.

Finally, I express my appreciation to Neil Elliott at Fortress Press and his editorial team for the opportunity to write this book and for their skilled work in its production.

The book is dedicated to its readers.

1

What Are We Reading and Why Does It Matter?

I sort the last couple of days' mail. Seven items. I recognize two items as marketing cards. No envelope. Bright colors. Beaming faces. A firm wants to fix the A/C, but it's not broken so I drop it into the recycling. A local church is advertising talks on Revelation that will explain how Revelation predicts and interprets today's news stories. I read a few of the details—obviously the speaker has not read my book on Revelation.[1] Also into the recycling. Then there's an envelope addressed with neat, small handwriting. I recognize the name and address on the envelope. I guess it's a birthday card. The fourth item is a long envelope with a window. I recognize the name and address of the sender in the top left corner. Printed, not attached stamp. It's a bill from my doctor's office. I don't get many bills these days, with online payment. Next is the weekly copy of *Time* magazine. Interesting cover. Then another long envelope with a window. The envelope declares, "Important: Do not discard." From the company logo in the top left corner, I guess it's a credit card offer. I discard it into the recycling.

1. Warren Carter, *What Does Revelation Reveal? Unlocking the Mystery* (Nashville: Abingdon, 2011).

Finally another long envelope. The top left corner identifies the sender as a local car dealer. No window. The address is in fake personal handwriting. The name is not mine but that of a previous owner of our house. Two owners ago. Into the recycling.

I haven't opened an envelope yet. I've made these decisions, these classifications, simply by observing features of the envelopes: their size, style of print, graphics, and content.

We're scrolling through Netflix looking for a movie. What are we in the mood for?

A comedy would be light and amusing. Not demanding too much from us as viewers, but not so silly or pathetic that we lose interest. Good for a Friday night. Amusing situations in touch with daily life. Some distortions and/or surprising turns of events. Clever, witty, insightful dialogue. Engaging and interesting characters. Misunderstandings and obstacles, conflicts and competition. Maybe a love story with heartwarming outcome. Satisfying resolutions. Lighthearted, upbeat ending that ties all the pieces together.

Or we could go for the stimulation of a political thriller. We'd expect power plays and conflicts. Issues of national importance. The nation's security under threat from sophisticated, technologically smart villains who challenge fundamental values. Ambiguity about good and evil. Secrets to protect. Corruption in high places. Public order or morale to maintain. Things and people not as they seem. Conflict among the power players as to how to respond. A hero—often broken or controversial or unlikely. Perhaps a love interest. Satisfactory resolution. The good guys win; evil is under control; security prevails.

We expect each type of movie to have different features. Sometimes movies combine genres, complexifying expectations and features (comedy *and* romance). Each type of movie requires different participation from us as viewers and has a different impact on us.

Genre matters. Recognizing genres is something we do every day. Whether printed material, social media, oral media, or visual material, we have to determine what we are engaging and what sort of engagement and/or action or participation is expected or required from us. Some genres we enthusiastically embrace, others we might happily avoid (reminder emails about dentist appointments!). Sometimes we identify genres correctly; sometimes we're not sure what to expect or get it wrong. Posting inappropriate comments on social media, as numerous sports and entertainment people have done, is often a matter of not taking the public nature of this genre seriously. What someone thinks in their head or even speaks to a trusted friend is not always appropriate for public consumption. Paying for an unsatisfying movie, not recognizing an envelope that must be opened and requires follow-up action (paying a bill), choosing a book by its cover but finding it unsatisfactory, not noticing a text or email that expresses important information or makes a request of us, signing a contract without reading it—they are all decisions that involve miscues about genre.

We can think of genre, then, as employing a number of predictable and recognizable features that are crucial for communication between ourselves and a text or movie. Recognizing a genre creates a set of expectations for us as readers and/or viewers. Genre sets up a contract that guides our appropriate engagement.

1.1 More Than Four

Throughout this chapter, I refer only to the four Gospels in the New Testament canon. By one count, some thirty-four gospels were produced in early Christianity:

Four canonical Gospels: Gospel of Mark; Gospel of Matthew; Gospel of Luke; Gospel of John
Four complete noncanonical Gospels: Infancy Gospel of James; Secret Book of James; Gospel of Thomas; Infancy Gospel of Thomas
Eight fragmentary noncanonical Gospels: Egerton Gospel; Gospel of Mary; Gospel Oxyrhynchus 840; Gospel Oxyrhynchus 1224; Gospel of Peter; Dialogue of the Savior; Gospel of the Savior; Gospel of Judas
Four Gospels known only from early quotations: Secret Gospel of Mark; Gospel of the Ebionites; Gospel of the Hebrews; Gospel of the Nazoreans
Two hypothetical Gospels: Q; Signs Gospel
Twelve known by name alone: Gospel of the Four Heavenly Regions; Gospel of Perfection; Gospel of Eve; Gospel of the Twelve; Gospel of Matthias; Gospel of Bartholomew; Gospel of Cerinthus; Gospel of Basilides; Gospel of Marcion; Gospel of Apelles, Gospel of Bartimaeus; Matthew's logia collection[2]

What, then, is the genre or genres of the four Gospels in the New

Testament? What are we reading? How do we read? What do we expect from a Gospel? And in reading them, what might they require of us?

Some might think such questions are inappropriate. After all, the Gospels are Scripture; they are holy writings. Some have argued that gospels are a unique genre, that they are one of a kind (*sui generis*, "of its own kind," is the Latin term). But if we think about it, claims of the uniqueness of a genre make no sense. As we have seen, genre is about communication by means of recognizable features that create expectations for readers or hearers or viewers. A unique genre, even if it existed, would be incomprehensible. A writer or artist might create a strange or unusual genre using features from an unusual mix of media in an exciting and creative way. I have, for example, read some mystery novels that feature a crime-solving chef—the novels include recipes! But in order to communicate, such a work must rely on readers or viewers recognizing some of the features and using them as points of engagement with the work. Without some familiar and recognizable features, whatever the mix, there is no communication. The unusual genre is going to look like something else in some form.

So in reading the Gospels, what are we reading?

An Eyewitness Historical Account of Jesus' Life?

In popular imaginations and piety, the Gospels are often understood as eyewitness, historical accounts of Jesus' activities and teachings written by four of his male followers. The scenario posits that these men accompanied Jesus, recorded what they saw, and passed it along in writing. This has been a common, though not universally accepted, view throughout the church's history. Whether wittingly or unwittingly, to this day preachers often reinforce this scenario when they talk about Gospel scenes.

2. I follow Charles Hedrick, "The Thirty-Four Gospels: Diversity and Division among the Earliest Christians," *Bible Review* 18 (June 2002): 20–31, 46–47, with one exception, the Gospel of Judas.

1.1 The Four Gospel Writers, from the studio of Jacob Jordaens. It has been customary to imagine the four Gospel writers as eyewitnesses who even cooperated in composing their different narratives, but this is hardly likely. Sint Janeskirk, Mechelen, Belgium; Commons.wikimedia.org.

But just a little investigation shows this view not to be convincing. I mention five factors.

1. First, two of the names associated with the Gospels were not "disciples" of Jesus. Neither the name "Mark" nor the name "Luke" appears in any of the lists of Jesus' twelve chosen male

disciples (see Matt. 10:2-4; Mark 3:16-19; Luke 6:13-16; John's Gospel does not have a list).

2. Second, if being an eyewitness is a key qualification for writing a Gospel, then both Matthew's Gospel and John's Gospel fail the test. A disciple, Matthew, is named in the three lists of disciples just mentioned, but outside those lists he is referred to in only one other place, namely Matt. 9:9. In Matt. 9:9 Jesus calls a tax collector called Matthew to follow him, but Matthew then disappears from the story. He is not mentioned again except in the list of Matt. 10:2–4. The Gospels of Mark and Luke include a call scene involving a tax collector, but the tax collector has a different name. He is called Levi, not Matthew (Mark 2:14; Luke 5:27). How did he get the name Matthew in Matthew's Gospel when two Gospels call him Levi? That seems like a suspicious piece of editing! If being an eyewitness is the basis for the historical credibility of the Gospels, why does Matthew not have a pervasive presence throughout the Gospels? And why is there no claim in the Gospel somewhere that this Matthew is writing the Gospel?

   The Gospel of John raises the same issue. This Gospel, strangely, does not include a disciple named John. The Gospel refers nineteen times to John the Baptist and four times to Peter's father by that name ("son of John": John 1:42; 21:15-17), but there is no disciple called John. At 21:2 it mentions "the sons of Zebedee" but does not name them. At 13:23, it mentions a disciple "whom Jesus loved" but does not name him either. Later, this disciple was identified by some as John. If we are to understand the author "John" as an eyewitness of Jesus' ministry, why is he not present in the Gospel and not presented as a constant companion of Jesus?

3. This last question raises a third problem. Among the disciples who are identified as Jesus' associates, several seem to form an inner circle as special companions of Jesus. In Mark's Gospel, for example, Peter, James, and John are exclusively associated with several narratives like the transfiguration and Gethsemane (Mark 1:16-20; 9:2; 10:35; 13:3; 14:33). But none of the four Gospels claims

authorship by either Peter or James, and, as we have seen, John does not appear in John! It is surprising that these links are not made if eyewitness authority was paramount for authorship.

4. There is a fourth problem. As I will show later, the Gospels are probably written in a time period between the years 70 CE and 100 CE or so. Jesus is crucified around the year 30 CE. The prospect of an eyewitness account of Jesus' activity appearing some forty to seventy years after Jesus' ministry is not high, though not impossible. The issue is life span. For example, at a minimum, a reliable eyewitness would need to have been, perhaps, twenty years old during Jesus' ministry. That would make him between sixty and ninety when the Gospels were written. But average life spans in the first-century Roman world, affected by unhealthy living conditions and poor nutrition for much of the population, don't support such odds. Bruce Frier points to the table of the third-century-CE Roman jurist Ulpian, to census returns from Egypt, and to gravestone studies that suggest the average life expectancy at birth was twenty-one to twenty-two years, and at age ten, about thirty-five further years.[3] Ann Hanson suggests that "about half the babies born died before reaching their fifth birthday." Of those who reached age ten, nearly half reached age fifty and about a third reached sixty. In overall terms, "less than 20 percent" reached sixty.[4] So while it is not impossible, it is unlikely that adult eyewitnesses of Jesus' activity would have still been alive to write Gospels in the period of the 70s–100 CE. But there is a further question: why would eyewitnesses, if they existed, wait that long to write?
5. Fifth, none of the New Testament Gospels identifies its author. This might seem like a strange statement when we know them as the Gospels of Matthew, Mark, Luke, and John. Yet it is true. The earliest evidence we have for these names being associated with the Gospels comes from around 180 CE, some hundred years

3. Bruce Frier, "Roman Demography," in *Life, Death, and Entertainment in the Roman Empire*, ed. D. S. Potter and D. J. Mattingly (Ann Arbor: University of Michigan Press, 2001), 85–109, esp. 87–88.
4. Ann E. Hanson, "The Roman Family," in Potter and Mattingly, *Life, Death*, 19–66, esp. 27.

after the Gospels were written. Irenaeus, the bishop of Lyons, provides the earliest evidence for these links. Irenaeus wrote a work called *Against Heresies* in a time of ecclesial controversy and diversity. Irenaeus sought to defend and define an expression of Christianity that was distinct from groups whose practices and thinking he considered outside acceptable limits. Part of his attack is to discredit their writings and interpretations of Scriptures. He upholds the reliability and authority of the four canonical Gospels by seeking to guarantee their origin with the apostles.

1.2 Irenaeus's Claims regarding the Gospels (ca. 180 CE)

Matthew also issued a written Gospel among the Hebrews in their own dialect, while Peter and Paul were preaching at Rome, and laying the foundations of the Church. After their departure, Mark, the disciple and interpreter of Peter, also did hand down to us in writing what had been preached by Peter. Luke also, the companion of Paul, recorded in a book the Gospel preached by him. Afterwards, John, the disciple of the Lord, who also had leaned upon His breast, did himself publish a Gospel during his residence at Ephesus in Asia. (Irenaeus, *Ante-Nicene Fathers* 3.1.1)

There is much to debate in this passage from Irenaeus. But it is sufficient to note that this text, written around 180 CE, is the earliest identification we have linking the four Gospels with these four authors. We can also note how vague are the connections Irenaeus makes to establish apostolic origins for the Gospels. Matthew's link with Peter and Paul consists of nothing other than Matthew writes "while Peter and Paul were preaching at Rome." Irenaeus does not say Matthew was in Rome, or that he heard Peter and Paul's preaching, or, if he did, that he represented it in the Gospel! Irenaeus says that Mark writes what Peter had preached, but he does so after Peter has departed from Rome and he writes as an interpreter of Peter. What sort of interpreter? How much liberty did he take? Luke writes, according to Irenaeus, the Gospel preached not by Jesus but by Paul! For these three Gospels, it seems that Irenaeus is more interested in suggesting (not establishing) links with Peter and Paul, not Jesus.

With John, however, Irenaeus creates several links with Jesus. First, Irenaeus identifies John as "the disciple" of the Lord, even though, as we have seen, John's Gospel does not include any references to a disciple John! And second, Irenaeus identifies John as "the one who "leaned upon [Jesus'] breast," a reference to the "disciple whom Jesus loved." This disciple, though, is not named in the Gospel—it is Irenaeus, a century later, who identifies him with John. Irenaeus also links the Gospel to Ephesus.

Irenaeus's material, then, indicates the first link between the Gospels and the four figures we know as their authors. Yet it is very clear that his information is not historically reliable. It originates some hundred or so years after the Gospels were written. His claims are vague in their attempt to link authors and apostles. It seems he is more interested in suggesting apostolic links to Peter and Paul than in establishing reliable historical information and connections to Jesus. His purpose is not to establish accurate eyewitness accounts but to assert Gospels that bear apostolic authority.

Over a century later, Eusebius, bishop of Caesarea (d. 340 CE), makes some similar claims in an account that is vulnerable to numerous objections. Eusebius quotes a figure called Papias who was bishop of Hierapolis around 125–150, several decades before Irenaeus, and, more importantly, several centuries before Eusebius himself. Papias's testimony constitutes what he passes on from an earlier figure, an "elder" or "presbyter," called John, but whose identity is not clear. So the first problem is that Eusebius's material is thirdhand—he is quoting Papias who is quoting the elder. And the second problem is the time gap of some two hundred years! Further, we have no independent source for either Papias or the elder, so we cannot compare the accuracy of what Eusebius transmits thirdhand and secondhand. Fourth, nor is it always clear in Eusebius's account what comes from Papias and what comes from the elder. The passage has been much debated, and most scholars think it cannot be relied on for accurate testimony. According to Eusebius's account (*Hist. eccl.* 2.15.1–2; 3.39.15), Mark is Peter's "interpreter" and writes "accurately what he remembered" what he heard from Peter but "not in order." This is an ambiguous statement that pulls in two directions—toward defending

Mark's accuracy while also allowing for inexactitudes from his interpretation and memory, and concerning the order of material in Mark's Gospel. Its meaning has also been much debated. We should also note that Eusebius himself seems to discredit Papias, referring to him elsewhere as "not very intelligent." And Eusebius's own accuracy is not beyond scrutiny. He says, for example, that Matthew wrote in Hebrew, something that seems most unlikely (see the discussion in chapter 5). Eusebius's statements, then, do not support the claim that the Gospel was an eyewitness account of Jesus' ministry.

1.3 Eusebius's Testimony regarding the Gospels (*Ecclesiastical History* 2.15.1; 3.39.15)

And so greatly did the splendor of piety illumine the minds of Peter's hearers that they were not satisfied with hearing once only, and were not content with the unwritten teaching of the divine Gospel, but with all sorts of entreaties they besought Mark, a follower of Peter, and the one whose Gospel is extant, that he would leave them a written monument of the doctrine which had been orally communicated to them. Nor did they cease until they had prevailed with the man, and had thus become the occasion of the written Gospel which bears the name of Mark.

This also the presbyter (Papias) said: "Mark, having become the interpreter of Peter, wrote down accurately, though not in order, whatsoever he remembered of the things said or done by Christ. For he neither heard the Lord nor followed him, but afterward, as I said, he followed Peter, who adapted his teaching to the needs of his hearers, but with no intention of giving a connected account of the Lord's discourses, so that Mark committed no error while he thus wrote some things as he remembered them. For he was careful of one thing, not to omit any of the things which he had heard, and not to state any of them falsely." These things are related by Papias concerning Mark.

In terms of genre, then, we cannot approach the Gospels expecting them to give us eyewitness historical accounts of the activity of Jesus. Two Gospels are not linked with disciples of Jesus (Mark, Luke), two make nothing of any eyewitness claims (Matthew, John), and none employs disciples from the inner circle (Peter, James). The dating of the Gospels largely rules out the likelihood of eyewitnesses still being alive, and the first evidence for linking the four names with the Gospels comes from Irenaeus, some one hundred or so years after the Gospel's writing. Irenaeus's concern seems to be more with establishing apostolic authority than with historical accuracy.

Gospels as Ancient Biographies

Another option exists for identifying the genre of the Gospels, that of ancient biographies.[5] I begin by noting some important features of the Gospels, then I identify features of ancient biographies and discuss the Gospels as belonging to this genre—though with a twist or two.

What do the four canonical Gospels have in common? Here are some features:

- They are prose narratives (not poems or theoretical discourses).
- Their focus is almost exclusively on Jesus as the main character. There are very few scenes from which he is absent. Other characters (disciples, Jerusalem leaders) are positioned in relation to him and interact with him. He is the subject of around 20 percent of the verbs. When not the subject, he is usually the object of the action, especially in the accounts of his death. Events leading to and involving his death and resurrection occupy about 15 to 20 percent of the Gospels.
- The Gospels narrate Jesus' activity in chronological and geographical sequence, starting with John's baptism of Jesus (Matthew and Luke begin with a birth account). Three of them, Matthew, Mark and Luke, present his activity in Galilee involving teaching, healings, feedings, and exorcisms. Then the action moves to Jerusalem. John narrates the events differently, with Jesus going back and forth between Galilee and Jerusalem. All four Gospels end with Jesus' death by crucifixion and his resurrection.
- Jesus' character is displayed through his teachings and particular actions rather than stated in generalized descriptions. His words are recounted and his actions narrated in short episodes. From these episodes emerge his virtues—compassion with crowds and outsiders,

5. I rely, with a slight modification of language, on the excellent discussion of Richard Burridge, *What Are the Gospels? A Comparison with Graeco-Roman Biography*, 2nd ed. (Grand Rapids: Eerdmans, 2004). See also Warren Carter, *Matthew: Storyteller, Interpreter, Evangelist* (Peabody, MA: Hendrickson, 2004), 30–46; Carter, *John: Storyteller, Interpreter, Evangelist* (Peabody, MA: Hendrickson, 2006), 3–20.

verbal dexterity with opponents, faithfulness to God's will, and so on. Jesus' interactions with other characters reveal both Jesus' character and the characters of those who have contact with him.

- Generally the Gospels' tone is serious and their presentation of the main character Jesus respectful.
- They function to teach readers about Jesus and to shape the identity, practices, and lifestyle of his followers. In so doing, they oppose false or uninformed views about Jesus, offer their own views, and encourage faithful following.

A lot more could be said about each of these features, but this list is sufficient to establish some of the main features of what we find in the Gospels. The use of these features together in a literary work—a prose narrative, focus on a main character, a chronological sequence of events, significant attention on the character's death, display of his character through words and actions, serious and respectful tone, didactic and hortatory functions—was by no means unique in the ancient world. These features appeared together in and constituted a genre that ancient readers would have recognized, which we call "ancient biography." I am suggesting that ancient readers would have identified the Gospels as using the genre of ancient biography.

The adjective "ancient" matters in this designation. There are several key difference between modern "kiss-and-tell" biographies and ancient biographies. Modern biographies, post-Freud, focus on a person's internal processes and the growth and development of their particular personality. Modern biographies often like to dish the dirt concerning scandalous and shocking relationships and behaviors. Ancient biographies did not rule out some development in their main character, but their focus was much more on external actions and words as expressions of a person's somewhat fixed and usually virtuous character. They were more interested in parading virtues for an audience to admire and aspire to and imitate than in dishing up dirt to boost sales. Moreover, the eminent subjects of biographies were commonly presented not primarily as unique individuals but as representatives of elite group values and virtues.

We have a number of examples of ancient biographies from before, around, and after the time when the Gospels were written. Some are written in Greek and some in Latin. For example, we have Tacitus's biography of his father-in-law Agricola, written in 98 CE, just five years after Agricola's death. Agricola, one of the senatorial ruling elite, held various military and political positions, much of them in Britain, where he rose to be governor for seven years. Tacitus presents Agricola very positively. He notes the elite origin and accomplishments of his ancestors. He celebrates his great deeds, which result from his political and military skills, especially in subduing and ruling the difficult province of Britain, which did not welcome Roman rule. And he spends about 10 to 15 percent of the work on Agricola's death. Especially important is his emphasis on how Agricola was able to make his way successfully through the dangers posed by the emperor Domitian. In the biography, Tacitus criticizes the recently deceased Domitian for being jealous of senatorial leaders like Agricola and threatening their liberty. Yet Agricola was able to overcome Domitian's threats and jealousy by being virtuous in his military and administrative duties in Britain on Rome's behalf, without regard for Domitian's responses. This virtuous faithfulness meant subjugating and "civilizing" local Britons under his rule. Tacitus ends the biography by highlighting this theme and urging (other elite) readers to imitate Agricola's virtuous example of not being intimidated by a tyrannical ruler.

Sometime around the beginning of the second century, Suetonius, who would work as a secretary for the emperors Trajan and Hadrian, wrote twelve biographies under the title *Lives of the Caesars*. The first biography concerns Julius Caesar, and the last one is about Domitian, who died in 96 CE. In constructing his prose narratives, Suetonius frames the biographies chronologically by discussing the ancestries, births, and deaths of the emperors, but he uses a thematic approach for the rest of the material, often narrating short and lively scenes involving an emperor. This approach allows him to cover the "great deeds" and virtuous actions typical of the genre. In terms of length, the biographies are around fifteen thousand words, similar to the length of the Gospels.

1.2 A first-century bust of Julius Caesar, the first subject of Suetonius's Lives of the Caesars, an example of the ancient biographical genre. Altes Museum Berlin; Commons.wikimedia.org.

What, then, are the features a reader would expect to find in an ancient biography? We can identify four groups of features.

1. Opening features: These include perhaps a title and an opening formula, or preface, or prologue.
2. Subject: The focus is on the main character, as evidenced by being

the main subject and/or object of the work's verbs and the focus of its content.

3. Features of form: these include the use of prose narrative, size on average between ten to twenty thousand words for medium-length works, chronological structure, focus on a main character who is usually an elite figure (ruler, military commander, king, etc.), use of short episodes, use of sources, and presentation of characters by displaying actions and words.
4. Features of content: characterization controls the use of settings; topics cover ancestry, birth, education, great deeds, virtues, death and its consequences; a straightforward style; and serious atmosphere. Characterization includes a tension between the real and the stereotype; a social setting; and a purpose of informing and teaching, and at times attacks on enemies and opponents, which distinguish the virtues and accomplishments of the central figure.

The Gospels exhibit these features, as we can briefly note.

1. Opening features: Each of the four Gospels begins with either an opening *formula* as in Mark ("The beginning of the good news of Jesus Christ, the Son of God") and Matthew ("An account of the genealogy of Jesus the Messiah, the son of David, the son of Abraham") or somewhat longer *prologue* as in Luke (Luke 1:1-4) and John (John 1:1-18).
2. Subject: the Gospels present Jesus as the central *character*. In Mark, Jesus is *subject* of about 25 percent of the verbs, in Matthew and Luke about 17 percent, and John over 30 percent. As with other ancient biographies, the Gospels give comparable *significant attention to Jesus' death* (about 15–20 percent of the work). So in Mark, Jesus enters Jerusalem in chapter 11 and after increasing conflict, the long chapters 14–15 narrate his death, and chapter 16 his resurrection.
3. Features of form: as we have noted above, the Gospels employ a *prose narrative* and are in *length* between eleven to nineteen

thousand words (average for medium-length biographies). They use a *chronological structure* for the story of Jesus. Matthew and Luke begin with accounts of his conception and birth. Mark and John begin with John the Baptist and his baptism of Jesus. Three Gospels (Mark, Matthew, Luke) shape the story with an initial focus on Galilee and then movement to Jerusalem. John has Jesus going back and forth between Galilee and Jerusalem. Within this chronological-geographical structure, the Gospels maintain the focus on Jesus with *both short episodes and collections of teaching* for his followers. The short episodes comprise miracle stories of healings, exorcisms, and feedings; call stories that summon someone to follow Jesus; and conflict stories with opponents. His teachings are presented as parables (Mark 4; Luke 15), pithy and witty one-liners (Mark 2:17, "I have come to call not the righteous but the sinners"), extended metaphors (John 10, the good shepherd; John 15, the vine and the branches), lengthy discourses about being disciples (the Sermon on the Mount, Matthew 5–7) or about the eschatological establishment of God's reign (Mark 13), judgment statements against opponents (Matthew 23), and instructions for church life about mission and community (Matthew 10; 18), especially in Jesus' absence (John 13–17). Like ancient biographies, Gospels use *sources* in presenting their accounts. Luke's Gospel begins by referring to many previous accounts and the passing on of material: "Since many have undertaken to set down an orderly account of the events that have been fulfilled among us, just as they were handed on to us by those who from the beginning were eyewitnesses and servants of the word, I too decided, after investigating everything carefully from the very first, to write an orderly account for you" (Luke 1:1-3). And as the next chapter will show, it seems most likely that Matthew and Luke used both Mark as a source and another collection of Jesus' sayings. Throughout, the Gospels do what ancient biographies do: they most often *display or demonstrate*

Jesus' character through actions and teaching rather than describing it.

4. Features of content: Like ancient biographies, the Gospels use various *geographical settings* (wilderness, lake, town, synagogue, houses, temple, etc.) but without moving the focus from Jesus. They also employ similar *topics* in presenting Jesus: his *ancestry* (especially in Matt. 1:2-17 and Luke 3:23-38, but with much less attention in Mark 6:3; John does a variation in emphasizing Jesus' origin with God who sent him; see, for example, John 6:39-44); *birth* (Matt. 1:18-2:23; Luke 1:5-2:40); *boyhood and education* (only in Luke 2:41-52); *great deeds and teachings* that form most of the Gospel narratives and display his *virtues* of character; and his *death and its consequences*, which include the resurrection stories (minimal in Mark 16 but more protracted in Matthew 28, Luke 24, and John 20–21). Their literary *style* is straightforward and direct, with Mark being perhaps the simplest and Luke more sophisticated and varied. Their *atmosphere* is generally serious and respectful, though there are instances of joy and humor. As with ancient biographies, their characterization combines *the typical* (Jesus as healer, teacher) along with *the real*, such as Jesus being tired and thirsty (John 4:6-7), and the inclusion of various emotions, for instance, of grief (John 11:35), anger (Mark 3:5), and compassion (Matt. 9:36). Gospels, like ancient biographies, emerge from and address particular *social settings*, notably the circumstances of groups of Jesus-followers. These circumstances can be reconstructed to some extent. Attending to the sociopolitical conditions and experiences of late first-century urban life provides some insights. So too does carefully noticing the contours and details of each Gospel's presentation of the story of Jesus and contemplating how it might *function* for followers in particular circumstances. Possible functions might include holding up Jesus for praise or as an example or inspiration, informing or teaching how to live as his follower, and countering misunderstandings or false charges.

There is, then, a considerable degree of similarity between the features of ancient biographies and the Gospels.

Ancient Biographies—with a Couple of Twists

Yet while ancient readers or hearers of the Gospels would have recognized from these features that the Gospels belonged to the genre of ancient biographies and would have expected to be informed, inspired, and taught by them about a significant person, there were a couple of surprises for them and for us.

One surprise concerns the main character Jesus. Ancient biographical literature typically celebrated important and powerful figures such as rulers, military commanders, and philosophers. Elite readers expected a character of a certain gender (male) and social status (elite). They expected this male character to exhibit and represent elite masculine cultural values and imperial claims, namely, ruling over and dominating others. So Philo presents Moses as a king. Tacitus presents Agricola as a governor and as a successful military commander. In fact, he devotes about a quarter of the biography to the victory Agrippa won over the united British tribes in 84 CE at Mt. Graupius (*Agricola* 29–39).

By comparison, Jesus is not presented as an elite individual. He comes not from a great center of power but from a small village in an unimportant part of a minor province of the Roman Empire. His family is not a member of the high-status elite with great wealth and important connections. He does, though, exhibit considerable power in his miraculous actions and in his summoning of followers whom he instructs about how to live. The title the Gospels give him, Lord, is one of power and authority, as are the titles king and Son of Man. He is also presented as manifesting the kingdom or reign or empire of God in his words and actions. His "great deeds" combine elements of subjection (he asks others to "follow me") with life-giving transformations. In an age of pervasive diseases of deprivation and contagion, his healings effect new life. In an age in which demons and spirits were understood to cause people all sorts of woes, his exorcisms offer people freedom from fear and bondage. In an age of material deprivation for many, his forming of a community of followers, committed to practical love for one another with whatever limited resources they had, is a godsend. In an age dominated by the empire of Rome, Jesus' manifestations of the empire of God imitate some imperial structures while also creating a space for different priorities and communal experiences.

The Gospels, then, were biographies with a twist—written primarily not for elite audiences but for nonelites, not to celebrate a socially high-status individual who furthered dominant elite values and practice, but about a paradoxical figure of low social status and marginal within Rome's world, yet who is presented as central to God's purposes for the world.

Second, readers of ancient biographies expected considerable attention to the main character's death, as we have noted. A subject's "good" death meant the noble acceptance of its circumstances, facing the inevitable with courage, being honored for one's accomplishments by one's friends and underlings, and dying bravely. The Gospels depart from the script somewhat at this point. Jesus' death is by crucifixion, the shameful and dishonorable death of a lowly provincial criminal at the hands of the ruling Jerusalem and Roman elite. He approaches his death with some ambivalence—resolved to it and not trying to escape it, yet asking God if "this cup" might be removed from him (Mark 14:36). His followers run away and abandon him to his fate. The power figures mock him as a kingly wannabe, a treasonous threat to Roman power. His death reveals a fundamental antipathy between him and the ruling elites. And it seems to be their victory.

But even more surprising, this is not where the Gospels end. The ruling elites cannot keep Jesus dead. The Gospels claim God's power to be at work and revealed in his resurrection. The death-dealing power of the elites is not as strong as God's life-giving power. Resurrection follows crucifixion. Rome does not have ultimate power; there is a greater power—for life—at work in the world.

Third, these ancient biographies of Jesus gained another name, that of Gospel. The term literally means "good news." The Greek noun and related verb form are used in writings from before and around the time of these accounts to refer to various forms of messages or reports. In the Greek translation of the Hebrew Bible, the verb expressing the announcing of good news appears twice in Isa. 40:9, where it refers to a person or "herald of good tidings." The "good tidings" consist of the presence of God with power as a warrior to overcome Israel's enemies and to nurture the flock of Israel. Along similar lines, in Isa. 52:7, it refers twice to one who announces peace and salvation, namely, that "your God reigns," signifying God's control of events whereby those in exile under Babylonian rule return to the land of Israel. In Isa. 61:1, quoted in Luke 4:18, the good news is also of deliverance "to the oppressed." The language of "good news" also appears in inscriptions concerning Roman power, notably the news of military victory, the enthronement of an emperor, and to celebrate the birthday of the emperor Augustus and the benefactions that his rule brought to the world.

1.4 "Good News" in the Priene Inscription

The Priene Inscription, from 9 BCE, uses the plural of the Greek word that is translated "good news" in the Gospels, here translated "good messages":

> . . . and since the Caesar through his appearances has exceeded the hopes of all former *good messages*, surpassing not only the benefactors who came before him, but also leaving no hope that anyone in the future would surpass him, and since for the world the birthday of the god was the beginning of his *good messages*, may therefore be decided that. . . .[6]

The "good news" celebrated here is associated with rule and the blessings of "peace," which means subjugation to Roman power.

The same language is used in Paul's Letters, where it designates the proclamation of God's action in Jesus. Paul can talk of both "the gospel of God" (Rom. 1:1) and "the gospel of Christ" (Rom. 15:19), and he describes his own mission as being "to preach" or, more literally, "to announce good news" (1 Cor. 1:17). He uses the language of "good

6. Quoted in Helmut Koester, *Ancient Christian Gospels: Their History and Development* (Philadelphia: Trinity Press International, 1990), 3–4.

news" to refer to a proclamation and message, but not to a written account of the life and actions of Jesus.

It is clear that during the second century, these written ancient biographies that we know as Matthew, Mark, Luke, and John were widely known as Gospels. Early in the second century, the letter of Ignatius to the Smyrnaeans (5.1) and the anonymous writing called the Didache (8.2; 11.3; 15.3–4) seem to refer to Matthew as a written Gospel. By around 140, Marcion refers to Luke's writing as Gospel. Justin Martyr (ca. 100–165 CE) refers to Matthew and Luke as "memoirs of the apostles" and "Gospels" (*1 Apol.* 66.3; *Dial.* 10.2; 100.1).[7]

Were these, though, the earliest references? What about the Gospel writers? Do they refer to their ancient biographies as Gospels?

Mark's Gospel, the first of the four to be written, uses the term *gospel* and its cognates seven times (Mark 1:1, 14, 15; 8:35; 10:29; 13:10; 14:9). Most of these references refer to proclamations or announcements of good news. So in 1:14-15, Jesus is located in Galilee and identified as "*proclaiming the good news* of God, and saying, 'The time is fulfilled, and the kingdom of God has come near; repent, and believe *in the good news*.'" But what about 1:1, which reads, "The beginning of *the good news* of Jesus Christ, the Son of God"? Scholars debate whether this reference to good news is a title for the whole Gospel as a written work or whether it maintains the meaning of a message or proclamation. The latter meaning sees a close connection to verses 2-8 and the proclamation made by John the Baptist in preparation for Jesus' coming. But the written proclamation about Jesus continues all the way through this written work to chapter 16. It seems reasonable to suggest, then, that the term *gospel* in 1:1 refers to the written account of all of Jesus' activity that follows and so would refer to the written work that we know as Mark's Gospel.[8]

7. Koester, *Ancient Christian Gospels*, 37-43.
8. For discussion, ibid., 10–14; Graham Stanton, "Matthew: BIBLOS, EUAGGELION, or BIOS?," in *The Four Gospels 1992*, ed. F. van Segbroeck et al. (Leuven: Leuven University Press, 1992) 1187–1201, esp. 1193; Adela Yarbro Collins, *Mark*, Hermeneia (Minneapolis: Fortress Press, 2007), 130–32.

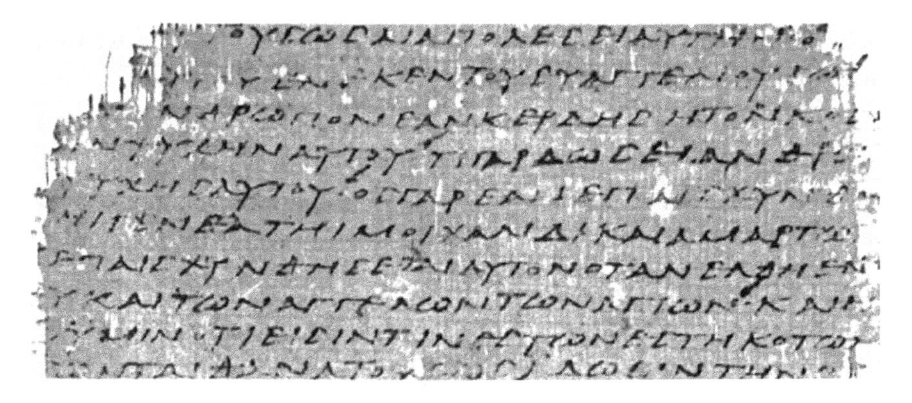

1.3 Third century CE Mark. A section of the papyrus manuscript P45, from about 200 CE, showing Mark 8:35–9:1; the Greek word for "gospel" appears in the second line.

Matthew's Gospel also seems to refer to his written work as a "Gospel." In 26:13, the account of the woman's action of anointing Jesus is included in "this good news" that is to be proclaimed to the whole world. The use of the demonstrative adjective "this" (not present in Mark 14:9) changes what seems to be in Mark a reference to oral proclamation to a reference to Matthew's written account of the incident. A similar change occurs in Matt. 24:14 ("this gospel will be proclaimed"; compare Mark 13:10, "the gospel . . .") in relation to Jesus' teaching about the "end times." These instances of Jesus' teaching and actions are part of "this Gospel," the written account of "good news" of God's action in Jesus that we know as Matthew's Gospel. Neither Luke nor John uses the noun, though John does refer to his biography as a "book" (John 20:30).

Conclusion

The Gospels, then, employ the genre of ancient biography to tell the story of Jesus. This genre sets up expectations for readers and hearers of these writings about what will follow—an account of the life and death, the great deeds and the teaching, of a noble and virtuous man. This is what the Gospels deliver—but with a twist. Jesus is not a socially elite man. In fact, he comes from nobody parents in a nothing place, but, the Gospels claim, he is absolutely central to God's purposes for the world. And his death is far from noble. He is crucified as a rebel wannabe king that threatened Roman power. Yet Rome could not keep him dead; God's life-giving power was exhibited in a victory over Roman death-dealing power when God raised him from the dead. God's life rules. And all of this these writings call "Gospel"—good news!

Questions for Review and Reflection

1. Why does genre matter? How do we recognize genres? Can you recall instances when you have misidentified or confused genres in selecting a movie or book? To what effect?
2. Concerning the genre of the Gospels, summarize the five factors that the chapter identifies to suggest the Gospels are not eyewitness historical accounts of Jesus' life.
3. What are the main features of ancient biographies? What features do Gospels share with ancient biographies?
4. The chapter suggests that the Gospels make several twists to the genre of ancient biography. What are they?
5. What impact does it make to read the Gospels as ancient biographies? What can we expect and not expect from them?
6. What meanings does the word *gospel* have?
7. As you think back over this chapter, what have you learned so far? What questions are emerging for you?

2

Telling Stories about Jesus Prior to the Written Gospels

In the last chapter, we established that the Gospels belong to a type of writing in the ancient world that we call ancient biography. How did they come to be written? What material about Jesus did they use? How did material about Jesus circulate among Jesus-followers in the time after Jesus' death up to the time of the writing of the Gospels?

Gospels were not written during Jesus' ministry or immediately after his death. Rather, there is a gap of some forty years between Jesus' death and the writing of the first Gospel. What was happening to stories about Jesus in this interval?

For starters, we need to get in view two key dates—30 CE and 70 CE.

First, 30 CE. Jesus was crucified around this date. We don't know for sure. No one has discovered the big book of Roman crucifixions in which each governor entered the name, offense, and date of each crucifixion. But we do know from the Gospel accounts, from Acts (3:13; 4:27; 13:28), from 1 Timothy (6:13), and from the Roman writer Tacitus (*Annals* 15.44) that Jesus was crucified by the Roman governor Pontius

Pilate. Pilate was governor of Judea between 26 CE and early 37 CE. That gives us a ten-year window for Jesus' crucifixion. Within this time span, scholars argue for various dates for Jesus' crucifixion—27 CE, 30 CE, and 33 CE. For our discussion in this chapter, we don't need to establish an exact date. For the sake of a nice round figure, let's settle on 30 CE.[1]

2.1 Nero's Persecution of Christians

The historian Tacitus offers a gruesome report of how the emperor Nero sought to shift suspicion for the terrible fire of 64 CE from himself to the Christians of Rome.

> To get rid of the report, Nero fastened the guilt and inflicted the most exquisite tortures on a class hated for their abominations, called Christians by the populace. Christus, from whom the name had its origin, suffered the extreme penalty during the reign of Tiberius at the hands of one of our procurators, Pontius Pilatus, and a most mischievous superstition, thus checked for the moment, again broke out not only in Judaea, the first source of the evil, but even in Rome, where all things hideous and shameful from every part of the world find their centre and become popular. Accordingly, an arrest was first made of all who pleaded guilty; then, upon their information, an immense multitude was convicted, not so much of the crime of firing the city, as of hatred against mankind. Mockery of every sort was added to their deaths. Covered with the skins of beasts, they were torn by dogs and perished, or were nailed to crosses, or were doomed to the flames and burnt, to serve as a nightly illumination, when daylight had expired. Nero offered his gardens for the spectacle, and was exhibiting a show in the circus, while he mingled with the people in the dress of a charioteer or stood aloft on a car. Hence, even for criminals who deserved extreme and exemplary punishment, there arose a feeling of compassion; for it was not, as it seemed, for the public good, but to glut one man's cruelty, that they were being destroyed. (*Annals* 15.44)

Second, 70 CE. When were the Gospels written? Just as the Gospels themselves do not claim authorship, they similarly do not tell us directly the date and place of their writing. We know from several early second-century writings that the Gospels had to have been written by the early second century. So, for example, the letters of Ignatius of Antioch and the Didache, both probably written in the first decade of the second century, quote from Matthew's Gospel. Matthew had to have been written by around 100 CE.[2]

1. We could write this date as c. 30 CE, with the *c* being an abbreviation for the Latin word *circa*, meaning "about."
2. Ignatius writes to the church in Smyrna and begins by listing their beliefs, including that Jesus was baptized by John that "all righteousness might be fulfilled by him" (*Smyrn.* 1.1), a quote from only Matthew's version of the baptismal story (Matt. 3:15). The Didache 8.1–3 includes the Lord's Prayer in the form that appears in Matthew's Gospel (Matt. 6:9-13), not the form that appears in Luke 11:2-4. There is no version of the Lord's Prayer in Mark or John.

The best clue for the earliest date for their writing comes from references in the Gospels to the destruction of the city of Jerusalem and its temple in the year 70 CE by the Romans at the end of the 66–70 war. A number of references to the fall of Jerusalem are placed in Jesus' mouth. These words were probably not spoken by Jesus. During the time of his ministry, in the decade of the 20s, a war between Rome and Judea did not seem likely, and the destruction of Jerusalem and its temple even less so. More likely, these verses reflect the time and circumstances of the Gospels' writing in a post-70 world of shock, mourning, and starting over without the temple.

Note the following references to the fall of Jerusalem:

- Matthew 22:1-10 and Luke 14:15-24. Luke's parable of a great feast or dinner appears in Matthew's Gospel as a parable about a wedding feast that a king gives for his son. The king sends his slaves to invite guests to the banquet, but they refuse (Matt. 22:3-5). Some even mistreat and kill the slaves (22:6). In verse 7, the king becomes very angry: "The king was enraged. He sent his troops, destroyed those murderers, and burned their city," declaring that the invited "were not worthy." He then sends the slaves "into the main streets [to] invite everyone you find to the wedding banquet" (22:9). Verse 7 is the crucial verse for our purposes. The verse is not in Luke's account: compare Luke 14:21. And its inclusion here creates an unlikely scenario of a king destroying his own city and then holding the wedding feast for his son in its smoking ruins. Moreover, if we read from verse 6 to verse 8 and ignore verse 7, the story makes good sense (just as it does in Luke 14:21-22). When the invitations are rejected, the king sends out other slaves to invite anybody and everybody to the wedding. What might verse 7 evoke? The most obvious candidate is that the reference to burning the city evokes the fate of Jerusalem and its temple in 70. When the Romans broke into the city after a lengthy siege, they burned it, along with the temple. By recasting the parable in terms of a king and the elite's refusal to attend a wedding feast for his son, Matthew's Gospel presents an allegory of God's anger at the rejection of his Son Jesus by the Jerusalem elite, and interprets the destruction of Jerusalem in 70 CE as God's judgment on them. Interestingly, the Jewish historian Josephus also sees the temple-burning as an act of God's judgment, though from a different perspective, one not at all concerned with Jesus.

2.2 Josephus on the Burning of the Temple

The Jewish historian Josephus claims that the burning of the temple was God's judgment on the temple (*Jewish War* 6.249–250, 267):[3]

> So Titus [the Roman general] retired into the tower of Antonia, and resolved to storm the temple the next day, early in the morning, with his whole army, and to encamp around the holy house [Jerusalem temple]; but as for that house, God had, for certain long ago doomed it to the fire; and now that fatal day was come according to the revolution of ages. . . . Now, although anyone would justly lament the destruction of such a work as this was, since it was the most admirable of all the works that we have seen or heard of, both for its intricate structure and its size, and also for the vast wealth bestowed upon it, as well as for the glorious reputation it had for its holiness; yet might such a one comfort himself with this thought, that it was fate that decreed it so to be, which is inevitable, both as to living creatures, and as to works and places also.

- Mark's Gospel also has Jesus speak about the temple: "Then Jesus asked him, 'Do you see these great buildings? Not one stone will be left here upon another; all will be thrown down'" (Mark 13:2).
- In Luke's Gospel, Jesus approaches Jerusalem.

> As he came near and saw the city, he wept over it, saying, "If you, even you, had only recognized on this day the things that make for peace! But now they are hidden from your eyes. Indeed, the days will come upon you, when your enemies will set up ramparts around you and surround you, and hem you in on every side. They will crush you to the ground, you and your children within you, and they will not leave within you one stone upon another; because you did not recognize the time of your visitation from God." Then he entered the temple. (Luke 19:41-45)

As with Matt. 22:1-10, the verses provide a theological interpretation of Jerusalem's destruction in 70 CE. The "visitation from God" presumably

3. See Josephus, *Jewish War*, 6.249–280 for his account of the fire.

refers to God's response to the elite's rejection of God's agent or Son, Jesus.

- Or again in Luke: "When you see Jerusalem surrounded by armies, then know that its desolation has come near. Then those in Judea must flee to the mountains, and those inside the city must leave it, and those out in the country must not enter it; for these are days of vengeance, as a fulfillment of all that is written" (Luke 21:20-22).
- In John's Gospel, the Jerusalem leaders say: "If we let him go on like this, everyone will believe in him, and the Romans will come and destroy both our holy place and our nation" (John 11:48). Here Rome's allies, the chief priests and leading Pharisees, observe the danger Jesus poses to their social order and to Roman interests. The irony of the Gospel is that they do not "let him go on" but they crucify him. Or so it appears. In John's Gospel, the narrative presents Jesus as giving himself to be crucified (John 10:11, 15, 17-18), popping the illusion that the chief priests and Pharisees are in control. Further, their act of crucifying him, of course, does not prevent the Romans' destroying Jerusalem in 70 CE, an event that must have happened in order for this verse to expose the error of their thinking and actions. It is precisely because they do crucify him, the Gospel suggests, that this act of judgment on the city takes place.

The Gospels, then, refer to and interpret the shocking event of 70 CE, when Jerusalem and its central temple institution were destroyed by the Romans. While various Jewish writings interpreted this event as an expression of God's punishing anger, the Gospels present a Christian perspective and interpret it as punishment for the rejection of Jesus.

2.1 Roman soldiers carry the menorah from the Jerusalem temple destroyed by the Romans (70 CE) in this panel from the Arch of Titus in Rome; Commons.wikimedia.org.

Such talk of God's judgment might be strange or disconcerting for us. The Gospel writers, however, are employing biblical traditions that frequently see both God's blessing and God's curse taking place in everyday, human life. Seeing God's punishing purposes in historical events runs deep in the scriptural tradition. A speech given to Moses in Deuteronomy 28 articulates this perspective of God's judgment taking place through international events:

> Because you did not serve the Lord your God joyfully and with gladness of heart for the abundance of everything, therefore you shall serve your enemies whom the Lord will send against you, in hunger and thirst, in nakedness and lack of everything. He will put an iron yoke on your neck until he has destroyed you. The Lord will bring a nation from far away, from the end of the earth, to swoop down on you like an eagle, a nation whose language you do not understand, a grim-faced nation showing no respect to the old or favor to the young. It shall consume the fruit of your livestock and the fruit of your ground until you are destroyed. . . . It shall besiege you in all your towns until your high and fortified walls, in which

> you trusted, come down throughout your land; it shall besiege you in all your towns throughout the land that the Lord your God has given you. (Deut. 28:47-52)

And the writers of 2 Kings interpreted the destruction of Jerusalem in 587 BCE by the Babylonians in the same terms:

> In his days King Nebuchadnezzar of Babylon came up; Jehoiakim became his servant for three years; then he turned and rebelled against him. The Lord sent against him bands of the Chaldeans, bands of the Arameans, bands of the Moabites, and bands of the Ammonites; he sent them against Judah to destroy it, according to the word of the Lord that he spoke by his servants the prophets. Surely this came upon Judah at the command of the Lord, to remove them out of his sight, for the sins of Manasseh, for all that he had committed, and also for the innocent blood that he had shed; for he filled Jerusalem with innocent blood, and the Lord was not willing to pardon....Indeed, Jerusalem and Judah so angered the Lord that he expelled them from his presence. (2 Kgs. 24:1-4, 20)

Six hundred years later, in circumstances involving Rome, not Babylon, the Gospel writers draw on the same tradition. Yet they modify the tradition a little. Their perspective on the fall of Jerusalem is that they see the rejection of Jesus as the sin that is being punished.

So What?

The years 30 CE and 70 CE: The death of Jesus and the destruction of Jerusalem—after which the Gospels are written. Here are the questions that will concern us in the rest of this chapter: What was happening between 30 and 70 CE to stories about Jesus? How were stories of Jesus being told and passed on in the time after Jesus' death and before the Gospels were written? What role did communities of Jesus-followers play in this period of time?

Scholars have put forward several different models. We will look at two—one that concentrates on the roles of communities of believers and forms or patterns of the traditions, and one that focuses on the oral nature and performance of the material about Jesus. The former held sway among scholars for a long time; the latter is a more contemporary approach.

Form Criticism

This first model, known as form criticism, emphasizes several interrelated characteristics.[4] It sees the Gospels as the end of a process of development that took place over forty to fifty years. The model posits that during this time period, material about Jesus inevitably developed from simple and short sayings or units into longer, more complex forms that were eventually combined to form the written Gospels. Short became long; simple became complex. To examine this process, scholars start with the final product—the Gospels—and take the Gospel accounts apart, breaking them down into the individual units and sayings that make up the Gospel accounts. These individual units are readily recognized in the Gospels from the often simple and nonspecific ways that sayings or scenes are joined together ("And immediately"; "Then"; "After Jesus had . . ."). The sayings are often the punch lines of scenes. Then scholars tried to trace the development of the form of each unit or saying back to recover an "original form" spoken by Jesus, or to communities of followers of Jesus who had developed the form across several decades. Added details, or the apparent additions of contexts for sayings or combinations of sayings or combinations of types of material (for example, healings and controversy stories), were all understood as signs of the development of traditions over time.

So, for example, the parable of the lost sheep appears in two Gospels with two quite different functions. In Matt. 18:10-14, it instructs disciples on caring for one another, and in Luke 15:4-7, along with other parables, it shows something of the welcoming, loving mercy of God manifested by Jesus. The parable can be easily detached from these different Gospel contexts. This suggests that before the Gospels were written, the parable existed independently and was associated with

4. The classic contribution is Rudolf Bultmann, *The History of the Synoptic Tradition* (New York: Harper & Row, 1963). Other helpful discussions include Werner Kelber, *The Oral and the Written Gospel: The Hermeneutics of Speaking and Writing in the Synoptic Tradition, Mark, Paul, and Q* (Philadelphia: Fortress Press, 1983), and E. P. Sanders and Margaret Davies, *Studying the Synoptic Gospels* (London: SCM, 1989).

these different contexts, perhaps before the Gospels were written or by the Gospel writers themselves.

2.3 Parable of the Good Shepherd in Matthew and Luke	
Matthew 18:10-14	*Luke 15:4-7*
Take care that you do not despise one of these little ones; for, I tell you, in heaven their angels continually see the face of my Father in heaven.	
. . . What do you think? If a shepherd has a hundred sheep, and one of them has gone astray, does he not leave the ninety-nine on the mountains and go in search of the one that went astray? And if he finds it, truly I tell you, he rejoices over it more than over the ninety-nine that never went astray. So it is not the will of your Father in heaven that one of these little ones should be lost.	Which one of you, having a hundred sheep and losing one of them, does not leave the ninety-nine in the wilderness and go after the one that is lost until he finds it? When he has found it, he lays it on his shoulders and rejoices. And when he comes home, he calls together his friends and neighbors, saying to them, "Rejoice with me, for I have found my sheep that was lost." Just so, I tell you, there will be more joy in heaven over one sinner who repents than over ninety-nine righteous persons who need no repentance.

Form criticism emphasizes the creative and important role of communities of Jesus-followers before the Gospels were written. These communities were said to be responsible for this expanding, evolving tradition. These anonymous folks were committed to the risen Jesus and understood material about him through the perspective of the resurrection. They shaped units of material about Jesus in typical situations or "settings in life" involving preaching, teaching, arguments with opponents, and ethical instruction. These units developed, so this model posits, in typical forms and in predictable ways to address needs in their ecclesial communities.

What did these forms look like? I will discuss five: apothegms or *chreia*, stories about Jesus, sayings of Jesus, miracle stories, and parables.

The first form, apothegms or *chreia*, comprised short scenes that highlighted a brief and memorable saying. This form developed from a short but significant saying attributed to Jesus, such as the following:

> Follow me. (Mark 2:14)
>
> Those who are well have no need of a physician, but those who are sick; I have come to call not the righteous but sinners. (Mark 2:17)
>
> Is it lawful to do good or to do harm on the sabbath, to save life or to kill? (Mark 3:4)

Each saying gained a brief narrative context or setting, sometimes from Jesus and sometimes from communities of followers. This context often involved conflict and criticism or sometimes friendly instruction. The scenes and their sayings highlight examples of discipleship, and address matters of importance to communities of followers: honoring Sabbath, forgiveness, how to follow Jesus, welcoming sinners, the role of the Spirit, alienation from families, welcome to the vulnerable (e.g., children), relations with the empire.

2.4 Apothegms and *Chreiai*

The Greek word *apophthegma* means "saying" or maxim. *Chreiai* (the plural of *chreia*) were "helpful" sayings attributed to particular characters. Examples include Mark 2:1-12, 13-14, 15-17, 18-22, 23-28; 3:1-5, 20-30, 31-35; 10:13-16; 12:13-17; Luke 9:57-62.

We can elaborate several subcategories of these sayings.

One category of scenes, known as "conflict stories," presents Jesus disputing with nonbelieving opponents. These scenes usually involve Jesus, followers, and hostile outsiders. So in Mark 2:23-28, for example, the scene provides a context of conflict for two of Jesus' teachings about the Sabbath. Outsiders, comprising some Pharisees, accuse the disciples who had plucked some heads of grain while they walked through a grain field of violating the Sabbath. Jesus defends the disciples' actions by declaring that actions that ensure human welfare are appropriate ways of observing the Sabbath:

> The Sabbath was made for humankind, and not humankind for the Sabbath. (Mark 2:27)

In the scene, Jesus speaks this memorable and brief saying, the punch line of the scene. The conflict scene provides a means of providing teaching for later followers on appropriate Sabbath observance. In the scene, the disciples who are criticized function as representatives of the church.

Subsequently, so the model says, *another* saying from Jesus about the Sabbath has been added to the punch line of verse 27. Verse 28 reads:

> so the Son of Man is lord even of the sabbath.

In this model, this second saying about Jesus having authority to determine how the Sabbath should be observed as "Lord of the Sabbath" has been attracted to and added to the saying about the Sabbath existing for the good of human beings. The unit has grown to provide further teaching in a claim about Jesus' authority.

Another example comprises "teaching or school sayings." These present Jesus' teaching for his followers in a friendly or nonconflictual context. So in Matt. 18:21-22, Peter, representing the disciples, asks Jesus how many times one should forgive a member of the Jesus-community. Jesus answers, "seventy-seven times." This is the punch line around which the scene involving Peter's question has subsequently been created. In other words, according to this model, the answer existed before the question. But beyond this, more material has expanded this very brief scene. A parable follows—not about forgiveness but about what happens if one does not forgive (18:23-35)—suggesting that another independent unit that has been added here, perhaps before the Gospel was written or at the time of writing the Gospel.

Another type of expansion involves the combining of different forms. In Mark 2:1-12, we have two types of material in one scene. Taking apart the scene's elements, we can see that part of the scene is a conflict and part of it is a miracle story. The healing story involves Jesus healing a paralyzed man (2:1-5, 11-12). The conflict involves Jesus in dispute with the scribes about who can forgive sins (2:6-10). These two forms existed separately, but at some point they were combined. Notice that the "join" remains rather awkward: in mid-sentence, Jesus pivots from speaking to the scribes to speaking to the paralyzed man (vv. 10-11). Perhaps the healing story raised questions about Jesus' authority to heal. The saying about the Son of Man having authority to forgive sin was introduced along with the controversy involving the scribes to assert Jesus' authority. The result is that Jesus' healing of the paralyzed man also attests to Jesus' forgiveness of his sin.

A second type of material consists of stories about Jesus. Sometimes called "legends," these stories offer some information about Jesus. Examples include Jesus in the temple as a boy instructing the teachers (Luke 2:41-49), Jesus' baptism (Mark 1:9-11), and his temptation (Mark 1:12-13). The scene involving Jesus' baptism is an interesting example. None of the Gospels uses the scene to instruct followers to be baptized. It is not a teaching or example story. Rather, the scene gives information about Jesus as God's agent more than it instructs disciples about their own baptism.

A third type of material comprises sayings of Jesus. These sayings are usually not dependent on a narrative framework as are the apothegms or *chreia*. Rather, they are sayings that are often drawn together with other teachings to form a block of teaching on a particular subject or theme. In 6:25-34, for example, several different types of sayings have been combined.

- Proverbs or declarative sayings such as Matt. 6:34, "Do not worry about tomorrow" (see also Matt. 12:34; 22:14).
- Questions such as Matt. 6:27, "And can any of you by worrying add a single hour to your span of life?"
- Exhortations as in Matt. 6:33: "but strive first for the kingdom of God," and "Follow me, and let the dead bury the dead" (Matt. 8:22; also Luke 4:23). These sayings from Matt. 6:25-34 have been grouped together around a theme of trusting God.

Or in other sections of the Sermon on the Mount (chapters 5–7 of Matthew's Gospel), Jesus' instructions for church life and practices have been collected, including the command to reconcile with your brother or sister before offering a gift at the altar (Matt. 5:23-24); instruction on almsgiving (Matt. 6:2-4), prayer (Matt. 6:5-6, 7-13), and fasting (Matt. 6:16-18); and commands on reproving a church member (Matt. 18:15-17).

Sayings on related themes occur through the Gospels. Jesus makes prophetic and apocalyptic statements about the arrival of God's reign: "The time is fulfilled, and the kingdom of God has come near; repent, and believe in the good news" (Mark 1:15). He also predicts his imminent future coming (Matt. 24:37-41). These sayings include declarations of the blessing of God's salvation ("Blessed are you who are poor, for yours is the kingdom of God," Luke 6:20) as well as threats (Matt. 23:37-39) and woes on those who are perceived to be resistant ("But woe to you who are rich, for you have received your consolation. Woe to you who are full now, for you will be hungry," Luke 6:24-25).

Jesus also speaks about his own mission, work, and destiny. These "I-sayings" include Matt. 5:17 ("Do not think that I have come to abolish the law or the prophets; I have come not to abolish but to fulfill"), Matt. 15:24 ("I was sent only to the lost sheep of the house of Israel"), and Luke 19:10 ("The Son of Man came to seek and to save the lost").

Fourth, miracle stories abound in the Gospels. They include Jesus' healings (Simon Peter's mother-in-law, Mark 1:19-31; blind Bartimaeus, Mark 10:46-52), exorcisms (in the synagogue at Capernaum, Mark 1:21-28; the demons called "legion," Mark 5:1-20), and nature miracles such as calming the storm (Mark 4:35-41), walking on the water (Mark 6:45-52), feeding the five thousand and the four thousand (Mark 6:30-44; 8:1-10), the big catch of fish (Luke 5:1-11), and cursing the fig tree (Mark 11:12-14, 20). Healing stories and exorcisms often follow a basic three-part form: The circumstances of a person's affliction are described; then Jesus heals the person; the healing is demonstrated in some way, and onlookers confirm it and testify to it.

The brief account of the healing of Simon Peter's mother-in-law shows these three elements very clearly.

- Her affliction is described. Mark 1:30: "Now Simon's mother-in-law was in bed with a fever, and they told him about her at once."
- Jesus heals her by taking her hand. Mark 1:31a: "He came and took her by the hand and lifted her up. Then the fever left her."
- The healing is confirmed by her action. Mark 1:31b: "and she began to serve them."

Other healings have many more details—the length of the illness; the ineffectiveness of other healers, conversation between Jesus and the afflicted, descriptions of various means of healing (words, touch), various types of confirmations. Such details suggest, in this model, elaborations in transmitting the stories.

A fifth form of material involves parables. The word literally means to set one thing beside another, thereby forming a comparison. Most commonly, parables comprise a short narrative of a simple situation (a growing mustard seed, Mark 4:31-32) or a more complex and interesting or surprising situation (invited guests decline to come to a feast, Matt. 22:1-14; Luke 14:16-24). It is told in relation to God or to God's reign or to Jesus. Individual parables grow from very concise stories by enriching details. Parables tend to be collected together with other parables, as the collections in Mark 4, Matthew 13 and 21:28-22:14, and Luke 15 attest. Some parables gain allegorical interpretations whereby one-on-one equivalencies are made between details in the story and aspects of God's activity or discipleship. So in Matt. 13:3-9, the parable of the sower who sows seeds on four types of ground with varying yields is interpreted in 13:18-23 so that each kind of soil represents a different person's response to preaching the gospel.

2.2 Jesus heals a woman who touches his garment (compare Mark 5:25-34); fourth-century fresco from the Catacomb of Saints Marcellinus and Peter, Rome. Commons.wikimedia.org.

How was material about Jesus transmitted between the time of Jesus' death and the writing of the Gospels? This model suggests that communities of Jesus-followers played a key role in transmitting and developing material from Jesus. It also suggests that material developed in a variety of forms. These forms addressed situations and circumstances of these followers. It further suggests that across the decades, material expanded. The simple became more detailed and complex. The scattered and diverse units were drawn together in the Gospels.

There is much in this model that is speculative. That is to be expected since no one was keeping a video record. But while this model has been very influential, aspects of it are not convincing. For example, while material about Jesus was without doubt transmitted by his followers, it is by no means clear that transmission happened by means of set forms and isolated units and individual sayings. It is quite possible that material Jesus taught was transmitted in collections organized by theme or similar type of material and that sayings were passed on in narrative accounts. Nor can we be at all clear about the circumstances or settings in communities in which material supposedly developed when we know little about such communities. The claim that material began in recoverable "original forms" that then expanded and became more complex is by no means certain. Material about Jesus that did not continue to be useful or was not memorable no doubt was abbreviated, merged with other accounts, reformatted, forgotten, and disappeared. Speech is, as we know, much more flexible and creative than such set patterns suggest.

Orality and Performance

A different model for the transmission of traditions about Jesus has been proposed.[5] This model emphasizes the transmission of material not in isolated fragments and units created by communities of Jesus-followers, but in clusters of sayings or speeches attributed to Jesus. Moreover, this approach has emphasized the importance of transmission by oral performance. It recognizes that the culture transmitting Jesus material before the Gospels was a predominantly oral culture and that practices of performance—recitation usually from memory—significantly influenced the transmission process. Literacy, the ability to read and write, was very much a minority skill, associated with locations and personnel of power, namely cities and elites or educated slaves and scribes. Artisans and peasants had little use for it, preferring to utilize oral agreements, oaths, and witnesses.

5. I draw on the work of Richard A. Horsley and Jonathan A. Draper, *Whoever Hears You Hears Me: Prophets, Performance and Tradition in Q* (Harrisburg, PA: Trinity Press International, 1999); and Horsley, *Jesus in Context: Power, People, and Performance* (Minneapolis: Fortress Press, 2008), 231–45.

One focus of attention for this model has been a collection of Jesus' teachings known as Q. This abbreviation has nothing to do with James Bond. Rather, it is short for the German word *Quelle*, which means "source." There is good reason for thinking that the Gospels of Matthew and Luke used this collection of Jesus' teaching as a source for their Gospels.

A written copy of this source has never been found. Why? Perhaps very few written copies of it existed because it was recited orally, so the chances for written copies surviving the millennia were slim. Or perhaps a written version did not exist at all in an oral culture. It is likely that it was an oral collection of Jesus' teachings, transmitted and even composed as it was performed in assemblies of Jesus-believers.

The source has been reconstructed, however, from the speeches of Jesus that appear only in Matthew and Luke but not in Mark. Often these teachings appear in the same order in these two Gospels, and some of the material is word-for-word the same. These similarities point to a common source for the material, perhaps written, or perhaps with some fixed order and wording from regular oral performance.

But in what form did the teaching exist—as individual sayings or as clusters of sayings or speeches? This model points to the latter option. What is at stake is meaning. Communication and meaning depend on context, something that is missing from a focus on isolated sayings. Sayings mean things in the context of a particular speech and in the context of a sequence of speeches.

This approach understands Q, then, not as a collection of individual sayings (as in form criticism), but as a sequence of speeches. One analysis identifies at least the following speeches:[6]

- Q 6:20-49 Covenant Renewal
- Q 7:18-35 The Coming and Presence of the Kingdom of God in Jesus' Action
- Q 9:57-10:16 Sending Out Prophetic Envoys for the Renewal of Israel

6. Ibid., 231–45.

- Q 11:2-4, 9-11 Prayer
- Q 11:14-20/26 In Jesus' Exorcism of Demons, the Kingdom of God Is Come
- Q 11:39-52 Woes against the Pharisees and Scribes
- Q 12:2-12 Bold Confession When Brought to Trial
- Q 12:22-32 Anxiety about Subsistence and Single-Minded Pursuit of the Kingdom
- Q 13:28-35; 14:16-24 Prophetic Oracle against Jerusalem Rulers
- Q 17:23-27 The Day of Judgment

2.5 Citing Q Material

It is conventional to cite likely Q material in this way. First, the letter Q signals that Q material is being referred to. This matters because the numbers that follow reference Luke's Gospel. As we noted above, Q is the source for material common to Luke and Matthew (but not in Mark). But neither Luke nor Matthew uses this material in a "pure" form. That is, they both edit the material, sometimes expanding it, sometimes abbreviating it. Scholars generally think Luke does less editing than Matthew, so when they refer to Q material they do so by citing chapter and verses in Luke's Gospel. Readers know there is a parallel passage in Matthew's Gospel. So, Q 17:23-27 means "Q as we find it in Luke 17:23-27." The reference to Luke's Gospel, though, does not mean that everything in that section or verse is from Q because Luke (and Matthew) have edited the Q material. So scholars try to identify those editings and reconstruct a text that they think approximates Q.

This list of speeches is not the whole of Q, but it constitutes a significant part of the collection of Jesus' teaching. It probably began, for example, with an account of John the Baptist (Q 3:7-9, 16-17, 21-22) and of the testing of Jesus in the wilderness (Q 4:1-13). Most of the rest of it comprised speeches of Jesus.

How was meaning created in the oral performance of Jesus' teaching? These speeches were recited or performed in particular contexts of gathered communities of followers of Jesus. They resonated with and evoked the cultural context or traditions that performer and audience shared. Q probably developed in Galilee, given its references to places such as Bethsaida, Capernaum, and Chorazin and its common agrarian imagery. Performed in Galilee, the content of Q evokes popular Israelite traditions involving movements led by Moses, Joshua, and David, as well as the activity of prophets who announced God's judgment against oppressive rulers and set about renewing the life of the people.

For example, the speech in Q 6:20-49 evokes various aspects of the covenant traditions associated with Moses (Exodus 20–23; Deuteronomy; Leviticus 19, 25) and Joshua (Joshua 24).[7] It particularly concerns itself with basic economic issues and social conflicts that folks in village communities experienced: hunger, debt, poverty, conflict, animosity, oppressive rule. Addressing these concrete situations, it declares God's favor for the poor and instructs its hearers to live out covenant commitments to support one another for each other's good.

So the opening blessings and curses (Q 6:20-26) evoke the blessings and curses for obeying and disobeying the covenant in Deuteronomy 27–28. The command in Q 6:36, "Be merciful, just as your Father is merciful," echoes the covenant principle of imitating God in Lev. 19:2 ("be holy for I, the Lord your God, am holy"). It establishes mercy, not oppression or inflicting injury, as the norm for social interactions. The commands in Q 6:27-36 elaborate social and economic interactions: love your enemies; give to everyone who begs; do to others as you would have them do to you; do good, and lend, expecting nothing in return. These commands evoke covenant commands in Lev. 19:17-18 that include love for one's neighbor. The exhortation to love your enemy (repeated for emphasis in Q 6:27 and 35) evokes the covenant teaching to care for the livestock of one's neighbor and one's enemy (Exod. 23:4-5; Deut. 22:1-4). The repeated command to lend freely (Q 6:30, 34, 35) echoes Exod. 22:25 and 25:35-38 as a basic strategy for enabling others to live. And the speech ends in Q 6:46-49 with a blessing on those who "hear my words and act on them" and a curse or judgment on those who do not act on them, elements that recall the blessings on those who obey the covenant and sanctions or curses on those who disobey it (Deuteronomy 27–28).

7. Ibid., 71–88.

It is also important to note that this speech in Q 6:20-49 does not comprise just individual sayings but forms a well-organized speech. It follows and employs a basic three-part structure found in the covenant traditions in Exodus, Leviticus, and Deuteronomy. There, the covenant is grounded in an act of deliverance by God (part 1). Then (part 2) the teaching and demands of the covenant are set out. The teaching ends (part 3) with exhortations to be faithful and obedient to the covenant in the form of motivations (often blessings) and sanctions (often curses). The same structure can be seen in Q 6:20-49. The speech begins by declaring God's deliverance for the poor from the rich (Q 6:20-36; part 1). Then (part 2) it sets out teaching for social and economic interaction such as loving enemies and not judging others (6:27-42). Then (part 3) it concludes with motivations and sanctions by observing that like a tree, the fruit of a person's life, whether good or evil, shows what kind of person they are (Q 6:43-45). Their actions reveal, like a house in a storm, whether they have founded their life wisely on the teaching of Jesus or have foolishly ignored it (Q 6:46-49).

Or as another example, we can look at a couple of cultural resonances in Q 9:57—10:16.[8] This speech concerns the commissioning of envoys or prophetic workers to continue Jesus' work of manifesting God's kingdom in words and healings among the villages and towns of Israel. The speech begins with three brief scenarios of people who want to continue Jesus' work but make excuses to delay. The second and third scenarios, in which Jesus instructs the inquirers to "let the dead bury their own dead" and warns against putting "a hand to the plow and looking back," echo the scene of Elijah commissioning Elisha. Elisha is to assist and succeed Elijah in renewing Israel against the oppressive king Ahab (1 Kings 18–19). Then Jesus talks of a great "harvest but the laborers are few; therefore ask the Lord of the harvest to send out laborers into his harvest" (Q 10:2). The repeated image of "harvest" is common in the prophets to describe the fate of imperial nations punished for threatening Israel (Babylon, Jer 51:33; many nations, Mic. 4:11-13) and to describe the ingathering of Israelites

8. Following Horsley and Draper, *Whoever Hears You Hears Me*, 228–49, esp. 240–45.

scattered among the nations (Isa. 27:12-13; cf. 43:5-7). This is the work of the envoys. Yet, in a subsequent image, Jesus' envoys are depicted as being sent as "lambs among wolves" (Q 10:3). This image echoes Israelite traditions of the danger that rulers and the Jerusalem authorities posed to prophets in rejecting their calls for justice (see Ezek. 22:23-27; Zeph. 3:1-3). It depicts the danger these envoys of Jesus faced from Herodian and Roman rulers.

Since these rulers were dangerous and were not likely to be receptive to a call to just community and renewal, it's not surprising that two speeches are directed against Israel's rulers: Q 11:39-52, Woes against the Pharisees and Scribes, and Q 13:28-35; 14:16-24, Prophetic Oracle against Jerusalem Rulers.[9] The speech against the Pharisees and Scribes repeatedly employs a form of speech known as "woes." This "woe" form appears in prophets such as Amos 6:1-6, Mic. 2:1-5, Isa. 5:8, and Hab. 2:6-15. The form is frequently directed toward rulers. It names their violation of the covenant traditions in exploiting and manipulating peasants and announces punishment on them. So a woe in Mic. 2:1-5 identifies their violations as seizing fields and houses and oppressing households. Habakkuk similarly condemns the unjust taking of property. Isaiah announces woes on those who "call evil good" and take bribes in legal proceedings. The lament in Q 13:34-35 against Jerusalem's leaders evokes judgments spoken against Israel's leaders of old by prophets as the mouthpiece of God. Amos speaks as God's mouthpiece in Amos 5:2-3 and 16-17. The complaint that powerful rulers regularly kill prophets evokes situations such as the prophet Elijah's conflict with King Ahab and Queen Jezebel in 1 Kings 18–19, death threats to Jeremiah (Jer. 26:7-11), and the death of Uriah the prophet by means of a death squad sent by King Jehoiakim (Jer. 26:20-23).

In contrast to form criticism, this approach to the transmission of Jesus' teaching in the time between Jesus and the writing of the Gospels emphasizes

9. Ibid., 277–91.

- The importance of intentionally shaped and themed speeches as the means of communicating material, rather than individual sayings;
- The importance of the oral performance of these speeches among communities of Jesus-followers;
- The importance of evoking cultural traditions in the form of covenant teaching and prophetic speech in making meaning of Jesus' teachings.

In this discussion, I have focused on just a sample of material about Jesus as it developed in the time before the Gospels. However, this very helpful focus on the transmission of material as part of a larger collection provides an important insight into the transmission of other types of material. It may well be that other collections of similar materials also developed through oral transmission and performance. For example, Mark's Gospel includes several instances of material that scholars have suggested already existed in a coherent collection before the Gospel was written. One such collection comprises Mark 2:1—3:6, a series of conflict (and in several instances healing) scenes.

- Mark 2:1-12 Jesus healing the paralyzed man on the Sabbath
- Mark 2:13-17 Jesus associating with undesirable people
- Mark 2:18-22 dispute about fasting
- Mark 2:23-28 dispute about how to observe the Sabbath
- Mark 3:1-6 dispute about healing on the Sabbath

Another example of material possibly collected together before the Gospel was written comes in Mark 4. Here we have a series of parables with four of the five possible units concerned with growing seeds.

- Mark 4:2-9 parable of the sower, seeds, and soils
- Mark 4:14-20 explanation of the parable of the sower, seeds, and soils

- Mark 4:21-25 parable of the lamp (not concerned with seeds)
- Mark 4:26-29 parable of the growing seed
- Mark 4:30-32 parable of the mustard seed

Possibly both the form (parables) and the content (seeds) assisted the joining of the material into one memorable collection.

Another example of material possibly collected together in some form before the Gospel was written concerns the account of Jesus' death. This account forms chapters 14–15 of Mark's Gospel. It is very likely that during this time period, some followers of Jesus told a version of the story of his death and therefore set about making meaning of his shameful and dangerous death by crucifixion. Mark's Gospel includes an edited (redacted) form of this account.

Conclusion

In this chapter, we have considered how material about Jesus might have been transmitted in the time between Jesus' crucifixion (c. 30 CE) and the writing of the first Gospel in the early 70s CE. We do not know for sure how this might have happened. We have looked at two different models that have been proposed as ways of trying to understand this important but elusive period, one based on developing forms of material, and one based on oral performances of material. Now we will discuss each of the four canonical Gospels in turn, starting with the first to be written, the Gospel of Mark.

Questions for Review and Reflection

1. The chapter begins by highlighting two dates. What are they? Why do they matter? What is the significance of the "gap" between them for the writing of the Gospels?
2. What evidence is there for dating the writing of the Gospels to after 70 CE?
3. The first of two models for how material about Jesus developed in the time between Jesus and the writing of the Gospels is called

form criticism. What are the characteristics of this model? (Be sure you understand that the word *criticism* does not mean "attack" but refers to a way of understanding or discerning the process by which material about Jesus developed).

4. The chapter identifies five forms of sayings linked to Jesus. Describe each one and check out the examples from the Gospels.
5. What are some of the strengths and the weaknesses of this first model?
6. What is the second model the chapter offers for the transmission of tradition about Jesus? What are its distinctive features? What are some of its strengths and weaknesses?
7. There is a lot that is speculative in this chapter because we do not know for sure how traditions about Jesus were transmitted. What insights do you find helpful? What questions does the chapter raise?

3

The Tale Mark Tells

In the next two chapters, we think about the tale of Jesus the Gospel of Mark tells. In this chapter, I discuss the Gospel's plot and characters. I also highlight some of the distinctive features of Mark's presentation of Jesus, his strange command for secrecy, the identity and functions of the Jerusalem leaders with whom Jesus conflicts, and the significance of Jesus' death. In the next chapter, we will take up some further aspects of Mark's story, particularly asking about the possible contexts that this story originally engaged.

> **3.1 A Word to the Wise**
> Reading this chapter on Mark will make much more sense if you read along in Mark's Gospel at the same time.

One thing should be very obvious from the outset. The story of Jesus that Mark tells is not the same as that told in the other Gospels. The giveaway is length. Mark's story takes sixteen chapters, John, twenty-one chapters, Luke, twenty-four, and Matthew, twenty-eight. In subsequent chapters on the Gospels of Matthew, Luke, and John, we will have to think about why and how they present longer stories.

For now, it is sufficient to note that differing lengths mean different stories.

The ways the Gospels begin and end provide further points of difference. Mark's story begins with the activity of the adult Jesus at 1:14-15. Luke and Matthew begin with stories—different stories—of Jesus' conception and birth. Mark's story ends with an eight-verse account of Jesus' resurrection in which Jesus does not appear! Matthew, Luke, and John end with much longer accounts in which Jesus appears.

3.1 Russian icon (1657) of St. Mark the Evangelist, receiving heavenly inspiration to write; he sits upon a lion, his ecclesiastical symbol. By the hand of Emmanuel Tzanes. Commons.wikimedia.org.

We read, then, the Gospel or good news *according to Mark*—similar to, but not the same as, the Gospels according to Matthew, or Luke, or

John. That phrase "according to" expresses the importance of each Gospel writer's point of view in shaping their telling of the story. Paying attention to the contours of Mark's story alerts us to Mark's interpretation of the significance of Jesus and is an important task in this chapter.

Introduction (1:1-13)

Mark's account of Jesus' public activity begins promptly in verse 14 in chapter 1. In the Gospel's opening thirteen verses, five voices introduce Jesus.

The first voice is that of the Gospel narrator. The narrator names Jesus and with the use of two terms declares Jesus' identity as one commissioned by God, God's agent or representative (1:1). The term "Christ" is the Greek version of the Hebrew term "messiah." It literally means "anointed one." Anointing signifies a person is set apart for a particular role in God's purposes. But here's the catch. There was no clearly defined "job description" for the messiah. Expectations of a messiah were not widespread. And those waiting for a messiah did not have a common expectation. So calling Jesus "Messiah" or "Christ" affirms he is commissioned by God, but it does not specify *what* God has commissioned Jesus to do. How will we know? We'll have to read on.

3.2 "Anointed" Figures

Check out these characters anointed or set apart by God to serve God in their various roles: kings (Ps. 2:2), prophets (1 Kgs. 19:16), priests (Lev. 4:3-5), and even the gentile Persian ruler Cyrus (Isa. 44:28—45:1). In a writing not in the Bible, Psalms of Solomon 17, a king from the line of David is called the Messiah. He will send the Romans out of Jerusalem nonviolently.

The narrator's second term for Jesus, "Son of God," is similar. This term restates God's selection of Jesus as God's representative or agent. In the Hebrew Bible, this term designates people who are agents of God's will and purposes. So kings are designated God's Son, not because they were divine but because they exercised great power and rule on behalf of and in close relationship with God (2 Sam. 7:14; Ps. 2:7). Israel is called God's Son not because Israel was divine but because it enjoyed special covenant relationship with God (Hos. 11:1). Likewise the wise person who does God's will is God's Son or child (Wisd. of Sol. 2). Jesus is introduced as God's agent. What is he to do? Yep, you guessed it. Read on!

The narrator declares this announcement of Jesus' identity "good news" (1:1). This is contested language. The Hebrew Bible uses "good news" to announce God's rule expressed in delivering Jerusalem from its sixth-century-BCE Babylonian oppressors (Isa. 52:7; 61:1). Its use here suggests that we might look for some experience of God's saving rule to be manifested in Jesus' activity in the world under Roman rule. But the language of "good news" is also empire talk. It announces Rome's good news—the birthday and gifts of the emperor Augustus's rule; victories in battle. God and Rome: How will the "good news" of the story of Jesus intersect with Roman power? Are God's purposes and rule identified with or opposed to Rome's empire and rule over some sixty million people? How will we know? Yep, you guessed it. Read on!

The second voice we hear (1:2-3) is identified as the sixth-century prophet Isaiah—though in actual fact, portions of Mal. 3:1 and Exod. 23:20 are included along with Isaiah 40 in verse 2b. Here, the citation from Isaiah refers either to Jesus as a messenger who declares God's coming or to John the Baptist as a messenger declaring Jesus' coming. Either way, the Scripture from Isaiah is read as bearing witness to Jesus' identity in God's purposes. Of course, Isaiah was not originally talking about John or Jesus. But the Gospel makes the link to underscore continuity between what God has done previously and what God is doing in Jesus.

Voice three (1:4-8) belongs to John the Baptist, who prepares people for Jesus' coming. Like Isaiah (and Malachi and Moses), he witnesses to Jesus. These male figures ensure Jesus is center stage.

Voice four (1:9-11) belongs to God. Jesus is baptized by John. The Spirit comes upon Jesus. God from heaven declares Jesus' identity as "my Son, the Beloved." God's declaration repeats and confirms the narrator's announcement of Jesus' identity as agent or Son of God (1:1).

Voice five (1:12-13) is muted but powerful in its cosmic opposition to Jesus as agent of God's purposes. Driven by the Spirit into the wilderness, Jesus confronts Satan or the devil, who "tempts" or "tests" him. We don't hear the devil's voice, but by definition it is opposed to God's purposes. Presumably the devil's "test" comprises trying to turn Jesus away from his identity as God's Son or representative agent.

Thirteen verses and five voices later, we have learned Jesus' identity as God's agent (Christ, Son of God) in accord with the Scriptures, but we do not know yet what he is commissioned to do. And we have learned that while God's purposes are at work in the world, so too are other forces, those of imperial Rome, and the oppositional cosmic force of the devil. How will these various, even competing purposes be resolved? Yep, you guessed it. . . .

Jesus' Powerful and Transforming Activity as God's Agent (1:14–8:30)

Jesus' public activity begins in Galilee, part of the Roman province of Syria. In the first half of the Gospel, his activity is marked by continual displays of power that transform people's lives. These displays of power comprise:

- Preaching: Verses 14-15 refer to Jesus preaching "the gospel [or "good news"] of God" and announcing "the kingdom [or "empire" or "rule"] of God is at hand." Public rhetoric was regarded as a manly activity whereby important men exerted power over people's lives. Jesus' preaching comprises the "gospel/good news of God." The little word "of" signifies the good news comes from God and is about God. More particularly, it concerns God's rule or empire among human beings in Jesus' preaching. What happens when Jesus preaches this good news of God's rule? From 1:14, we learn that it involves a change of direction in thinking and living ("repent") and entrusting oneself to or being faithful to God ("believe"). In

1:38-39, Jesus declares that such proclaiming throughout Galilee is the purpose of his mission. Again, we have to read on to see what impact God's kingdom, manifested by Jesus in Rome's world, has among humans.

- Claiming followers: One impact of God's kingdom is experienced in human lives as Jesus calls people to follow him. So he disrupts the lives of four fishermen, calling them to leave their business, father, and homes to follow him (1:16-20). In 2:13-14, he summons Levi, a tax collector. Subsequently Jesus has twelve followers (3:13-19; 6:7-13). Initially, it seems Jesus only calls men—initially four men (1:16-20), then Levi (2:13-14), then eight more (3:16-20; Levi is not named). But other clues indicate many more followers: in 3:31-35, all those who do the will of God, and in 4:10, "twelve," and "those who were around him." Late in the Gospel, the narrator indicates that women were also among Jesus' followers and were financial supporters (15:40-41). We have to imagine their presence with Jesus throughout the whole narrative as disciples. From all these folks, Jesus demands loyalty, exercising authority over their lives, commanding them to be with him, sending them out to proclaim good news and to cast out demons (3:13-15; 6:7, 12-13), extending Jesus' mission.
- Exorcisms: Jesus exercises authority over evil spirits who control human beings in destructive ways. Demons are agents of the cosmic power Satan, who is at work in the world opposing Jesus' proclamation (4:15). Jesus regularly confronts these spirits, dismisses them, and reclaims the person's well-being (1:21-28, 32; 3:20-27; 7:24-30). These demons are presented as powers active in Rome's rule, including its military. In 5:1-20, the demon who controls a "wild man" living among the tombs introduces itself by the name Legion. A legion was the central unit of the Roman army, comprising some six thousand men. In exorcising legion, Jesus asserts power over the demon and over the demonic powers manifested in Rome's military. He has great power and authority that threaten Rome's power.

- Healings: The Gospel narrates scenes in which Jesus heals sick individuals: Simon Peter's mother-in-law (1:29-31), a leper (1:40-45), a paralyzed man (2:1-12), a man with a withered hand (3:1-6), a woman with a hemorrhage (5:21-43), a dead girl (5:21-43), a deaf man who could not speak (7:31-37), a blind man (8:22-26). Summary scenes narrate many more healings (1:32-34; 3:10; 6:54-56).
- Teaching: Jesus' teaching exercises power over people's thinking. He claims authority to speak on behalf of God, declaring a man's sins to be forgiven (2:1-12), permitting good and life-saving actions on the Sabbath (3:1-6), explaining in parables how God's rule or empire is at work in the world (4:1-34), warning about human traditions that are at odds with God's commandments and explaining that evil comes from the human heart (7:1-23), and claiming the power not of Satan but of the Holy Spirit for his own actions (3:20-30). Not every character welcomes his teaching.
- Creation: Jesus demonstrates great power over the Sea of Galilee twice calming the wind and sea (4:35-41; 6:45-52). These actions recall God's act in creation of taming the sea's chaotic force and setting it in its boundaries (Gen. 1:6-10; Ps. 69:1-3). His walking on the water recalls the image of God controlling the sea by walking on the water (Job 9:8; Ps. 77:16-20). In addition, Jesus twice exhibits power in multiplying limited supplies of bread and fish to feed large crowds (6:30-44; 8:1-10). In each instance, he over-caters, with abundant food left over.

Throughout these first eight chapters, Jesus displays great transforming power. The narrative regularly emphasizes Jesus' authority demonstrated in teaching (1:22, 27), forgiving sin (2:10), and authorizing his followers to cast out demons (3:15; 6:7).

Telling Secrets?

This emphasis on Jesus' great power might explain another element in these first eight chapters. Frequently, when Jesus performs a work of power, he tells the beneficiary and witnesses not to tell anyone. For example, after healing the leper, Jesus says, "See that you say nothing to anyone" (1:44). He gives similar commands to be silent in 3:12 (after many exorcisms), 5:43 (after raising a dead girl), 7:36 (after healing a deaf man), and 8:26 (after healing a blind man).

Why does Jesus at times have a "don't speak, don't tell" policy? Readers have offered various interpretations. Perhaps the writer of the Gospel presents Jesus trying to contain reports of his power (see 1:28). Perhaps he's encouraging people to spread reports about him. As we know, telling someone a secret is a sure way of spreading the news. And the narrator observes that "the more he ordered them to tell no one, the more zealously they proclaimed it" (7:36). Perhaps there is more to be told than accounts of his power. And then, sometimes he commands people to tell their transforming story (5:19).

Threads of Opposition

Another dynamic is in play in the narrative. Whenever power and influence are asserted—as happens through Jesus' actions and words—there is always resistance.

For instance, in chapter 2, the Jerusalem-based, Rome-allied authorities comprising scribes and Pharisees (2:6, 16, 18, 24) dispute with Jesus over observing the Sabbath and over food and eating practices (2:1-3:6). These scribal men occupied positions of power and social status as members of the local ruling group and interpreters of the law. With their teachings and rulings, they shape how society operates and how people live their lives. As far as they are concerned, they are the legitimate interpreters of God's purposes and defenders of the nation's customs and laws. They do not ascribe any legitimacy to a low-status man like Jesus who lacks connections of birth, wealth, literacy, education, and office. They resent his influence.

The conflict begins with their disparaging thoughts about Jesus (2:7)—which Jesus makes public. It escalates with questions to Jesus' disciples about his behaviors (like spies, 2:16). Then they challenge Jesus directly (2:18). Then they make a charge against Jesus' disciples

(2:24). Then they conspire with the supporters of Herod to destroy Jesus (3:6). Subsequently, they again complain to Jesus about the behavior of his disciples (7:1-23). And they demand from Jesus a "sign," a way of speaking about his credentials, that might justify his actions (8:11-13). Jesus refuses to play their game.

3.3 The Roles and Socially Elevated Position of a Powerful Scribe (Sir. 38:24—39:11)

Who are scribes and what roles do they perform?

The wisdom of the scribe depends on the opportunity of leisure;
only the one who has little business can become wise.
How can one become wise who handles the plow,
and who glories in the shaft of a goad,
who drives oxen and is occupied with their work,
and whose talk is about bulls?
He sets his heart on plowing furrows,
and he is careful about fodder for the heifers.
So it is with every artisan and master artisan
who labors by night as well as by day. . . .
So it is with the smith, sitting by the anvil, intent on his iron-work. . . .
So it is with the potter sitting at his work and turning the wheel with his feet. . . .
All these rely on their hands,
and all are skillful in their own work.
Without them no city can be inhabited,
and wherever they live, they will not go hungry.
Yet they are not sought out for the council of the people,
nor do they attain eminence in the public assembly.
They do not sit in the judge's seat,
nor do they understand the decisions of the courts;
they cannot expound discipline or judgment,
and they are not found among the rulers.
But they maintain the fabric of the world,
and their concern is for the exercise of their trade.
How different the one who devotes himself
to the study of the law of the Most High!
He seeks out the wisdom of all the ancients,
and is concerned with prophecies;
he preserves the sayings of the famous
and penetrates the subtleties of parables. . . .
He serves among the great
and appears before rulers;
he travels in foreign lands
and learns what is good and evil in the human lot. . . .
Many will praise his understanding;
it will never be blotted out.
His memory will not disappear,
and his name will live through all generations.
(Sir. 38:24—39:9 NRSV, selections)

Of course, this conflict will become deadly in the second part of the Gospel. But already in this first half, there is an indication that the alliance of ruling authorities will not tolerate challenge to its power and influence over people's lives. This note is sounded right at the beginning of the account of Jesus' public activity. His activities are introduced in 1:14 with a very short clause, "Now after John was arrested, Jesus came to Galilee" (1:14a). The narrator does not tell us what John has done until chapter 6, but the reference casts a shadow over the narrative. John's arrest is significant because John has been allied with Jesus in preparing people for his ministry and in baptizing Jesus (1:4-11). A threat to John signals danger to Jesus.

3.2 Salome with the Head of John the Baptist, by Caravaggio (1610). National Gallery, London. Commons.wikimedia.org.

In chapter 6, we learn what happened to John the Baptist. He has spoken truth to power and pays the price for criticizing the Roman puppet "king" Herod Antipas. Herod was the Rome-appointed ruler, or tetrarch, of Galilee and Perea (4 BCE–39 CE). John rebukes Herod for marrying his brother's wife, a marriage prohibited in Lev. 18:16; 20:21 as adulterous (Mark 6:18). The rest of the scene narrates the hows and whys of the consequence—John is executed. The scene anticipates Jesus' fate.

Jesus' Wobbly Followers

Another sort of resistance emerges. This resistance undermines the picture of Jesus' power that carries all before it. As we have noted, Jesus calls followers (3:13-19) who leave behind jobs and families (1:16-20, 29-31; 2:13). They take Jesus' teaching seriously and ask questions to gain more understanding (4:10, 34). They boldly and bravely go out in mission to proclaim and exorcize (6:7-13). All of this seems good and virtuous.

Yet all is not well. The last name in the list of twelve male disciples is Judas. It has a descriptor, "who betrayed him" (3:19). Within Jesus' inner circle exists a traitor.

There is more trouble. At times, his followers seem to have no clue as to who Jesus is. After Jesus calms the storm the first time, they respond: "Who then is this, that even the wind and sea obey him?" (4:41). And they seem unable to learn. When Jesus appears to them in the second storm, they do not cry out, "Jesus, we knew we could rely on you to rescue us." Instead, they "were terrified" at his appearing and "utterly astounded" when he calmed the wind and sea (6:50-51).

Likewise, Jesus multiplies bread and fish for a hungry crowd (6:30-44). Two chapters later, faced with another hungry crowd, we might expect the disciples to say to Jesus, "Jesus, you fed that last crowd—do it again." Instead, showing no understanding, they say, "How can one feed these people with bread here in the desert?" (8:4; cf. 6:52). Subsequently when Jesus quizzes them about the feedings, they remember they had witnessed them but have no insight into their significance (8:14-21).

3.3 The Storm on the Sea, ca. 1020. The disciples fear being capsized while Jesus sleeps. From The Gospels of the Abbess Hitda of Meschede; Hessische Landes- und Hochschulbibliothek, Darmstadt. Commons.wikimedia.org.

Yet when Jesus has another quiz for them about his identity, the group's spokesperson, Peter, offers the correct answer: "You are the Messiah" (8:30). This is Jesus' identity that the narrator declared in 1:1. Peter's correct answer contrasts with the false answers given by others that confuse Jesus with John the Baptist, Elijah, or a prophet (8:28). Yet immediately, Jesus "sternly ordered them not to tell anyone about him." Why does he order their silence? Why the secrecy? The command suggests that they have more to learn about what this term "messiah" means (8:30). We have to read on.

By the end of this first part of the Gospel (8:30), then, we have seen frequent demonstrations of great power from Jesus. His rhetoric is powerful. He makes claims on human lives. He casts out demons. He heals diseases. He resists the power of the Jerusalem-based, Rome-allied authorities. He calms stormy seas and multiplies limited supplies of bread and fish into abundant feasts. Yet with the assertion of his power and influence among the people, opposition and resistance begin to emerge involving the Jerusalem-based ruling alliance and his often nonunderstanding disciples. While they have responded positively to Jesus' call to follow him, a betrayer is in their midst and they seem at times slow to learn.

Jesus Commissioned to Suffer, Die, and Rise Again (8:31—16:8)

Things change significantly in the second half of the Gospel story. We get new information in 8:31. The verse functions in effect as a plot summary for the rest of the Gospel:

> Then he began to teach them that the Son of Man must undergo great suffering, and be rejected by the elders, the chief priests, and the scribes, and be killed, and after three days rise again.

Twice more, Jesus declares his approaching death in Jerusalem and resurrection, first in 9:30-32, and then again in 10:32b-34:

> He took the twelve aside again and began to tell them what was to happen to him, saying, "See, we are going up to Jerusalem, and the Son of Man will be handed over to the chief priests and the scribes, and they will condemn him to death; then they will hand him over to the Gentiles; they will mock him, and spit upon him, and flog him, and kill him; and after three days he will rise again."

The repetition underscores the importance of this new information. The declarations explicitly identify two key players—Jesus and the opponents—who are central to the second half of the Gospel. They also imply a third key player, God, whose purposes Jesus carries out.

Jesus' declaration that he must die brings a contesting response from Peter. While he confesses Jesus to be the Messiah, he does not know what the term means. Jesus rebukes Peter for misunderstanding, for focusing on "human things" instead of being open to the revelation of "divine things" (8:32-33). Jesus then goes on to announce that his followers must be willing to take up their cross—the first indication that he will die on a cross—and that he as the Son of Man will return in glory to establish God's rule or empire in power (8:34—9:1).

3.4 Son of Man

The term "Son of Man" embraces Jesus' death, resurrection, and return (8:31). The term can mean simply a "human one" or a "mortal" (so Ezek. 2:1-3), and can be another way of referring to oneself as a person with authority ("I," see 2:10, 28). But the term also occurs in the book of Daniel, where it refers to a heavenly figure to whom God entrusts "dominion and glory and kingship . . . that shall never be destroyed" and which "all peoples, nations, and languages serve" (Dan. 7:13-14). The Gospel's presentation of Jesus as the resurrected and returning Son of Man presents Jesus anticipating these future roles as God's agent and ruler after his death.

In the following transfiguration scene (9:1-8), Jesus momentarily displays this glorious power. Echoing his words at Jesus' baptism (1:11), God confirms Jesus' teaching and again asserts Jesus' identity: "This is my Son, the Beloved" (9:7). And underscoring Jesus' teaching in the previous scene about his death and resurrection, God adds, "Listen to him."

In chapter 10, Jesus acts on his declaration about his upcoming fate. He leaves Galilee with his disciples and heads to Jerusalem. In chapter 11, he enters Jerusalem, the setting for the rest of the Gospel, where conflict between Jesus and the Jerusalem leadership centered on the temple escalates. Jesus is welcomed into the city by a crowd (11:1-11). He goes to the temple and drives out those involved in the commercial and monetary transactions typical of ancient temples. He protests these bank-like activities, condemns the temple as a "den for robbers," and, citing Isa. 56:7, declares it should be "a house of prayer for all the nations." Such actions criticize the elite's leadership and bring a predictable response. The chief priests and scribes regard him as a rival with increasing influence over the crowd; they look to kill him (11:18).

The conflict escalates. The temple-based Jerusalem leaders—chief priests, scribes, and elders—demand to know by what authority Jesus carries out his activity (11:27-33). They have not sanctioned his activity, but the Gospel's audience knows that God has sanctioned him (1:11; 9:7). They, though, do not recognize God's presence in his activity. He gets the better of them in the verbal sparring and refuses to answer their question.

Jesus then tells a parable of the vineyard and its tenants who refuse to pay rent to the owner. This parable is directed against the leaders. It shows them to be leaders who have refused to render to God the allegiance and "fruits" of faithful leadership that they owe to God. They reject God's messengers, including God's Son or agent, Jesus. Jesus concludes this stunning attack by asserting that God will destroy them. They hear Jesus' condemnation and seek to arrest him (12:12).

Thereafter, through chapter 12, Jesus verbally spars with them. Jesus wins the contests; by verse 34, "no one dared to ask him any questions." The chapter ends with Jesus denouncing the scribes who, according to Jesus' criticism, love societal honor and exploit widows economically (12:38-40).

In chapter 13, Jesus continues the attack. While he talks *about* his opponents and their world, he does not talk directly *to* them. Instead, he talks to his disciples. In response to their questions, he announces that the world shaped and governed by these Rome-allied and Rome-sanctioned leaders will end. Their temple will be destroyed (13:1-8) and his followers will be persecuted (13:9-23), but he will return in power to establish God's reign (13:24-27). He warns his followers to be alert and watchful for that day, whose timing no one knows (13:32-37).

Perspectives on Jesus' Death

Chapters 14 and 15 show the conflict to be a matter of life and death. But these chapters interweave a range of perspectives. Jesus' death is multilayered and complex.

The Power Group: Jerusalem Leaders and Pilate; Jesus' Death as His Defeat

At first glance, Jesus' death seems to be the victory of the ruling elite, who eliminate this challenge to their power. In 14:1-2, the chief priests and scribes seek to arrest and kill the popular Jesus, but they have to be careful. Such an action during the festival of Passover, when many visitors have come to Jerusalem, might stir up the crowds against the leaders. Jesus has, of course, previously named these leaders as the ones who will put him to death (8:31; 10:32-34). And the conflicts of chapters 11–13 set up their actions against him. With Judas' help, they arrest Jesus (14:43-51), condemn him for speaking against the temple and claiming to enact God's purposes and power (14:53-65), and hand him over to the Roman governor Pilate for crucifixion as "king of the Jews" (15:1-5). That, at least, is one of the things that Pilate chooses to focus on among the "many things" of which the leaders accuse Jesus (15:3-4).

Pilate's involvement is crucial. Rome commonly ruled territories like Judea through governors appointed by the emperor or Senate in Rome. These governors, though, did not and could not rule alone. They often respected local ruling structures already in place, so they made alliances with local ruling elites. Both parties needed each other to rule. But these relationships were often tense, with the two parties contesting power and trying to gain an advantage over each other. Governors sought to maintain Rome as the supreme power over provincial leaders. In Judea, for example, the governor appointed the chief priest who thus needed to keep the governor happy in order to keep his job. And the governor retained the right to decide on the use of the death penalty. Hence the Jerusalem elite have to bring Jesus to Pilate for execution (15:1).

Pilate of course knows that any enemy of his local allies is an enemy of his. He and his allies have a common interest in protecting their power, wealth, and status. The Jerusalem leaders charge Jesus with being "king of the Jews" (15:2). This serious charge amounts to sedition. The charge is not unlikely. Jesus has announced from the beginning that he manifests the presence of the kingdom or empire of God. Kingdoms always have kings or rulers. The problem is that only local kings or rulers appointed by Rome are legitimate rulers. While Jesus is sanctioned by God, he is not sanctioned by Rome. Rome executed unsanctioned kings as threatening Roman power. That's what the Jerusalem leaders ask Pilate to do with Jesus.

However, if Pilate automatically and immediately consents to their request, he has made himself their lackey and conceded too much power to them. So Pilate plays a game with them. He first offers to release Jesus (15:9), but when the crowd, manipulated by the chief priests, shouts for Barabbas's release and Jesus' crucifixion, Pilate makes them beg even more by asking about Jesus' crimes (15:14). Then, posing as a ruler sensitive to public pressure, Pilate hands Jesus over to be crucified (15:15). In the process, Pilate has gained power by making the leaders beg for Jesus' crucifixion, reinforcing their dependence on him to get this task accomplished, and by seeming to yield to their demands when Jesus' death also serves his interests.

3.4 *The Merciful Christ* (between 1500 and 1700); from the Franciscan Monastery in Pjrzemyśl, Poland. Christ mocked and scourged has been one of the most prevalent themes in Christian art. Commons.wikimedia.org.

They immediately crucify Jesus as "king of the Jews" (15:21-39), taunting and mocking him (15:29-32). They have won. They have removed a threat to their control among the people. Or so it seems.

Jesus' Death as His Victory

Chapter 16 offers yet another perspective. The eight verses of chapter 16 demonstrate that Jesus' death is not the end of the story. The Jerusalem-based elites have not won. Several women find Jesus' tomb empty. A "young man" looking like an angel (16:5) announces that Jesus has been raised from the dead and plans to meet with the rest of the disciples in Galilee. God's raising of Jesus from the dead reveals that the power of the ruling elite is limited. It is not infinite. They can't keep Jesus dead. And the language of being "raised" or "resurrection" signifies that a new age has begun that will end the injustice and oppression of Rome's rule (chapter 13) and inaugurate a new age of justice.

3.5 Resurrection Is an Eschatological Event

The notion of resurrection emerges very clearly in the second century BCE in the context of faithfulness to God's will in the midst of political-religious oppression. The book of 2 Maccabees narrates the deaths of several martyrs who refuse the edict of the Seleucid ruler Antiochus IV Epiphanes to abandon observance of the law. In 2 Maccabees 7, a mother witnesses the faithful resistance and torture of her seven sons before she herself is killed. Their tongues are cut out, they are scalped, their hands and feet are cut off, and they are literally fried in a pan. During their torture, they assert their confident faith that God will raise up to new life the faithful who die in this way (2 Macc. 7:9, 14, 23). In the resurrection, God will restore their bodies (2 Macc. 7:10-11) and their family relationships (2 Macc. 7:29). Resurrection, then, is somatic and social, an eschatological event, one of a cluster of events linked to the new age when God will establish God's reign in full. It is an act of God's justice that honors faithfulness to death in oppressive circumstances when God did not rescue people before death. So in declaring that God has "raised" Jesus (Mark 16:5), the angel points to the beginning of the time when God completes God's purposes.

This announcement that God has raised Jesus does not come as a surprise. In his predictions of his imminent death, Jesus also announced that he would be raised "after three days" (8:31; 9:31; 10:34). That is, Jesus goes willingly from Galilee to Jerusalem knowing that death *and* resurrection are ahead of him. He goes trusting that God will raise him from the dead. Demonstrating the same trust, on several occasions he announces that as the victorious Son of Man, he will return in power and glory to set up God's kingdom or empire in its fullness (8:38—9:1; 13:24-27; 14:62).

Jesus' Death as Inevitable

A very different perspective on Jesus' death emerges in the scene immediately after the leaders' plot to kill Jesus (14:1-2). In 14:3-9, an unnamed woman crashes the party in the house of Simon the leper. She breaks open a bottle of oil and pours it on Jesus' head as an action of anointing (14:3). Some of the (male) guests complain about a waste of money (14:4-5). But Jesus defends and praises her action as "a good service for me" (14:6).

What has she done? The Gospel scene does not describe her motivation, but her action of anointing Jesus is significant. It expresses the recognition that he is a king or emperor, who represents God's rule or empire among humans. Her action reflects the understanding that God's reign or kingdom is drawing near in Jesus and his actions. She anoints him as a new and true emperor who represents God's empire that challenges, imitates, and will eventually replace Rome's empire when Jesus returns in power and glory (13:24-27).

Of course, such a claim is treasonous. Not surprisingly, the scene presents Jesus interpreting her action—without asking her—as anointing him for burial (14:8). Jesus has announced three times previously that he must die (8:31; 9:31; 10:32-34). He has expressed the realistic conviction that those who challenge imperial power often pay the price. In Jesus' view, she has understood what the male disciples were not able to understand (8:32; 9:32).

In his predictions and the scene with the woman who anoints him, Jesus seems to accept his fate serenely. Yet at other moments, it is not so. The Gospel also presents Jesus' trust wavering in Gethsemane when, "distressed and agitated . . . and deeply grieved," he asks God three times to remove from him "this cup"—a symbol of suffering (14:32-42).

But he resolves his doubts by consenting: "not what I want but what you want" (14:36). In consenting, Jesus gives himself to die trusting God's power and purposes. He does not avoid this confrontation with the ruling elite. He does not run away. He does not hide. He is not taken by surprise nor defeated by their greater power. He participates actively in his own death—and experiences God's life-giving power in his resurrection.

The Paradigm of the Righteous Sufferer

This claim of the inevitability of Jesus' death needs more reflection. Some have understood Jesus' announcement that he "must" die (8:31) as expressing the view that God has preplanned and predestined Jesus to suffer and die. This view interprets Mark 10:45 ("the Son of Man came not to be served but to serve and give his life a ransom for many") as conveying that Jesus' death carries out God's plan to pay the penalty for sin in the place of others.

Yet numerous interpreters have been troubled by this view. This theological claim constructs God as a murderer who is also guilty of child abuse involving God's own Son. Such a God who consigns God's own agent to death does not seem worthy of worship, nor compatible with other biblical emphases on God's love and mercy, nor on God's life-giving power in the world. Nor does the verse use the language of paying a penalty.

Another view interprets "must" to mean that Jesus' death is a political inevitability. That is, it highlights human involvement in Jesus's death rather than divine purposes. Without Pilate and the Jerusalem leaders, without Judas' betrayal and the fickleness of the disciples, it would not have happened. Jesus dies because he has challenged the powers that be, and the empire always strikes back to remove its opponents.

This view recognizes that the biblical tradition includes scenarios of prophetic figures whose lives are threatened or taken by ruling figures who resent their challenges to unjust uses of power. We might think of Pharaoh's pursuit of Moses and the slaves (Pharaoh's workforce!)

fleeing Egypt (Exodus 14), or Ahab and Jezebel's death threats against Elijah (1 Kings 19), or Daniel tossed into the lion's den by king Nebuchadnezzar, or the martyrs who resisted Antiochus Epiphanes (1 Maccabees 1; 2 Maccabees 6–7). In Mark's Gospel, we can recall John the Baptist's death in chapter 6 and the parable Jesus told in 12:1-12 against the Jerusalem leaders that identifies them as killing a long line of slaves (read "prophets") sent by the owner (read "God") to the tenants (read "Jerusalem leaders"). Jesus' death is politically inevitable, a certain result of his challenge to and rejection by the political leaders.

This view interprets Jesus' giving his life in Mark 10:45 in terms of a moral confrontation with oppressive rulers (so 10:42-43). His death reveals the destructive force of their rule and its self-interested nature in protecting their own privilege. Jesus' resurrection shows their power to be limited and not ultimate, freeing people to live against it as a community of solidarity and resistance with the realization that its power is limited and temporary. Moreover, with the demonstration of God's power over evil and death, people live in this power, anticipating the completion of God's purposes.

Yet while this second view makes considerable sense of the Gospel story, it does not adequately account for the Gospel's conviction that Jesus' death is part of God's will. So a third view has tried to bridge aspects of both positions.

It claims that Jesus' death is a political inevitability that is embraced within God's purposes, but without claiming it is predestined and preplanned by God. This view affirms Jesus' death as both a political consequence and of theological significance. It recognizes that the Gospel employs a Hebrew Bible paradigm or form of spirituality called "the righteous sufferer" to interpret Jesus' death.

Woven into the narrative of Jesus' arrest, condemnation, and death in chapters 14 and 15 are a number of motifs from Psalm 22. This psalm was not written about Jesus. It had existed in the Jewish tradition and had been used in worship for hundreds of years without reference to Jesus. The writer of the Gospel, though, uses echoes or motifs from it to interpret Jesus' death.

The most well-known of these motifs comes in Mark 15:34 with Jesus' cry from the cross, "My God, my God, why have you forsaken me?" This comes from the opening verse of Psalm 22, as the psalmist laments his suffering and God's apparent absence from and indifference to it. The psalmist's suffering comes primarily from an unidentified third party and comprises social hostility. He describes how he is surrounded by enemies (22:6-8, 12-13), that people mock him (22:6-8) and shake their heads at him (22:7). In addition, he suffers physically. His body is out of joint and his mouth dry (22:14-15). He also suffers psychologically and materially since he is surrounded by evildoers (22:16), who gloat over him and divide his clothing (22:18).

God initially seems uncaring and unresponsive; yet toward the end of the psalm, somehow God intervenes (though the psalm does not say how) and the psalmist celebrates God's saving presence (22:22b-26). He declares that even all the nations will join in the worship of God (22:27-28).

There are extensive points of contact between this psalm of the righteous sufferer and Mark's account of Jesus' suffering and death in Mark 14–16. A table demonstrates the echoes between the two texts.

Psalm 22	**Description of Circumstances**	**Instances in Mark 14–16**
22:1	Cry of Godforsakenness	15:34 Jesus from the cross
22:6-8, 12-13	Surrounded by enemies	14:1-2, 10-11, 18-21, 26-31, 43-65; 15:1-38
22:6-8	Mocking	14:65; 15:16-20, 29-32
22:7	Shaking their Heads	15:29
22:14-15	Dry mouth and needing drink	15:23, 36
22:16	Company of evildoers	14:43-65; 15:1-38
22:18	Dividing clothing by casting lots	15:24
22:22b-26	Announcement and celebration of God's saving intervention	16:1-8
22:28	Gentile acknowledgement	15:39

What is the impact of these connections with Psalm 22 and its presentation of the righteous sufferer rescued by God? Mark 14–16 present Jesus as a righteous person, one who is faithful to God's will yet suffers at the hands of the wicked, namely, the Jerusalem leaders and their ally Pilate. The chapters present God's intervention to save or vindicate Jesus in his resurrection. He has not been abandoned by God, but God acts justly, mercifully, and powerfully to intervene in raising him. Even a gentile centurion acknowledges Jesus' identity ("Son of God"), consistent with the narrator's declaration of Jesus' identity (1:1) and with God's declaration (1:11; 9:7). Jesus' death, then, is accounted for as a political action carried out by powerful leaders in Jerusalem to secure their own position and advantages, but embraced within God's purposes as a demonstration of God's justice and life-giving power.

Other Characters and Other Dimensions of Jesus' Death

While the Gospel narrative shows Jesus to be resolute in his tasks of proclaiming and manifesting the "good news of God" amid opposition that leads to his death, the same cannot be said for others who accompany him in chapters 14–15.

First is the group of twelve male disciples. Peter, James, and John fail to stay awake and support Jesus as he faces death (14:32-42). Judas, identified as Jesus' betrayer at his first mention (3:19), allies himself with Jesus' enemies, the chief priests. They pay him money in return for his handing over of Jesus (14:10-11). Subsequently, Judas identifies Jesus with the prearranged sign—a kiss—and Jesus is arrested (14:43-49).

The arrest of Jesus causes the male disciples to flee (14:50). On several previous occasions, they have chosen to act on the basis of fear rather than faith. They do so twice, for example, when they are in the boat in the storms (4:40; 6:50). Here again, fear seems to be the basis for their action. They abandon Jesus, even though previously they had declared that they would always remain loyal to him (14:31).

Peter follows the arrested Jesus at a distance to a meeting of the chief priests, elders, and scribes (14:54). Outside in the courtyard warming himself at a fire, he is three times identified by a servant girl as being "with Jesus." Each time, Peter denies the association (14:66-72). Ironically, back in 3:14, Jesus appointed the disciples to be "with him"; Peter denies the very core of his calling and identity as a disciple. After the third time, he leaves, weeping (14:72). Peter's fall is great. He had vowed "vehemently" that even though all the disciples abandon Jesus, he would not (14:29-31). Jesus had not believed him, predicting that Peter would behave like all the rest (14:30).

In similar style, a young man—described with the disciple buzzword of "following him"—also runs away (15:51-52). His clothing, a "linen cloth," connects him to Jesus' death. Jesus is buried in a "linen cloth" (15:46). The young man escapes the attempts to capture him and runs off naked. His fear has been laid bare.

Other characters are caught up in the drama. Barabbas, a rebel against Roman order who has been taken prisoner, becomes a pawn in the political power games involving Pilate and the Jerusalem leaders, and gets an unexpected reprieve (15:6-15). Simon of Cyrene, coming into Jerusalem, finds himself compelled to carry Jesus' cross. Jesus had previously instructed his followers that "taking up their cross" was the way of discipleship (8:34). The image refers to embracing a way of life marked by opposition to Roman imperial values and structures, as well as by harsh rejection from the imperial status quo, even to the point of death. Simon carries out a quintessential discipleship action.

A centurion on guard at Jesus' cross—probably a gentile soldier, though the verse does not say so—witnesses Jesus' death and announces, "Truly this man was God's Son" (15:39). This is the first time in the Gospel narrative that a human being has announced Jesus' identity as God's Son, thereby echoing God's announcements of Jesus' identity (1:11; 9:7).[1] But what does the centurion mean? Interpreters have long debated whether this is a confession or an ironic sneer. If it is the former, it signifies a climactic moment in the story. Only at the cross, only after reading the whole Gospel account that spans both Jesus' life-giving power *and* his weakness and death, can anyone

1. Notice that in 3:11 and 5:7 (cf. also 1:24) demons use this term for Jesus. We might say that a confession only in terms of Jesus' power and without reference to his death is demonic.

confess Jesus' identity accurately. Understanding Jesus as commissioned to manifest God's power and suffer death at the hands of powerful humans makes sense of Jesus' lack of warm response to Peter's confession in 8:29 ("you are the Messiah") when Jesus tells him not to tell anyone. A confession made only in response to Jesus' power is inadequate.

On the other hand, it might be a sneer with which the centurion, a representative of Roman power, marks the victory of Roman power over a troublemaker. If so, it is nevertheless significant. As we have seen above, it is only an *apparent* victory since Rome can't keep him dead and Jesus will return to establish God's empire over all—the end of Rome's rule. And the sneer is ironic—the centurion would speak more truly than he knows, agreeing with God's verdict on Jesus' life *and* death.

If it is a sneer at the dead Jesus, the actions of Joseph of Arimathea provide a significant contrast (15:42-47). Joseph is a wealthy and powerful Jerusalem leader, a member of the council that had gathered with the chief priest to condemn Jesus (14:53-65). He is described as one who is waiting for God's kingdom, precisely what Jesus has been announcing and enacting throughout. For some reason that is not specified, he decides now to honor the body of Jesus, crucified as a political rebel and wannabe king. He honors him with an honorable burial.

One group of followers, though, has not run away. The women who are identified in 15:40-42 as Jesus' followers in Galilee and who had provided support for him are at the cross. They had come to Jerusalem and witnessed his crucifixion. Several of them come to his tomb after the Sabbath to anoint Jesus' dead body (16:1). Ironically, this action suggests that they had not understood Jesus' teaching about resurrection. At the tomb, they learn Jesus has been raised (16:6). An angel sends them to Galilee to tell the "disciples and Peter" that he will meet them there. The angel commissions the women to be the first preachers of the resurrection gospel. But "they went out and fled from the tomb, for terror and amazement had seized them; and they said nothing to anyone, for they were afraid" (Mark 16:8).

It seems that the women disciples also choose fear rather than faithfully carrying out their commission. At the end of the story we, the Gospel audience, are left with the angel's commission to "go and tell" and with the same choice—faithful telling or fearful silence.

Questions for Review and Reflection

1. What is the significance of the phrase "according to" in identifying the Gospel as "the Gospel according to Mark?"
2. Read the opening thirteen verses of Mark. What features in these verses does the chapter identify? What else do you notice in these introductory verses?
3. The chapter identifies Mark 1:14—8:30 as the story of Jesus as "God's Powerful and Transforming Agent." Of what/whom is Jesus an agent, and how does Jesus do his transforming work?
4. But also in this first section of the Gospel up to 8:30, there are some other emphases. What do you make of the Gospel's emphasis on secrets? On threads of opposition? On wobbly followers?
5. In your reading of Mark 1:14—8:30, are there other features that you notice? Why are they important?
6. The chapter identifies the second part of the Gospel as the story of Jesus commissioned to suffer, die, and rise again (8:31—16:8). It suggests four perspectives on Jesus' death: as defeat, as victory, as inevitable, as that of the righteous sufferer based on Psalm 22. Review each perspective.
7. What do you think of the suggestion that Psalm 22 informs the narrative of Jesus' death in chapters 14–15? Why might only some parts of the psalm have been adapted in this way?
8. What other dimensions of Jesus' death do characters such as the disciples (including Judas and Peter), the young man, Barabbas, Simon of Cyrene, the centurion, and the women contribute?
9. What does it mean to say Jesus' resurrection is an eschatological event?

4

Mark: Roman Social Upheavals, Propaganda, and Urban Misery

Mark's Gospel, as I outlined in the last chapter, tells a story of Jesus that combines power and weakness, secrecy and disclosure, followers and opponents, life and death.

Along the way, it also tells the story of Jesus' male and female followers, often uncomprehending and often more fearful than faithful. They are privileged to be called to be with Jesus (1:16-20; 2:13-14; 3:14; 15:40-41). They are entrusted with the responsibilities of continuing and extending Jesus' mission—to proclaim, exorcize, heal (3:14b-15; 6:7-13; 13:10), and to feed hungry people (6:37). They are warned about the harsh realities and challenges of following Jesus. Awaiting them, according to Mark's Jesus, are troubles and persecution (4:17); pressures from "the cares of the world, the lure of wealth, and desire for other things" (4:18); appearances before councils, governors and kings, and beatings in synagogues (13:9-11); lives of self-denial and taking up the cross (8:34); foregoing the desire to be first or great (9:35; 10:43); divisions in families and betrayal by family members (13:12);

and experiences of hatred (13:13). And they are promised, if they persevere and remain alert (10:29-30; 13:13, 32-37), great reward in the present and in the future, namely, participation in the life of the age (10:30) or in the establishment of the fullness of God's reign at Jesus' return (13:26-27).

In this chapter, I ask about the circumstances from which the Gospel emerged and to which it was addressed. Or in other words, might this depiction of Jesus—which combines power and weakness with the Gospel's presentation of discipleship in terms of fear and the need for courageous faithfulness in facing troubles and hardships and in carrying out these responsibilities—be shaped by and address followers in similar challenging situations? Might we think of the Gospel of Mark as a story-sermon told to encourage and empower struggling or hard-pressed followers? Might the Gospel story be a word on target that does encouraging and empowering homiletical or preaching and pastoral work among followers of Jesus?

4.1 This *quadrans*, the lowest-value Roman coin, is mentioned in Mark 12:42 as the value of the coins the widow contributes to the temple treasury. Commons.wikimedia.org, courtesy of Classical Numismatic Group.

In asking these questions, I make an assumption that the Gospel was written in and for a specific set of circumstances and that those circumstances influence the telling of the story. I do not mean to suggest that the Gospel is contained by these circumstances or that it cannot reach beyond them to audiences of other times and places. Two thousand years of use in church communities—and counting—indicate that such a claim could not possibly be true. One of the signs of any influential creative work is its ability to touch people beyond its immediate circumstances of origin, even while it continues to bear the marks of its origin (language, subject, ideology, settings, or media). So here we think about possible interactions between the Gospel and its circumstances and audience of origin. This focus on circumstances that may have influenced the telling of the Gospel story in turn opens up some vistas for contemporary audiences to engage with the Gospel.

Time, Place, and Sociopolitical Structures?

The quest for the Gospel's circumstances of origin, however, is complicated. Unfortunately, we do not have original manuscripts, or "autographs," which identify the author, date, and place of writing. Conventionally, the Gospel has been understood to have been written sometime around 70 CE. This date is arrived at on the basis of Mark 13:1-2:

> As he came out of the temple, one of his disciples said to him, "Look, Teacher, what large stones and what large buildings!" Then Jesus asked him, "Do you see these great buildings? Not one stone will be left here upon another; all will be thrown down."

This passage presents Mark's Jesus predicting the downfall of the Jerusalem temple. It is of course possible that Jesus predicted the temple's destruction some forty or so years before it happened. Possible—but not very likely. Nothing around the year 30 CE suggested such a catastrophe. In fact, Herod was rebuilding it, and it seemed here to stay for quite some time! And 13:1-2 is very vague in details—nothing about when or how the destruction might happen. In a sense, everything will fall down sooner or later!

More likely, we have a *vaticinium ex eventu*. This Latin phrase literally means "prophecy from the outcome." It denotes a literary technique that attributes to a prominent past figure a prediction of a future event when in fact the event has already happened and the writer is looking back on the event. So Mark 13:1-2, then, more likely looks back on the recent destruction of Jerusalem and the temple by the Romans in 70 CE and after the event attributes a future prediction to Jesus. On this basis, I suggest a likely date of about 71–72 CE for the writing for Mark's Gospel.

As to the place of writing, there is no certainty, but we do have a couple of possible scenarios. One view locates the Gospel's composition in Syria or northern Galilee. Another view that circulated in the early church locates its composition in Rome.

To be quite honest, I do not think this matter of Mark's place of origin can be solved with any certainty one way or the other. Those in favor of Mark's origin in Syria or Galilee note the Gospel's focus on Galilee rather than Jerusalem or Judea for the initial setting of the story (1:9, 14-20, 28, 39) and for the resurrection (14:28; 16:7). They also appeal to the Gospel's numerous rural images such as sowing seed (14:3-20), ripening grain (4:26-29), mustard seeds (4:26-29), and vineyards (12:1-9). Especially important are connections suggested between chapter 13 and the war in Judea with the Romans that led to the destruction of Jerusalem in 66–70 CE.

But much of this is hardly convincing. Since Jesus performed his ministry in Galilee and Judea, the story has to be set there; this says nothing about where it was written. Many stories have settings far away from where a writer lives. Likewise, one can write about rural and agricultural practices without living in such an area. Much of the ancient world was rural, so many folks had at last some familiarity with agricultural practices. And one can refer to historical events without proximity of either time or distance.

The Gospel's connection with Rome appears in the writings of several early church figures. The late second-century bishop Irenaeus makes the claim, and it is passed along by subsequent writers. Irenaeus links the Gospel's writing with a character named Mark who is also linked in a vague way with the apostle Peter and with Rome.

4.1 Irenaeus's Testimony regarding Mark

While Peter and Paul were preaching at Rome, and laying the foundations of the Church. After their departure, Mark, the disciple and interpreter of Peter, did also hand down to us in writing what had been preached by Peter. (*Adversus haereses* 3.1.3)

There has been much debate as to the meaning and historical accuracy of Irenaeus's material. It may well be shaped by 1 Pet. 5:13, in which the author refers to "my son Mark." It is very doubtful, though, that the apostle Peter wrote the two letters that use his name. So perhaps the tradition linking Mark, Rome, and Peter sought to attribute authority to Mark's Gospel by associating it with a powerful imperial and ecclesial location (Rome) and a leading male apostle (Peter). Nevertheless, this traditional link with Rome has continued to exert strong influence.

Other factors have been suggested to strengthen a possible link to Rome. These include the Roman, not Jewish, practice of a woman being able to initiate divorce (Mark 10:12) and the Roman, not Syrian, coin, a *kodrantēs*, referred to in 12:42 ("penny," though there is some doubt about its use only in Rome). In addition, Latin terms appear—a *modios* in 4:21 as a measure of grain; *legiōn* in 5:9, 15; and *kentyriōn* in 15:39 (to note a few). Twice the narrative explains items by linking them to Latin terms. So in 12:42, the "two copper coins" are explained with the term *kodrantēs* to signify their minimal value, and in 15:16, the "palace or courtyard" is explained by the Latin term *praetorium* meaning "headquarters."

But how much these data tell us about the place of the Gospel's writing is dubious. They at least suggest an author and audience familiar with some Latin terms. Latin was, of course, not exclusive to Rome, and basic terms were widely known across the empire. And the terms used are mainly economic and military terms that probably had widespread recognition.

Pick One? Rome

So while both the Syrian and Roman setting have some plausibility, a case to prefer one over the other does not seem compelling to me. What to do? I am going to choose one location—the city of Rome—and think about how Jesus-followers living in the city in the early 70s might have engaged the Gospel. Why Rome? Its choice is not entirely arbitrary. I choose Rome not because I am persuaded the Gospel was *written* there—I don't know—but because we can be fairly sure that it was, at least, *read* there. The early church traditions that I mentioned above make a strong case for associating Mark's Gospel with Rome. And we know for sure that there were Jesus-followers in the city. Paul, writing perhaps in the late 50s, some fifteen or so years before Mark's Gospel, greets twenty-eight of them by name, both Jews and gentiles, men and women, and refers to others who seem to be members of house or apartment churches (Rom. 16:5, 14b, 15b). How might these Jesus-followers living in Rome have engaged Mark's story of the powerful yet suffering Jesus?

Reading Mark in Rome

I suggest that being a Jesus-follower—addressed by Mark's Gospel—was hard work in the early 70s CE because of at least three factors. (1) Rome had undergone various upheavals during the 60s that meant significantly challenging *sociopolitical* conditions for Jesus-followers. (2) In 71 CE, celebrations in Rome of Rome's victory over Judea in the 66–70 war posed *ideological or theological* challenges to Jesus-followers. (3) Living in Rome was not good for the physical and psychological-emotional well-being of many of its inhabitants with challenging *social* conditions. I am suggesting that these three arenas have significant resonance with Mark's story. They posed significant challenges for Jesus-followers in Rome even as the Gospel offers encouragement and empowerment for faithful living in the midst of these challenges.

Upheavals in Rome: Sociopolitical Challenges

The 60s CE saw a series of natural disasters and sociopolitical upheavals in Rome that significantly affected the daily lives of most of its million or so residents. Consider these six events:

4.2 *Nero Views the Burning of Rome*, by Karl von Piloty (1861). Commons.wikimedia.org.

- In 64 CE, a major fire lasting ten days devastated a large portion of Rome. It caused loss of life (Dio, who wrote an extensive history of Rome, says "countless persons perished": 62.18.2). There was extensive damage to property, and displacement of residents in eleven of Rome's fourteen districts. The fire was interpreted by some/many as a sign of the gods' displeasure with Rome and the emperor Nero. Tacitus reports that Nero propitiated the gods, scapegoated Christians, and devastated Italy and the provinces with demands for money for rebuilding the city (Tacitus, *Annals* 15.45–46). Rebuilding after the fire took years, though Nero found funds to build himself a massive and luxurious palace called the Golden

House (*Domus Aurea*). Dio says, furthermore, that Nero stopped grain distribution in the city and collected much money from citizens (62.18.2). Much social unrest and misery followed the fire.

- The scapegoating of Christians took place because rumors abounded that the fire had been deliberately lit, perhaps by Nero himself. Tacitus notes rumors that "the fire had taken place by [Nero's] order" (*Annals* 15.44) and Suetonius (*Nero* 38) says Nero "set fire to the city." Tacitus describes Nero's selection of the Christians, "loathed for their vices," as the culprits (*Annals* 15.44). They were arrested and convicted, "not so much on the count of arson as for hatred of the human race." That is, they were not persecuted for particular beliefs or practices as much as they were useful in taking attention away from Nero. They were put to death either by "being torn to death by dogs," crucified, or by fire. Tacitus declares that the harshness of the punishment backfired on Nero and drew forth "a sentiment of pity" for the plight of the Christians. Tacitus says that "vast numbers" were executed, but the claim is a great exaggeration since there weren't "vast numbers" of Christians in Rome in the first century. The exaggeration serves Tacitus's agenda to emphasize how terrible an emperor Nero was. Nor did the attacks last for any length of time, and they did not spread beyond the city of Rome. However many or few were executed, there is no doubting the impact of terror on surviving Jesus-followers in Rome.

- The year 65 CE saw political instability with Piso's conspiracy, which involved a significant number of elite figures who, very dissatisfied with Nero's style of ruling and living, sought to remove him as emperor. The conspiracy ended with the execution or forced suicide (including Piso, Lucan, and Seneca), or exile of significant numbers (Tacitus, *Annals* 15.47–62).

- Suetonius notes a plague in 65 CE that, he says, killed thirty thousand, though again the numbers may be exaggerated (*Nero* 39). In addition to this "deadly epidemic" that filled houses with "lifeless bodies," Tacitus identifies a destructive whirlwind in Campania. No admirer of Nero, he interprets these disasters as expressing the wrath and displeasure of the gods in punishing Rome for its wicked and shameful emperor. He describes the year 65 in these terms: "Upon this year, disgraced by so many deeds of shame, Heaven also set its mark by tempest and by disease" (*Annals* 16.13).

- In 66 CE, the province of Judea revolted, which clearly did not endear Jews to the imperial authorities in Rome. The war with Rome lasted until the defeat and devastation (by fire) of Jerusalem and its temple in 70 CE.

- The years 68 and 69 CE saw much civic instability in Rome, with civil war and a succession of four emperors. In 68, Vindex led a revolt against Nero in Gaul, and the army proclaimed Galba as emperor (Dio 63.22–23). Nero committed suicide shortly thereafter in June 68, and Galba ruled until being murdered in January 69. Otho became emperor for three months before he committed suicide. During Otho's reign, Rome experienced more social chaos, with severe flooding of the Tiber River causing bridges and *insulae* (apartment buildings) to collapse, and food shortages and famine to result (Tacitus, *Histories* 1.86, 89; Plutarch, *Otho* 5.1–2). With Otho's suicide, Vitellius became emperor. However, legions in the east declared Vespasian (who was fighting in Judea) emperor in July 69. More civil war between Vitellius and Vespasian followed. Rome saw continuing chaos with food shortages, clashes between Vespasian's and Vitellius' troops in the city, armed mobs looting the city, and the burning of the temple of Jupiter Optimus Maximus. Jupiter was understood to be Rome's patron deity, the most powerful god who sanctioned Roman power. Tacitus describes the burning of Jupiter's temple as "the saddest and most shameful crime that the Roman state had ever suffered" (Tacitus, *Histories* 3.72–86; 4.1; Dio 65.8–22, claiming fifty thousand dead, 64.15.2). Vespasian emerged from the civil war victorious and, completing an unlikely rise to power, was proclaimed emperor by the senate in December 69, returning to Rome in late 70.

Throughout all this sociopolitical and military unrest, there are, not surprisingly, indicators of significant levels of anxiety and "religious worry" during Nero's reign (54–68 CE).[1] The historian Tacitus reports an increasing number of strange happenings, or "prodigies," through the 50s and 60s. These happenings or signs included strange births (a woman giving birth to a snake), the appearance of comets in 60 CE and 64 CE, lightning strikes on temples and on a table at which Nero was dining, Nero falling ill, a statue of Nero melting, a theater collapsing just after Nero left (a good sign or bad sign?), and the great fire of 64. These happenings were often interpreted as expressions of divine displeasure or wrath and were often seen as portending imminent disaster for Rome. One historian argues that widespread popular attention to these happenings reveals that people were increasingly anxious about the immoral actions of Nero (incest with his mother, matricide, the murder of his wife, and other inappropriate/immoral behavior; Tacitus, *Annals* 15.37). They were fearful of the gods' disapproval and growing anger with Rome that would lead to disaster for the empire.

Tacitus begins his *Histories* by observing that "the gods are not concerned with our peace of mind, but rather with vengeance" (*Histories* 1.3). Such vengeance was not their disposition but was provoked by Roman folly: "The gods were ready to be propitious if our characters had allowed," but the shameful burning of the temple of Jupiter Optimus Maximus in 69 CE manifests "the mad fury of emperors" (Tacitus, *Histories* 3.72). And he seems to find numerous opportunities for discerning the gods' displeasure. He reports, for example, the view of rebellious Gauls that the burning of Jupiter's temple was a sign "from Heaven of the divine wrath (on Rome) and presages the passage of the sovereignty of the world to the peoples beyond the Alps" (*Histories* 4.54). Throughout, he continually sees "the anger of Heaven against the Roman realm" (*Annals* 16.16). Tacitus's verdict on the eve of 70 CE is that Rome's citizens were "downcast and anxious from many fears" with "false alarms" added

1. I follow John Hugo Wolfgang Gideon Liebeschuetz, *Continuity and Change in Roman Religion* (Oxford: Clarendon, 1979), 140–66.

> to "the actual evils that threatened them" (*Histories* 4.38).
>
> Similar views are found in the anonymous play *Octavia*, about Nero's wife whom he divorces and kills. Rome's inhabitants feared that they would absorb the gods' punishment for Nero's sins. The play includes a comment about Nero and the damage this behavior poses to the empire's survival: "Look, the very heavens are polluted by the fearful breath of our cruel emperor; the stars threaten unparalleled disaster to the people ruled by an impious leader" (*Octavia* 235–237).

How did Jesus-followers make their way in this world? Disastrous events—fires, epidemics, endangered food supply, floods, civil war, and looting mobs—affected all of Rome's residents, whatever their social level. Particularly affected were the large percentage of poor folks who had no social safety net and for whom the challenge to survive was especially difficult. Among these were Jesus-followers. Also, of course, they were severely affected by the deaths of group members under Nero. Nero's attack, short and sharp as it was, cast a long shadow of intimidation and warning of what could happen.

How did Jesus-followers who engaged Mark's Gospel negotiate the anxiety and fear of divine retaliation that pervaded Rome? Perhaps they found themselves sharing their neighbor's pervasive fear of impending disaster for the city from which they could not escape. Perhaps like the disciples in Mark they oscillated between fear and confidence or faith that God's reign or purposes would prevail. Perhaps they experienced suspicion and betrayal from friends and family who were worried that Jesus-followers were not loyal enough to Rome's gods and might bring retribution and disaster on the city. Perhaps like the disciples in Mark they experienced fragility in their discipleship in difficult circumstances that involved opposition or suspicion (4:16-17; 13:9-13; 14:66-72). Perhaps like Mark's disciples they found it hard to see God at work in the imperial world and struggled to identify God's reign present in their midst. Perhaps they found Jesus' displays of power narrated in the Gospel comforting and encouraging. Perhaps they gained strength from Jesus' struggle with the imperial authorities and his crucifixion and resurrection, knowing that their power, though very real, was not ultimate. Perhaps they found empowerment in the midst of "wars and rumors of wars" (13:8) by looking for Jesus' glorious and triumphant return (13:24-27).

We do not know for sure, but Mark's Gospel might have engaged these Jesus-followers and their circumstances in a variety of ways.

Roman Propaganda: Ideological and Theological Challenges

With this context of social unrest and anxiety, by the year 70 CE, folks in Rome needed some good news.[2] They got it in the form of Vespasian's accession as emperor in 69, his victory in Judea in 70, and the celebration of this triumph with his son Titus in July–August, 71 CE. Suetonius begins his biography of the deified Vespasian by remarking, "The empire, which for a long time had been unsettled and, as it were, drifting, through the usurpation and violent death of three emperors [Galba, Otho, Vitellius] was at last taken in hand and given stability by the Flavian family" (*Vespasian* 1.1). Vespasian's first task, Suetonius says, was "to strengthen the State which was tottering and almost overthrown, and then to embellish it as well" (*Vespasian* 8.1).

The Jewish historian Josephus, a client of the Flavian emperor Vespasian and living in Rome under his protection and patronage, predictably narrates much excitement and "universal goodwill" in anticipation of Vespasian's return to Rome in 70. Josephus constructs Vespasian's return and his "enthusiastic and splendid reception" as the opportunity for Rome's crowds, "exhausted by civil disorders," to put behind them their "miseries." Likewise, it was the opportunity for soldiers who had fought for Galba, Otho, and Vitellius to move beyond the "deep disgrace" of their defeats in the recent events and express loyalty to Vespasian, "confident that security and prosperity would again be theirs" (*J.W.* 7.63–71). Josephus thus presents Vespasian as the

2. Brian Incigneri (*The Gospel to the Romans: The Setting and Rhetoric of Mark's Gospel* [Leiden: Brill, 2003]) overemphasizes persecution; Adam Winn (*The Purpose of Mark's Gospel; An Early Christian Response to Roman Imperial Propaganda*, WUNT 245 [Tübingen: Mohr Siebeck, 2008]) overemphasizes messianic claims.

great uniter and reconciler, the cheerleader to restore Rome's fortunes in a renewed future. Josephus underscores that Vespasian is greeted as "benefactor," "saviour," and "only worthy emperor of Rome" (*J.W.* 7.71). Citizens of Rome "prayed God that Vespasian might himself long be spared to the Roman empire, and that the sovereignty might be preserved unchallenged for his sons and their descendants throughout successive generations" (*J.W.* 7.73).

Josephus presents Vespasian and his son Titus as "manly men" and successful warriors who embodied Rome's military power over the nations. In 70 CE, Titus, entrusted by his father Vespasian with command of the Roman troops in Judea, accomplished the major victory over the rebellious province of Judea, destroying and burning Jerusalem and the temple. Titus returns to Rome with captives/slaves and loot to join with his father in a "triumph" or victory celebration held in July–August 71 CE.

Central to the parade and parties in Rome was the depiction of Judea as a conquered and enslaved land and people. Before vast crowds, the parade displayed scenes from the war as well as loot and booty from Jerusalem and the temple. The captured rebel leader Simon bar Gioras was executed. Vespasian offered sacrifices at the temple of Jupiter Capitolinus, thereby publicly proclaiming the role of the gods, notably Jupiter, in choosing Rome and its emperor as the agents of the gods and ensuring Roman and Flavian military success (*J.W.* 7.153–155). The display of furnishings and scrolls from the Jerusalem temple attested Jupiter's superiority in defeating the Jewish God and the ending of worship in Jerusalem. It likewise constructed Rome as the superior and chosen people and Jews as a conquered people whose center and ways of worship were now obliterated and whose God was shown publicly to be powerless before Roman power. The Jewish historian Josephus likewise repeatedly recognizes that God's favor had passed to the Romans and the war and Rome's victory accomplished God's will and purposes (*J.W.* 2.390–391; 3.354; 4.104; 5.367–368, 412; 6.250; *Ant.* 20.166).

The parade also displayed loot from other conquered nations. The Judean conquest was set in a larger narrative of manly Roman military power that dominated and conquered weak, womanly subjugated nations. This narrative was displayed on *Judea Capta* coins, with conquered Judea presented as a weak woman towered over by a big manly Roman soldier. Vespasian and Titus, military opportunists now turned into a legitimate imperial dynasty, exhibit the "greatness of the rule of the Romans" (*J.W.* 7.133) over all nations with their rule sanctioned by the gods. The display delighted the crowds even while it intimidated Rome's foreign, and especially Jewish, populations. There were perhaps somewhere between twenty thousand and fifty thousand Jews in Rome around 70 CE.[3]

Gender therefore functions in the scene along with the performance of Roman ethnic superiority. Supporting Rome's gender and ethnic superiority, the victorious general Titus had selected some "seven hundred" of the numerous male Judean prisoners to be paraded. Josephus describes their manly warrior bodies—"being eminently tall and handsome of body"—as a way of highlighting the quality of Titus's victory over them (*J.W.* 7.118). Vespasian's masculinity is constructed in predictable elite terms through the performance of virtues.[4] He acts with self-restraint and dignity. He performs piously toward the gods, with prayers and sacrifices (7.128, 131, 153–155), rhetorically before the crowds with a brief address (7.129), generously toward his troops and others by providing abundant feasting (7.129, 156), dynastically and generatively in producing "an heir and a spare" (Titus and his younger brother Domitian) to establish civil order and a secure future after the civil war (7.152). And of course, all of this celebrates his military domination and courage before the nations in his victory over Judea. The celebrations construct and demonstrate his perfect manly identity as imperial ruler, able to exercise domination over Judea and the nations in effecting womanly defeat and enslavement.

3. David Noy (*Foreigners at Rome: Citizens and Strangers* [London: Duckworth with the Classical Press of Wales, 2000] 257) suggests "the region of 20,000-60,000 in the early first century." Harry J. Leon, *The Jews of Ancient Rome,* Updated Edition with a New Introduction by Carolyn Osiek (Peabody: Hendrickson, 1995; orig. ed. 1960) favors around 50,000, increasing after 70 CE (135-37).

4. Colleen Conway, *Behold the Man: Jesus and Greco-Roman Masculinity* (New York: Oxford University Press, 2008) 15-34; Maud Gleason, *Making Men: Sophists and Self-Presentation in Ancient Rome* (Princeton: Princeton University Press, 1994).

4.3 A Roman sestersius from the time of Vespasian, representing Iudaea Capta ("vanquished Judaea") as a subjugated and mourning woman beneath a palm tree. The message is clear: strong manly Rome has defeated weak womanly Judea. Commons.wikimedia.org, courtesy of Classical Numismatic Group.

Predictably, Josephus celebrates Rome's new future, built on victory over foreign enemies, the end of the "miseries" of civil war, and manly Flavian rulers: "for the city of Rome kept festival that day for her victory in the campaign against her enemies for the termination of her civil dissensions, and for her dawning hope of felicity" (*J.W.* 7.157). Josephus presents the victory celebration as marking a turning point, a leaving behind of a time of enemies and "civil dissensions," and a turning toward a hopeful future of "felicity." With "the empire of the Romans established on the firmest foundation" (*J.W.* 7.158), Josephus's narrative moves immediately to the Temple of Peace, which Vespasian built in 75 CE, four years later, which was now full of goods from around the world—including "vessels of gold" from the Jerusalem temple—that symbolized the Flavian accomplishment of successful control over all the nations (*J.W.* 7.158–162).

Vespasian's triumph in 71 CE openly displayed Roman imperial theology. Rome was chosen by the gods as their agent to accomplish their will and purposes in ruling and dominating the peoples of the world. How did Mark's Gospel address Jesus-believers, who followed a crucified but risen Jew, who witnessed this celebration of Roman imperial values and open display of Roman imperial theology? Perhaps they were intimidated, even terrified, by Rome's all-conquering power. Perhaps they were subdued by this convincing display of Rome's domination of the world and decided that they needed to keep a low profile and their commitment to Jesus a secret. Perhaps they were confused—or strengthened—by Mark's declaration that the empire of God was in their midst when all they could see was the power and apparent permanence of Rome's empire. Perhaps they were perplexed—or challenged—as to how they could live as Jesus' followers in this context. Perhaps they countered this display of Roman dominance by drawing on Mark's narrative of Jesus' powerful expressions of the good news of God's reign. Perhaps they were not surprised by this display of the great men's lording it over others, knowing that Jesus had rejected this way of being human and had commended another way of life, namely, seeking the good of the other (Mark 10:42-44). Perhaps they celebrated their alternative community, recognizing the importance of their new family of other followers for their survival (3:31–35). Perhaps they looked to and waited for Jesus' return and establishment of God's reign over all as the time of the inevitable demise of Rome's power (13:23-27).

We of course do not know for sure, but we can imagine numerous points of interaction between these followers of Jesus in these circumstances and Mark's Gospel.

Tough Living Conditions: Social Challenges

There is a further possible point of interaction between Jesus-believers living in Rome and Mark's Gospel. The Gospel is peopled with sick folks.

Numerous scenes involving individuals and crowds show Jesus' power in healing sicknesses and casting out demons. So Jesus exorcizes a man (1:21-28), heals a fever (1:29-31), heals and exorcizes "many" (1:32-34), exorcizes many (1:39), heals a leper (1:40-45), heals a paralytic (2:1-12), and heals a man with a withered hand (3:1-6). Then he exorcizes a demon-possessed man at Gerasa, heals a woman, and raises a dead child (5:1-43). He heals crowds of sick people (6:53-56), heals a deaf man (7:31-37) and a blind man (8:22-26), exorcizes a boy (9:14-29), and heals blind Bartimaeus (10:46-52). Jesus even performs such actions on the Sabbath, justifying them as actions that "do good" (not harm) and that "save life" (not kill; 3:4). In addition, twice Jesus commissions his disciples to exorcize and to heal, thereby extending the work of "doing good" and "saving life" (3:15; 6:7-13).

Why are there so many sick people in the Gospel? And how might the scenes of Jesus' exorcizing and healing activity engage Jesus-followers in Rome?

Living in Rome was unhealthy for many, especially the majority poor.[5] By one estimate, some 65–70 percent of city inhabitants lived at or below subsistence levels.[6] For these folks, population density was high and housing conditions generally poor.[7] Many lived in multistoried apartment buildings that often set in place a vertical social stratification, with more spacious and comfortable apartments on the ground level for the wealthier, and a significant decrease in size and number of rooms in the upper floors for much higher numbers of those of lower status and lesser economic means. Tenement buildings were proverbially poorly built with unsanitary living spaces. Juvenal refers to housing that is "ready to fall and the daylight begins to show

5. I follow Alex Scobie, "Slums, Sanitation, and Mortality in the Roman World," *Klio* 68 (1986): 399–433.

6. Steven Friesen, "Poverty in Pauline Studies: Beyond the So-Called New Consensus," *JSNT* 26 (2004): 323–61.

7. John E. Stambaugh, *The Ancient Roman City* (Baltimore: Johns Hopkins University Press, 1988), 337, estimates population density of 300 per acre. Rodney Stark ("Antioch as the Social Situation for Matthew's Gospel," in *Social History of the Matthean Community: Cross-Disciplinary Approaches*, ed. David L. Balch [Minneapolis: Fortress Press, 1991], 189–201, esp. 192) estimates a population density for Rome of 200 per acre (compared with Manhattan Island of 100 per acre, modern Kolkata of 122 per acre, and Bombay of 183 per acre).

between the cracks" (*Sat.* 11.11–12). The disgruntled Umbricius in Juvenal's third satire pays "a big rent for a wretched lodging" (3.166), fears that the building might come "tumbling down" (3.190–192), is alarmed by the prospect of fire and being burned to death (3.197–202), is exasperated by the lack of sleep due to noise (3.234–235), and fears being killed by the things people throw out the windows of tenement buildings onto the street at night, while hoping for nothing worse than "the contents of their slop-basins" (3.268–277). In addition, construction designs neglected adequate light, ventilation, water supply, and waste disposal. Peter Brunt declares, "We may fairly suppose that most of the inhabitants of Rome lived in appalling slums."[8]

4.4 An apartment building (insula) that commonly comprised shops, workshops, and apartments for non-elite folks from the Roman port of Ostia Antica; second century. Commons.wikimedia.org.

8. Peter A. Brunt, "The Roman Mob," *Past and Present* 35 (1966): 3–27, esp. 13.

Juvenal's Umbricius goes on to complain about too many foreigners in Rome (3.58–125), extensive poverty (3.126–189), the dangers of the city (3.190–231), crowding and traffic (3.232–267), accidents, drunken brawls and bullies, thefts, and murders (3.268–314).[9] Intense population density is also frequently accompanied by intense social scrutiny, conflicts, and violence.[10]

Living conditions were very unsanitary. Alex Scobie identifies various factors contributing to this environment. There is meager evidence for sewers and latrine/cesspits. There were "open cesspits in kitchens, a general lack of washing facilities in latrines, defecation and urination in the streets, the pollution of [street] water basins with carrion and filth, lack of efficient fly control, and inadequate street cleaning," along with corpses abandoned in streets, the presence of disease-carrying animals and insects such as vultures and dogs, the emptying of chamber-pots onto the street, the collection of urine by tanners, and the use of human feces as manure for food-producing fields and gardens. The "inhabitants of Rome lived in an extremely insanitary environment" in which disease and death were rife.[11]

Concerning Rome's water supply,[12] most residents collected water from 591 open, public water basins (called *laci*) distributed through the city. These water basins were subject to all the sources of contamination present in the streets noted above (sewage, trash disposal, animals, etc.). Water was also supplied to public baths. Often visits to baths were prescribed for medical treatment. Scobie cites Celsus, who details treatment in the baths for fevers, paralysis, headaches, dysentery, worm infestations, bowel and anus troubles, gonorrhea, rabies, and boils, among others.[13]

9. On violence, Garrett G. Fagan, "Violence in Roman Social Relations," in *The Oxford Handbook of Social Relations in the Roman World*, ed. Michael Peachin (Oxford: Oxford University Press, 2011), 467–95.
10. Scobie, "Slums, Sanitation," 427–33.
11. Ibid., 417, 421; also Neville Morley, "The Salubriousness of the Roman City,' in *Health in Antiquity*, ed. Helen King (London: Routledge, 2005), 192–204.
12. Scobie, "Slums, Sanitation," 422–24.
13. Ibid., 425–27.

4.5 Bread for sale; from the "House of the Baker," Pompeii. Naples National Archaeological Museum; Commons.wikimedia.org.

Compounding the challenges of daily survival was that of unstable food access. Access to adequate food supply, both in quality and quantity, typically reflected channels of power. Those in Rome with considerable power, wealth, and status generally ate well. Those with limited resources and standing had limited food access.[14] Hence diets expressed the hierarchy of the city's social structure. Supplying the city with nutritionally adequate and affordable food was a major challenge in having to overcome uncertainties of crop production, dangers and costs of transportation, difficulties in coordinating supply, providing adequate storage, and limited port facilities on the Tiber and

14. Greg Aldrete and David Mattingly, "Feeding the City: The Organization, Operation, and Scale of the Supply System for Rome," in *Life, Death, and Entertainment in the Roman Empire*, ed. David Potter and David Mattingly (Ann Arbor: University of Michigan Press, 1999), 171–204, esp. 172–77.

initially at Ostia. In addition, disasters such as the fire of 64 and the civil war of 68–69 further interrupted the food supply. Accordingly, as Peter Garnsey observes, "For most people, life was a perpetual struggle for survival."[15] He argues that while famines were rare, shortages of food and nutritionally inadequate diets were much more common, with malnutrition pervasive among poorer sections of the population, whose diets were based in poor-quality cereals, legumes, olives, and cheap wine.[16]

In addition, levels of stress were high, which severely corroded the mental health and physical well-being of many in the population. Jerry Toner identifies a range of stressors:[17]

- The frequency of death especially, with high death rates for infants
- Strenuous physical labor
- Periodic malnourishment and undernourishment
- Various economic challenges (debt, failed business ventures, fear of falling further into poverty, the precarious income for urban day laborers)
- Dangers from urban life (crime, overcrowding, fire, assault, lack social networks) and natural disasters (flooding, fire)
- Occupational accidents that prevented manual labor and slashed earning power
- Difficult social interactions (showing deference, avoiding public humiliation)
- Household pressures (close living, female submission, domestic violence)
- The vicissitudes of the large number of slaves (hard work, beatings,

15. Peter Garnsey, *Food and Society in Classical Antiquity* (Cambridge: Cambridge University Press, 1999), xi.
16. Ibid., 34–61, 113–27. Also Garnsey, *Famine and Food Supply in the Graeco-Roman World: Responses to Risk and Crisis* (Cambridge: Cambridge University Press, 1988), 3–39.
17. Jerry Toner, *Popular Culture in Ancient Rome* (Cambridge: Polity, 2009), 1–91.

limited food, coerced sexual availability, pregnancies, constant humiliation, break up of families)

Many knew the vulnerability and fragility of life, and some, of course, broke under such pressures both emotionally and physically. Such stressors were crazy-making.

One result of the unhealthy living conditions, the minimally sufficient diet, and high energy demands from manual labor outlined above was widespread disease. Peter Garnsey argues that in such conditions diseases both of deficiency, from a lack of nutrients and vitamins, and of contagion abounded.[18] Among diseases of deficiency were very painful bladder and kidney stones, numerous eye diseases, and rickets or limb deficiency. Deficiencies in vitamin A, for example, contributed to blindness, bone deformation, growth retardation, and lowered immunity. Vitamin D deficiency contributes to pain and muscle weakness, and skeletal deformities. If one is incapacitated or too weak to work, one does not eat. Diseases of infection, including diarrhea, dysentery, cholera, and typhus, of course, affected both elite and nonelite women and men, but with poorer diets and immunity, the latter suffered more.

Why, then, are there so many sick people in the Gospel? Because there were so many sick folks in the Roman world. The Gospel mirrors its society at this point. Indeed, the structures and practices of the empire made people sick and disabled the bodies of its inhabitants. We might say that the Roman Empire, like cigarette packets, should have come with a health warning! It was not good for folks' health. The disabled bodies in Mark's Gospel embody a world of harsh physical conditions, of diseases of deficiency and contagion, and of considerable daily stress. The paralyzed and lame, the blind and deaf, the pained and fevered, the lepers and epileptics, the demoniacs, and the sick somatically absorb and manifest the disabling damage of imperial structures.

And how might Mark's readers, well familiar with and indeed

18. Garnsey, *Food and Society*, 43–61, esp. 45.

participants in such a world, have engaged the Gospel story? What might they have made of the frequent stories of Jesus' exorcisms, healings, and miraculous feedings?

Clearly the Gospel does not promise immunity from these daily challenges and social woes. But it does narrate scenes of Jesus repairing and reversing the damage the empire inflicted on bodies. Jesus' frequent healings and exorcisms roll back the destructive impact and somatic damage of a world that ensured good food supply only for elites and limited food quantity and quality for nonelites, and subjected them to considerable societal stressors. In sending his followers into this world to heal and exorcize its somatic victims, the Jesus movement was to continue Jesus' work of repairing and reversing the damage to bodies and lives caused by imperial practices and structures (3:13–14). These healings, exorcisms, and feedings enact and embody God's reign. They make present God's kingdom among people and manifest God's purposes of a good somatic life for all people.

Perhaps Jesus-followers were overwhelmed by the challenges of survival in this harsh physical environment and paid little active attention to Jesus' miraculous and transforming engagement with it in the Gospel story. Or perhaps they experienced considerable encouragement and empowerment in hearing about Jesus' actions and experienced for themselves some healings and exorcisms as a result. Perhaps they prayed over limited food supplies in circumstances of want and need, asking God to multiply limited resources to feed hungry people just as happened when Jesus prayed to God to multiply limited resources (6:30-44; 8:1-10). Perhaps they obeyed Jesus' instruction to continue his mission and regularly and successfully performed acts of healing and exorcism. Perhaps in attempting to access this power, they experienced frustrations in praying to God for healings and exorcisms but encountered limited positive responses. And perhaps such experiences account for the Gospel's instructions about prayer and healing. In 8:22-26, even the very powerful Jesus needs two attempts to heal a blind man (8:22-26). In 9:14-29, the Gospel includes the account of disciples who are unable to cast out a spirit

(9:18). Jesus uses the experience as a "teachable moment" to exhort them to faith (9:24) and prayer (9:29).

Conclusion

We do not know for sure how members of the audience engaged Mark's Gospel. But in this chapter, we have imagined some possible interactions between the Gospel's audience and the Gospel narrative in the context of the difficult and complex circumstances of their urban environment.

Questions for Review and Reflection

1. The chapter explores the possible interactions between Mark's Gospel and its audience of origin, the audience for which it was written. Why does the chapter privilege a possible address to an audience living in Rome in the early 70s CE?
2. The chapter identifies three factors that suggest life in Rome in the 70s was tough for Jesus-followers: political upheavals in Rome, the celebrations of Rome's victory in Judea in 70, and tough urban conditions. It goes on to suggest how Jesus-followers might make their way in each of these circumstances. Review each of the three scenarios. Do you find the suggestions of how the Gospel might have addressed Jesus-followers in each scenario to be convincing? What other possibilities do you imagine?
3. Think of some contemporary church contexts: a prosperous (upper-)middle-class white suburban church; an inner-city ethnic community; a chapel service in a hospital or prison; a Bible study with a group of women in a shelter for women subjected to domestic violence; a youth group Bible study; and so on. Pick one and describe and elaborate this context. How might Mark's Gospel as a whole or a passage from it that you choose function in a pastoral way in this context?

5

The Tale Matthew Tells

In this chapter, we turn to the Gospel according to Matthew. As I noted in relation to Mark's Gospel, the words "according to" are very important in reminding us that each Gospel story is perspectival in offering its own particular account of Jesus' teaching and actions, life and death, resurrection and return. So in this chapter, I outline *Matthew's* tale, paying particular attention to its plot, which, as we will note, in places resembles and in other places differs from Mark's. Then, in the next chapter, we will look at some attempts to understand the significance of this different telling of the story of Jesus.

What Is a Plot?

From watching movies and TV programs, and reading novels, not to mention fourth-grade literature sessions, we know that stories have a beginning, middle, and end. More importantly, as Aristotle observed more than two millennia ago, satisfying plots have a unity of action. We as viewers or readers connect various scenes together in a sequence to form this unity of action. Causality is a vital part of this sequence. An event is the consequence of previous actions or the cause for subsequent actions. Matthew's Gospel uses connectives such as "and" or "but" (Greek *kai; de*), "for" (*gar*), "therefore/so" (*oun*), and "for/because" (*hoti*) to denote relations between scenes involving sequence, consequence, implications, explanations, and reasons.

5.1 *The Calling of Saint Matthew*, by Caravaggio (1599-1600). The painting draws the eye to a young tax collector seated at his table (although the character in Matt. 9:9-13 is likely not the Gospel author). Contarelli Chapel, Church of San Luigi dei Francesi, Rome; Commons.wikimedia.org.

5.1 What Is a Plot?

"The king died. The queen died" is not a plot. There is no unity, sequence, or causality. But "The king died. Then the queen died" is a plot. So too is "Because the king died, the queen died." Unity, sequence, and causality are evident in these two examples.

Plots also establish time relationships among events. These temporal relationships might be expressed by connectives ("then" [*tote*], "again" [*palin*]), by genitive absolute constructions designating simultaneous ("as," "while," "when"), and subsequent ("after") connections, and by specific time phrases ("on the third day"). Other techniques include foreshadowings (for example, Herod's opposition to Jesus' birth anticipates the opposition of the Roman governor Pilate and the Jerusalem leaders at his crucifixion), flash-forwards (the judgment of the sheep and the goats anticipates the final judgment), and frequency (repeated scenes of healings and teachings). By these and other techniques, time relationships are established among events involving order, duration, frequency, and repetition.

While there are many actions in a story, some events are more important than others. One indicator of this hierarchy of events is the phenomenon of "outtakes" associated with movies. Outtakes are scenes that were shot for a movie but don't make it into the finished form of the movie. While these scenes might have contributed something to the movie if they had been included, the director has decided for whatever reasons that they are not necessary for its story. Conversely, there are other scenes in any movie that are utterly indispensable and, if removed, would result in a plot that did not make much sense.

Not all events in a story, then, are created equal. There is a hierarchy of events. An audience must determine which events are central and which are subsidiary. The literary critic Seymour Chatman calls the most important events that form the plot "kernels" and the less important events "satellites."[1] While the language of "kernels" and "satellites" may not be especially appealing, the notion of events that are more important than other events is clear. Chatman argues that kernels, or central events, perform crucial functions in the plot:

1. They provide major "branching points" or "hinges" that advance the action of the plot.

1. Seymour Chatman, *Story and Discourse* (Ithaca, NY: Cornell University Press, 1978), 53–56.

2. They are consequences of earlier kernels in that they provide answers to questions that arise from previous plot actions.
3. In turn, they raise questions that subsequent kernels will address.
4. Kernels provide the central event of a larger narrative block comprising events that are linked to and derive from the kernel. Moreover, kernels provide the crucial scenes that are foundational for the whole narrative structure. If they were deleted, the narrative structure would collapse and not make sense.

Satellites, on the other hand, are minor events. They derive from the kernels, often elaborating or filling in kernels. If the kernels provide the skeleton of the plot, the satellites are the flesh. The kernel and its related satellites form a narrative block.

The Plot of Matthew's Gospel

I propose that the plot of Matthew's Gospel comprises six kernels (major branching points) with numerous satellites filling in and elaborating these kernels to constitute six narrative blocks.

1. Kernel: 1:18-25; Narrative Block: 1:1—4:16. God initiates the story of Jesus with the conception and commissioning of Jesus to manifest God's saving presence.
2. Kernel: 4:17-25; Narrative Block: 4:17—11:1. Jesus performs his commission to manifest God's saving presence in his public activity: announcing God's kingdom or reign or empire, calling and forming disciples, teaching, healing, and exorcising demons.
3. Kernel: 11:2-6; Narrative Block: 11:2—16:20. Jesus' public activity reveals his identity as God's commissioned agent and his transformative impact on the elite-controlled world. His activity necessitates a response from people of acceptance or rejection, recognition or nonrecognition.
4. Kernel: 16:21-28; Narrative Block: 16:21—20:34. Jesus teaches his followers that God's purposes and reign or empire, which he

reveals, will cost him his life and involve his death, resurrection, and return in power. This cluster of events also shapes discipleship.

5. Kernel: 21:1-17; Narrative Block: 21:1—27:66. In Jerusalem, Jesus conflicts with and is rejected by the leaders based in the temple, who are tensively allied with the Roman governor Pilate. He dies at their hands.
6. Kernel: 28:1-10; Narrative Block: 28:1-20. God's saving purposes are not thwarted by the elite's opposition. God overcomes their opposition by raising Jesus from the dead. Jesus commissions his disciples to worldwide mission, promising to be with them.

5.2 Reading Matthew

As with Mark's Gospel, this chapter will make more sense if you read along with Matthew's Gospel.

First Kernel (1:18-25) and Narrative Block (1:1—4:16)

I suggest the first kernel appears in 1:18-25, when God initiates the story of Jesus through the Holy Spirit's involvement in the conception of Jesus and his commissioning to manifest God's saving presence. Mary's conception of Jesus is new action. The scene is a branching point, a point of departure for the rest of the story. Without this action, there would not be a story of Jesus. Through the Holy Spirit, God, not Mary and Joseph (1:18c and d, 20d, 25a), gets the story underway. By means of the involvement of an angel and the witness of Scripture, God's purposes for Jesus are announced and signified by his names, Jesus and Emmanuel (1:21-23). From his conception, he is commissioned to save people from their sins and to manifest God's presence.[2] *How* Jesus is to carry out this task of manifesting God's saving presence will be elaborated in the second kernel.

2. See Warren Carter, "'To Save His People from Their Sins' (Matthew 1:21): Rome's Empire and Matthew's Salvation as Sovereignty," in *Matthew and Empire: Initial Explorations* (Harrisburg, PA: Trinity Press International, 2001), 75–93.

The choice of 1:18-25 as the kernel does not in any way slight the Gospel's opening scene, the genealogy (1:1-17). Rather it recognizes the contribution of this satellite as contextualizing God's initiative. By tracing generations in three groups (from Abraham to David, to the exile, to Jesus, 1:17), the genealogy presents a version of God's previous dealings with Israel and the world, with men and with women (note the inclusion of five women, 1:3-6, 16). It highlights God's promises to bless all the families of the world (Gen. 12:1-3, Abraham), the expression of God's rule and purposes through Israel's kings (2 Samuel 7; Psalm 72, David), and God's faithfulness to Israel through and beyond the disaster of exile to Babylon in 587 BCE, when God's covenant commitments to people, land, temple, and city seemed in vain. In this context, God initiates a new action in the person of Jesus to manifest God's saving presence.

The satellites of chapters 2:1—4:16 elaborate the impact of this initiative.

- Verse 1 of chapter 2 narrates Jesus' birth and thereby confirms the efficaciousness of God's word and purposes in 1:18-25.
- The arrival in Jerusalem of the "wise men" or magi, priestly-political-astrologer-advisors from the East, and the reference to "the days of King Herod" introduce two sets of characters who display two contrasting responses to God's initiative. Herod is immediately threatened by the naming of Jesus as "king of the Jews" while *he* is the Rome-appointed client or puppet king (2:1-3). He tries to turn the magi into spies in locating Jesus's birthplace and lies about wanting to worship him (2:8b). His real purpose, to kill Jesus, is revealed by an angel (2:13) and thwarted by the magi and Joseph and Mary (2:13-23), but not before he brings terrible grief to parents and siblings of male babies in Bethlehem and its surrounding regions with a nondiscriminating outburst of murderous violence (2:16-18). Ironically, while Herod tries to kill Jesus, the narrative declares Herod's death three times (2:15, 19, 20). The destructive threat of kings, though, continues in the rule of his son Archelaus (2:22-23).

5.2 Mothers beat their breasts in anguish as Herod orders his soldiers to massacre the children of Bethlehem; illumination from a 10th-century Gospel manuscript (Codex Egberti). Stadtbibliothek Trier; Commons.wikimedia.org.

- The magi, by contrast, travel to Bethlehem to pay homage to Jesus and refuse to spy for Herod (2:2, 9-12).
- The "chief priests and scribes" (2:4-6) appear for the first time. They are allies of Herod as part of the ruling elite. That is, they are partly religious leaders, but they are also Judea's native rulers who exercise sociopolitical power. Here they answer their ally Herod's question about where the Messiah might be born. But they fail to read this Scripture in relation to Jesus and fail to act on what they know. They do not travel to Bethlehem to honor him (as do the magi).
- Joseph plays a key role in protecting Jesus from Herod by receiving angelic direction in dreams and courageously traveling (with Mary) to and from Egypt.

Matthew 3:1-12 brings the witness of the strange prophetic figure, John the Baptizer. He prepares people for the encounter with God's saving presence manifested in Jesus, and he announces two further aspects of Jesus' mission, to baptize with the Holy Spirit (3:11) and to judge (3:12). Jesus comes to John for baptism (3:13-17). This scene provides an opportunity for God to confirm Jesus' identity as God's Son or agent of God's saving presence and for Jesus to accept this divinely commissioned role (1:21-23). Jesus' identity is challenged in the next scene by the devil (4:1-11). Twice, the devil raises the question of Jesus' identity as God's agent ("if you are the Son of God": 4:3, 6), three times the devil challenges Jesus to obey the devil's bidding rather than God's (4:3, 6, 9), and finally the devil demands that Jesus worship him (4:9). The scene sets the contest for Jesus' allegiance in a cosmic perspective; the dividend for Jesus is control of "all the empires of the world" (4:8). In rejecting the devil's commands, Jesus remains faithful to his God-given commission. The closing satellite of the block concerns Jesus' move to Capernaum in Galilee in anticipation of his public activity there (4:12-16). The scene cites Isa. 9:1-2 to emphasize Jesus' mission of manifesting God's saving presence that is about to get underway. God's saving presence ("light") shines into the darkness and death of imperial rule (4:16).

This opening narrative block, then, introduces Jesus in relation to God's purposes. In the kernel, God initiates the story in the conception and commissioning of Jesus as God's agent to manifest God's saving presence (1:18-25). The satellites of the block elaborate both God's action and Jesus' identity. They are contextualized in God's life-giving, ruling purposes (1:1-17). Jesus is presented as vulnerable to and opposed by Herod, homaged by the magi or wise men from the East, protected by Joseph, and attested by the Scriptures (2:1-23). He is witnessed to by John (3:1-12), sanctioned by God in baptism (3:13-17), tested by the devil (4:1-11), and located in Galilee and in the Scriptures (4:12-16).

5.3 Mark Watch

As we read through Matthew's Gospel, we will also keep an eye on Mark's Gospel, one of the sources for the Gospel. How does Matthew edit or rework Mark's version of the story of Jesus?

Matthew's Gospel begins the account of Jesus' public activity in 4:17. Mark's Gospel begins at 1:14-15. Much of Matt. 1:1—4:16, Matthew's introduction to Jesus, is not in Mark. Matthew has added the account of Jesus' origins (chs. 1–2) and expanded Mark's scenes involving John the Baptizer, Jesus' baptism, and the temptation. In the next chapter, we will consider where this added material originates.

The Second Kernel and Narrative Block (4:17—11:1)

In 4:17-25, a significant development or branching point occurs in the plot. Jesus now begins to perform his commission to manifest God's saving presence (1:21-23) in his public activity. He announces God's kingdom or reign or empire, calls and forms disciples, teaches, heals, and exorcizes demons.

This scene performs the functions of a kernel. (1) The scene provides a branching point that advances the action of the plot. The first narrative block has introduced and positioned Jesus as one commissioned by God to manifest God's saving presence. Now he takes up that commission in this public activity. (2) This scene, then, is a kernel in that it is a consequence of the first kernel, answering the question posed by the first kernel as to *how* Jesus might perform his God-given commission. (3) In turn, this scene raises a question that the next (and following) kernel(s) will specifically address: How do people respond when God's saving presence is manifested in various ways in their midst? (4) This kernel in 4:17-25 is the central event of the second narrative block and is elaborated by its numerous satellites.

Jesus begins his public activity in 4:17 by announcing that "the kingdom of heaven has come near." Jesus has demonstrated in the temptation scene that he is faithful to God's purposes, so as God's faithful Son (4:3, 6), he now carries out his commission to manifest God's saving presence (1:21-23). The language of "the kingdom of heaven" expresses this commission but in terms of God's reign, or rule, or empire. Given the Gospel's origin from and address to groups in the Roman Empire, the latter translation seems most appropriate. The little word "of" indicates the origin of this empire in heaven, which is God's dwelling place (5:34; 6:9-10). Jesus' task is to extend God's saving presence, God's reign or empire, to earth among humans (6:10).

The verb "has come near" has puzzled interpreters. Is God's empire already present among humans, or will it be encountered in the future? The Gospel's answer is yes to both options. God's empire is both present in Jesus' activity now (12:28), at least in part, and it remains to be established in its fullness in the future (13:47-50; 19:28).

What does this empire, God's saving presence, which Jesus is commissioned to manifest, look like in Jesus' activity? The rest of the kernel summarizes key expressions of God's saving presence or empire among human beings that will be elaborated in the satellites. In 4:18-22, Jesus calls four fishermen to follow him. That is, when God's empire comes among humans in Jesus' activity, it claims human loyalties, moves them to leave behind the claims and priorities of their social and economic worlds embedded in Rome's economy,[3] gives them a new identity as followers of Jesus, and commissions them to a new lifestyle of mission in creating other followers. In addition, Jesus manifests God's empire in teaching, preaching, and healing crowds "from Galilee, the Decapolis, Jerusalem, Judea, and from beyond the Jordan" (4:23-25).

This kernel, which demonstrates in summary form Jesus carrying out his God-given commission, is elaborated in the satellites that comprise this second narrative block (4:17—11:1). Having called followers, Jesus now instructs them about living in God's empire (5:3, 10; 6:10, 33; 7:21) in the Sermon on the Mount (chs. 5–7). Chapters 8–9 offer a series of scenes of Jesus' activities. To the fore are healings: a leper (8:1-4), a very sick servant (8:5-13), Peter's fevered mother-in-law (8:14-17), two demon-possessed men (8:28-34), a paralyzed man (9:2-8), a dead girl and a woman with a hemorrhage (9:18-26), two blind men (9:27-31), a mute, demon-possessed man (9:32-34). The final summary

3. See the important article by K. C. Hanson, "The Galilean Fishing Economy and the Jesus Tradition," *BTB* 27 (1997): 99–111.

scene highlights Jesus' much more extensive healing activity (9:35-38) and recalls a similar summary in the kernel at 4:23-24. As we observed in the last chapter on Mark, when God's empire comes among people, it repairs the physical and somatic damage that is so pervasive in Rome's imperial world.

Chapters 8–9 demonstrate the impact of God's empire or saving presence in other ways. Jesus provides a glimpse of its future vast reach (8:11-12), its continuing power to claim individual human lives (8:18-22; the tax collector Matthew, 9:9), and its reach to the created order to subdue the sea (8:23-27). Jesus also demonstrates its compassionate impact in forgiving sin (9:2-8) and in mercifully welcoming the socially marginalized "tax collectors and sinners" (9:10-13).

Chapter 10, a second sustained example of Jesus' teaching (4:23; 5:2), develops another aspect of the kernel in 4:18-22. There, Jesus calls the disciples to "fish for people" (4:19) but does not explain what this means. The satellites provide elaboration. The Sermon on the Mount declares that followers are "salt of the earth" and "the light of the world" (5:13-16). In 9:36-38, Jesus observes the scarcity of laborers among crowds that are "harassed and helpless." In chapter 10, he commissions his followers to continue his activities among the crowds. He sends his followers to do what Jesus has done in chapters 8–9 and demonstrate God's empire or saving presence among humans. So he authorizes them to exorcize unclean spirits, heal diseases, raise the dead, and proclaim that "the kingdom/empire of heaven has come near" (10:1, 8).

By the end of chapter 10, the second narrative block has demonstrated how Jesus carries out his God-given commission to manifest God's empire or saving presence among humans. But it has also raised a question: How do people respond to Jesus' activity? Will people recognize Jesus as God's commissioned agent, and will they encounter in his activity God's empire and saving presence?

5.4 Mark Watch

Matthew's second narrative block contains two big sections of instructional material, spoken by Jesus, that are not in Mark. The first is Matthew 5–7, the Sermon on the Mount. By comparing Mark 1:22 with Matt. 7:29, it is clear that Matthew adds these chapters right before Mark 1:22. Matthew 10 (the mission discourse) initially parallels the lists of male disciples in Mark 3:13-19; 6:7-13, but then Matthew constructs much of the rest of the discourse. We will discuss the origin of this added material in the next chapter.

The Third Kernel (11:2-6) and Narrative Block (11:2—16:20)

This third kernel moves the action forward by centering on the key question of whether those who encounter Jesus' activity are able to discern—and welcome—his God-given commission as agent of God's empire or saving presence (11:2-6). The issue is posed by the disciples of John the Baptizer, who ask Jesus if he, Jesus, is the Messiah, the "one who is to come." Jesus does not answer directly but provides the means whereby the question can be answered. Citing Isaiah 35, he points to his healing and preaching actions as disclosing his identity and blesses those who welcome him (11:6). He cites Isaiah because the prophet envisions God's purposes being established in the transformation of a sick world into a world of life and wholeness. Jesus carries out this agenda; this is God's empire at work. Those who discern in Jesus' activity the empire and saving presence of God welcome his transforming activity.

The satellites of the narrative block elaborate these issues. Jesus immediately praises John the Baptizer as one who discerned and bore witness to his identity (11:7-19), and then offers contrasting eschatological condemnation of the unrepentant cities of Chorazin, Bethsaida, and Capernaum (11:20-24), which failed to discern the significance of Jesus' actions as displays of God's empire and saving presence. Jesus goes on to frame these various responses as God's concealing and revealing work. God has concealed God's workings from "the wise and intelligent" (the powerful) but has revealed them, through Jesus the Son, to "infants" (the nonelite; 11:25-27). He subsequently identifies these "infants" as "all you that are weary [lit. "who labor"] and are carrying heavy burdens" and are in need of rest (11:28).

Interpreters have frequently interpreted these "burdens" as the demands of the law as taught by the Pharisees (cf. 23:4). But neither the requirements of the law nor the Pharisees have been in view in recent chapters. And the tradition did not regard the law as a burden. In fact, Deut. 30:6-14 regards it as "not too hard for you" and declares that it offers life. It is more realistic to understand those who are weary (or those who labor) and are burdened as referring to those—most of the population—who did hard manual work to survive in the Roman world. Jesus offers them a different yoke, one that is kind or good ("easy" is an inaccurate translation).[4] In other words, he speaks of God's empire or saving presence, which has a transformative impact in the world.

The "infants" who discern Jesus' identity and receive God's work in him encounter mercy and wholeness (12:1-8). So Jesus heals the man with the withered hand (12:9-14), exorcizes the blind and mute demoniac (12:22), feeds the hungry crowds (14:13-21; 15:32-39), exorcizes the faithful Canaanite mother's daughter (15:21-28), and heals many (12:15-21; 14:34-36; 15:29-31). He declares that those who do "the will of my Father in heaven [are] my brother and sister and mother" (12:50). They receive his teaching (13:10-17). He reveals the ways in which God's empire is at work in their midst even when it seems invisible or weak and powerless (the parables of ch. 13). He walks on the water (14:22-33), manifesting God's saving presence by doing what God does (see Job 9:8; Pss. 77:16-20; 107:23-32). He continues to manifest God's empire and presence in Godlike actions, overcoming the watery chaos and restoring the water to its rightful place (see Gen. 1:6-10), stretching out his hand to save Peter from drowning (Isa. 41:10, 13; Jonah 1–2), urging his followers not to fear (Isa. 41:10-11), and revealing himself with the same words God uses ("I am": Matt. 14:27; Exod. 3:14; Isa. 43:10-13). They recognize him as God's agent or

4. This perspective is elaborated in Warren Carter, "Take My Yoke Not Rome's: Matthew 11:28-30," in *Matthew and Empire*, 108–29.

Son (14:33), thereby sharing God's perspective on him as the one who manifests God's empire or saving presence (1:21-23; 2:15; 3:17).

By contrast, the Pharisees refuse to accept his merciful and valuing actions on a Sabbath as a revelation of God's will (12:1-14). They conspire to destroy Jesus (12:14). They declare that his actions are energized by the devil (12:24-32), not by God or God's empire or God's Spirit (1:21-23; 3:16-17). Because they cannot recognize it, they demand a sign that indicates God sanctions his actions (12:38-42). Jesus recognizes that various forces oppose his work—the evil one (13:19), trouble or opposition (13:21), the cares of the world and lure of wealth (13:22)—but evildoers will be destroyed at the end of the age (13:40, 48-50). His hometown folks reject his teaching and "deeds of power" (13:54). They identify him as the Son of the carpenter and of Mary, but they cannot discern his identity as the Son or agent of God. They "took offense at him" (13:57), the same language Jesus uses in the kernel of 11:6, "blessed is anyone who takes no offense at me." By taking offense, they condemn themselves. Their unbelief means Jesus does not work many deeds of power there (13:58). The Rome-sanctioned ruler Herod the tetrarch of Galilee and Perea beheads John the Baptizer, who witnessed to Jesus as God's agent (14:1-12). The Pharisees and scribes reject Jesus' teaching about the role of the tradition of the elders (15:1-20); the Pharisees and Sadducees demand a sign of God's validation of Jesus, which he refuses (16:1-4); and Jesus warns his disciples against the teaching of the Pharisees and Sadducees (16:5-12).

The satellite that closes the narrative block summarizes its central issue (16:13-20). Recalling the kernel (11:2-6), Jesus foregrounds the identity question, "Who do people say that the Son of Man is?" (16:13). Verse 14 summarizes four misunderstandings of Jesus' identity akin to the misunderstandings expressed by the elite leaders (12:14), the crowds (13:13), the people of Nazareth (13:53-57), and Herod the tetrarch (14:1-2). In verse 16, Peter makes the correct confession ("the Messiah, the Son of the living God"), which all the followers made in 14:33 and which agrees with God's declaration of Jesus' identity expressed previously (1:1, 17-18; 2:15; 3:17). In verse 17, Jesus blesses

Peter (recalling the kernel, 11:6), affirms that Peter's declaration results from God's revelation (cf. 11:27), and gives instructions about the community of disciples' future role (16:18-19). Jesus closes the narrative block by ordering the disciples "not to tell anyone that he was the Messiah" (16:20).

Why does Jesus give this command?

5.5 Mark Watch

The scene that ends this third narrative block (16:13-20) parallels, even as it expands, Mark 8:27-30. Matthew's extra material in the third narrative block includes the collection of parables (Matthew 13), which considerably expands Mark 4.

The Fourth Kernel (16:21-28) and Narrative Block (16:21—20:34)

The fourth kernel moves the action forward by disclosing a further aspect of Jesus' identity and commission (16:21-28). Jesus teaches for the first time that his commission as God's agent will result in his crucifixion in Jerusalem at the hands of the Jerusalem elite. Though he reveals the violent opposition of the powerful elite, this is not the end of the story. He also declares that God will raise him on the third day. Peter opposes Jesus' announcement, an action Jesus attributes to the influence of his opponent Satan (16:23). Jesus goes on to teach that his followers are to walk the same path of suffering and vindication. And he declares that he will subsequently return as Son of Man in powerful glory to establish God's empire. The kernel moves the action forward, adds to previous kernels in identifying a further dimension of Jesus' commission, and raises a question to be answered in subsequent kernels as to how this new development concerning Jesus' mission will unfold.

The satellites of this fourth narrative block develop both aspects of the kernel, one concerning Jesus and one concerning discipleship. In the next scene (17:1-8), the transfiguration, Jesus is presented in glory, an anticipation of his future powerful roles and a confirmation of what he announced in the kernel (16:21, 27-28). God also confirms Jesus' identity: "This is my Son, the Beloved" (17:5). And God confirms Jesus' declaration of his destiny and its implication for his followers: "Listen to him" (17:5). Jesus repeats his destiny of crucifixion and resurrection (17:12; 20:17-19) and explains his death as a "ransom," or benefit, that sets many free (20:28). In chapters 19–20, Jesus leaves Galilee and heads toward Jerusalem, where these actions are to unfold.

The satellites also develop the kernel's emphasis on discipleship. The soon to-be-crucified-raised-and-returning Jesus instructs his followers on how they are to live in God's empire until its completion (18:1, 23; 19:12, 23; 20:1). Chapter 18, the fourth concentrated collection of Jesus' teaching (after chapters 5–7, 10, and 13), addresses how the community of disciples is to sustain each other in this difficult existence. They are to relate with humility and mutual consideration (18:1-14) and forgiveness (18:21-35). In chapters 19–20, as Jesus leaves Galilee and heads south toward Jerusalem, he instructs followers on the households that are shaped by God's empire. Jesus resists the unlimited power of the husband over the wife (19:3-12), calls all disciples to live the marginal and vulnerable existence of children (19:13-15), opposes the rich man's quest for wealth and power (19:16-30), rebukes the "power over others" of Rome's "rulers . . . and their great men," and urges his disciples to imitate Jesus' self-giving death in being slaves of one another (20:20-28). In this instruction, Jesus to varying degrees resists (and, in places, imitates) imperial social practices and gender constructions.

However, his followers struggle to understand the different structures and values of God's empire (20:1-16). They resist Jesus' announcement of his imminent death (16:22-23; 17:23). They cannot heal the demon-possessed boy, and Jesus rebukes them for their "little faith" (17:14-20). They find his teaching on marriage and divorce hard to accept (19:10). They do not understand the special place the vulnerable and marginal have in God's empire (the children, 19:13-15). They are surprised that Jesus turns away the rich man (19:25). While Jesus promises them future reward for leaving everything to follow him (19:27-30), the mother of James and John lobbies for her sons' particular elevation (20:20-28). They have much to learn about the ways of suffering and vindication that comprise the rhythm of discipleship.

5.6 Mark Watch

This narrative block begins with the kernel of Matt. 16:21-28, which parallels Mark 8:31–9:1. While much of Matthew 17 parallels Mark 9, Matthew adds the fourth teaching discourse of chapter 18 (the community discourse), which from verses 10-35 (including the parable of the unforgiving servant) has no parallel in Mark. In Mark 10, Jesus sets out from Galilee to go to Jerusalem. This journey takes two chapters in Matthew 19–20.

The Fifth Kernel (21:1-27) and Fifth Narrative Block (Chapters 21–27)

The fifth kernel moves the action forward, answers a question raised by the previous kernel, and raises a question to be answered by the next kernel.

The kernel moves the plot forward toward Jesus' crucifixion at the hands of an alliance of the Jerusalem elite and the Roman governor Pilate. Jesus enters Jerusalem to be welcomed by a crowd (21:1-11). But the conflict with the ruling elite (the chief priests, scribes, elders) intensifies as he condemns their center of power, the temple, as a "den for robbers" that does not encourage prayer (21:12-17). He then curses a fruitless fig tree as a symbol of their failed leadership (21:18-22). They "become angry" (21:15) and counter him by demanding to know who or what authorizes Jesus' activity, but his response outwits them (21:23-27).

Such antipathy seals Jesus' fate, and the satellites will elaborate the fatal consequence of the conflict. The kernel thus performs a second function of answering a question raised by the fourth kernel (16:21-28). There Jesus announced his impending death at the hands of the Jerusalem elite. The fifth kernel not only confirms the reliability of Jesus' declaration but also supplies key pointers as to *how* this will come about. In turn, it raises a question for the sixth kernel to answer:

Will Jesus' death be the end of the story, and the victory of the power alliance based in Jerusalem that ends Jesus' God-given commission, or will God raise Jesus from the dead as Jesus predicted?

The conflict foregrounded in the kernel is elaborated in the satellites. Jesus immediately tells three parables against the chief priests and Pharisees, not all Israel (21:45), that accuse them of unfaithfulness to God, greed, and injustice. In the parable of the two sons, he declares that they do not do the will of the Father (God) and that tax collectors and prostitutes enter God's empire ahead of them (21:28-32). In the parable of the vineyard (21:33-45), he condemns them for killing God's Son and failing to pay the rent (fruit) to the owner (God). In the parable of the wedding banquet, he denounces them for spurning the king's son, for which their city is destroyed, and common folks from the streets take their place (22:1-14).

Then various groups from this leadership alliance—Pharisees, Herodians, Sadducees—engage Jesus in verbal sparring (22:15-46). They ask him questions about paying taxes, resurrection, the greatest commandment, and David's son. Jesus outwits them verbally, however, proving he is their superior, so that no one thereafter "dare[d] to ask him any more questions" (22:46). The conflict has increased so that all communication has broken down.

Unable to talk *to* each other, Jesus talks *about* them in very negative terms in chapters 23–25. In chapter 23, Jesus curses and condemns the Jerusalem-based, Rome-allied leaders. He repeatedly calls them "hypocrites," people who play a part but are not genuine, and enumerates their faults at length. For example, they neglect "the weightier matters of the law: justice and mercy and faith"; they are "full of greed and hypocrisy"; they are "full of hypocrisy and lawlessness"; they and their city Jerusalem reject the messengers God sends, including Jesus (23:23-39). This condemnation is not directed against all Jews for all time; it is specifically directed against this group of leaders.

In chapters 24–25, Jesus announces the end of the age in which these leaders and their Roman allies dominate, articulates signs of his return, and describes the future establishment of God's victorious empire. In 24:1-2, Jesus leaves the temple and predicts its downfall, a sign of divine judgment on the power base of the leaders. In 24:3-26, Jesus describes the difficulties of the hostile present for his followers, which requires their faithfulness, nonviolent resistance, and hopeful anticipation. He describes his spectacular return that affects the whole cosmos in its display of God's empire and power asserted over all things (24:27-31).

Two dynamics are operative in this scenario. On the one hand, the scene is seditious in that it depicts the end of the Roman order as it gives way to God's rule. Yet, ironically, on the other hand, it mimics and reinscribes the same sort of imperial structures of power that the Gospel simultaneously resists. It envisions God's empire, rather than Rome's, dominating all.

Jesus warns his followers to be watchful and ready for his return at an unknown time, faithfully attending to the master's business (24:32—25:30). The discourse finishes with a scene that anticipates the final judgment of the nations on the basis of whether they have attended to Jesus in the vulnerable and needy: the hungry, thirsty, the stranger, the naked, the sick, the imprisoned even though they did not perceive him to be present (25:31-46).

After these three chapters of denunciation that have demonstrated *why* Jesus and the imperial order are at odds, the narrative returns to the account of *how* the elite alliance effects Jesus' death. They plot his arrest and death, but hesitate, because of the festival of Passover and popular support for Jesus (26:1-5). With Judas' assistance in betraying Jesus (as predicted by Jesus), they arrest Jesus and his disciples flee (also predicted by Jesus, 26:14-56). The arrested Jesus appears before the chief priests, scribes, and elders and reveals his identity as the Son of Man who will return in power to establish God's empire in full (drawing on Daniel 7). This assertion brings cries of blasphemy. Blasphemy is of course also sedition in that it signals the end of the imperial order. They condemn Jesus to death (26:57-68). Because the Jerusalem leaders under Roman rule cannot condemn Jesus to death, they take him to the Roman governor Pilate. After playing power games with the Jerusalem leaders in which he makes them submit to him and beg for Jesus' crucifixion, he does as they wish and hands Jesus over for crucifixion (27:1-31).[5] The threat Jesus is understood to pose to the imperial order is evident in his being crucified with two bandits or armed rebels, and as an unsanctioned "king of the Jews" (27:32-56). Jesus dies and is buried by Joseph of Arimathea in a tomb, and Pilate and the Jerusalem leaders post a guard against Jesus' prediction that he would be raised on the third day (27:57-66).

5.3 Jesus before Pilate, who washes his hands, by Duccio di Buoninsegna (between 1308 and 1311). Museo dell'Opera metropolitana del Duomo, Siena; Commons.wikimedia.org.

While the main plot line has focused on the leaders securing Jesus' death, satellites present other characters who are involved in Jesus'

5. On the scene with Pilate, see Carter, *Matthew and Empire*, 145–68.

death and who offer various perspectives on his death. Jesus is not taken by surprise but affirms his death as imminent and inevitable (26:1-2), even as he struggles with it in prayer (26:36-46). He declares that his death secures a covenant marked by release from sins and anticipates the future establishment of God's empire (26:26-30). An unnamed woman anoints him as king or emperor and thereby prepares him for burial (26:6-13). Judas agrees to betray Jesus as Jesus predicts (26:14-25, 47-56). Jesus also predicts that Peter will betray him (26:31-35), and Peter does so (26:69-75). Peter, James, and John sleep instead of supporting Jesus in prayer in Gethsemane (26:36-46). Jesus' male disciples abandon him (26:56). Judas commits suicide (27:3-10). The women disciples who had followed Jesus from Galilee, though, gather near the cross, and two of them, "Mary Magdalene and the other Mary," watch the tomb (27:55-61).

This fifth narrative block ends with Jesus dead and buried. The last satellite of the block—the placing of a guard at Jesus' tomb—raises a question that the sixth kernel must address; can they secure the tomb against God's resurrecting power?

5.7 Mark Watch

Jesus enters Jerusalem in Mark 11 (Matthew 21). To intensify the conflict with the Jerusalem leaders, Matthew adds the parables of the two sons (21:28-32) and the wedding feast (22:1-14), and Jesus' cursing of or woes on the Jerusalem leaders in chapter 23. To emphasize the end of their Rome-allied world, Matthew doubles the eschatological and judgment material in Mark 13 to form two chapters (Matthew 24–25).

The Sixth Kernel (28:1-10) and Narrative Block (28:1-28)

The sixth kernel is a hinge, a branching point that advances the plot: God raises Jesus from the dead when the death of Jesus in the previous narrative block seems to be the end of the story. The story will continue. The kernel has also answered the question raised by the fifth kernel: Can the alliance of Jerusalem leaders and the Roman governor thwart God's work in Jesus? They do not have ultimate power. Jesus' death is not their victory over God's agent. It does not bring Jesus' commission to nothing. Jesus' prediction of his death and resurrection, made in the fourth kernel and its satellites (16:21; 17:23; 20:19), is shown to be reliable. The kernel also raises a question as to what impact Jesus' resurrection might have.

Women followers at Jesus' tomb await his resurrection (28:1). An earthquake (28:2), the presence of an angel of the Lord sitting on the tomb stone (28:3-4), and the angel's announcement that Jesus has been raised (28:5-7) attest a new divine act. Jesus' appearance to the women and his instruction to them to tell "my brothers to go to Galilee," where he will meet his male followers, confirm God's life-giving work that overcomes the alliance of leaders' death-bringing animosity (28:9-10).

Two satellites elaborate the kernel. In 28:11-15, the leaders confirm their rejection of Jesus. They continue to refuse to recognize any divine action in relation to Jesus and tell a story that differs from the angel's proclamation. They bribe soldiers to declare that his disciples stole Jesus' body.

By contrast, the second satellite focuses on the response of the eleven male disciples (28:16-20). Believing and doubting the resurrection proclamation, yet obeying Jesus' directive via the women disciples, they go to Galilee to encounter the risen Jesus (28:16-17). On a mountain, he declares himself the recipient (from God) of all authority "in heaven and on earth," thereby surpassing all Roman power (28:18). He commands his followers to teach, baptize, and make disciples of all nations, promising to be present with them in this mission activity until "the end of the age" (28:19-20).

5.4 The risen Christ appears to his disciples on a mountaintop in Galilee (Matt. 28: 16-20); Duccio di Buoninsegna. Museo del Opera metropolitana del Duomo, Siena; Commons.wikimedia.org.

This commission raises the question of whether Jesus' followers will be faithful in his task and how they will carry it out. That is, the sixth kernel announcing Jesus' resurrection must lead to subsequent kernels and satellites that continue the Gospel story.

5.8 Mark Watch

Mark's brief resurrection account consisting of only eight verses is expanded in Matthew 28 with an appearance of Jesus to the women (28:9-10), and the two satellites concerning the story of the disciples stealing the body (28:11-15) and the scene in which Jesus commissions the disciples to worldwide mission (28:16-20). The additions produce a less mysterious ending, and one that recognizes ongoing opposition from the leaders, as well as a connection between the risen Jesus and the continuing mission of his followers.

Questions for Review and Reflection

1. The chapter outlines an analysis of the plot of Matthew's Gospel. What are the six narrative blocks or sections that the chapter suggests? What are the six key scenes that are identified?
2. Read through the Gospel. Do you agree with the six key scenes identified in the chapter? Are there others you would select? Justify your choices.
3. The sidebars in the chapter draw your attention to comparisons between Mark's telling of the story of Jesus and Matthew's story. What similarities and differences do you note?

6

Matthew: Editing and Retelling Stories about Jesus

As we noticed in the last chapter, Matthew's telling of the story of Jesus is both similar to yet different from Mark's story. Explaining these similarities and differences has long occupied the attention of readers of the Gospels. How did they come about? What changes were made? Why were they made? The "how" question attends mainly to the mechanics of creating the similarities and differences. The "what" question concerns the content of the changes. The "why" question concerns their significance.

We begin this chapter with the how question, then take up the what and why questions.

How?

One long-held hypothesis for explaining how the similarities and differences in the Gospel accounts of Jesus were created was that Matthew was the first Gospel written and Mark was a later revised version that summarized and abbreviated Matthew and Luke. The problem with this hypothesis is explaining the omission of so much significant material about Jesus from Matthew and Luke. Why might Mark tell a story about Jesus that leaves out so much of his teaching (e.g., the Sermon on the Mount) and actions?

Another explanation—the most widely accepted current theory—is that Mark's Gospel, the shortest of the Gospels, was the first Gospel to be written. Matthew subsequently uses and expands Mark's story, as does Luke's Gospel. How does Matthew revise Mark to create an account almost twice as long? Where does the extra material originate?

First, Matthew incorporates nearly all of Mark's 661 (or so) verses, omitting approximately 55 verses. About half of these omitted 55 verses involve 8 of Mark's scenes that Matthew omits.[1]

Second, Matthew adds material to Mark's account. Some of this material is also found in parts of Luke's Gospel. Material common to Matthew and Luke but absent from Mark comprises over two hundred verses. Most of this material involves sayings of Jesus. It is possible that either Matthew or Luke borrowed this material from the other's Gospel. But the appearance of this common material in different contexts in the two Gospels and the presence of other material only in Matthew or only in Luke suggest that the accounts of Matthew and Luke were independent of each other.

A more likely explanation of this common material, then, was that there was a collection of sayings of Jesus that Mark's author did not know but that existed before either Matthew or Luke were written. Both Gospels used this collection, but independently of each other—so the theory goes—often preserving its wording, literary forms, and order, while also reconfiguring and reinterpreting it in places.[2] As I noted in chapter 2, scholars have called this source Q, after the German word *Quelle*, which means—yes, you guessed it—"source"! Scholars debate whether it was a written or an oral source, and whether it was

1. Mark 1:23-28, healing the demoniac in the synagogue; 1:35-38, Jesus leaves Capernaum; 4:26-29, the parable of the seed growing secretly; 7:31-37, Jesus heals a deaf mute; 8:22-26, healing a blind man at Bethsaida; 9:38-40, the strange exorcist; 12:41-44, the widow's mite; 14:51-52 the naked young man flees.
2. So, for example, the parable of the lost sheep in Luke 15:3-7 attacks the leaders who have criticized Jesus; Matthew relocates the parable to emphasize the responsibility of Jesus' disciples to care for one another (Matt. 18:10-14).

a fixed or flexible collection that developed over time through various versions. Nevertheless, similarities in order, wording, and forms in both the Matthew and Luke versions of this material that is not found in Mark suggest some form of common source for Matthew and Luke. This common (non-Markan) material largely comprises sayings or teachings attributed to Jesus.

Third, in addition to Q material, Matthew adds material that appears only in Matthew's Gospel and not in the other Gospels. This material is known—predictably—as M material. It comprises, by one count, some 380 verses, including Matthew 1–2; ten parables including 13:36-50; 18:23-35; 21:28-22:14; and chapter 25, and much of chapters 23 (attacks on the Jerusalem leaders) and 28 (resurrection).

How do we account for this M material? Does all of it or some of it come from a separate source or from several sources (an infancy story? collection of parables?)? And/or is the author of the Gospel responsible for creating all or some of it? One scholar, for example, identifies a collection comprising some forty-nine verses found mainly in chapters 5–6, 10, and 23.[3] A major challenge concerns how to determine whether material originates from a source or from the author. Most scholars argue that M represents an amorphous collection of material from multiple sources and from the author's editing or redactional work.

On this model, then, Matthew works with the outline of the story of Jesus provided by Mark's Gospel and elaborates it by adding Q and M material to create the new twenty-eight-chapter-long telling of the story of Jesus that I outlined in the last chapter.

3. Stephenson H. Brooks, *Matthew's Community: The Evidence of His Special Sayings Material*, JSNTSup 16 (Sheffield: JSOT Press, 1987), 160–65. Brooks identifies the following as M material: Matt. 5:19, 21-22, 23-24, 27-28, 33-35, 37, 36; 6:1-6, 16-18, 7-8; 10:5b-6, 23b; 23:2-3, 5, 8-10, 15, 16-22, 24, 33; 7:6; 12:36-37; 18:18, 19-20; 19:12. Brooks regards other material unique to Matthew such as the parable in 18:23-35 as originating not in a source but from the Gospel writer.

6.1 Who Is Matthew?

We do not know the identity of the person—or persons?—responsible for writing this Gospel. The earliest unambiguous link between the Gospel and "Matthew" occurs in the late second century in the writings of Bishop Irenaeus of Lyons, some one hundred years after the Gospel was written. Irenaeus does not offer any compelling evidence for the link. Rather, in a context of controversy and diversity involving those whom Irenaeus identifies as "heretics," his claim is part of his concern to underscore the reliability of the Gospels by associating them with apostles.

Why should the name Matthew be linked with this particular Gospel? Why not the name Peter, for example, since he is prominent in the Gospel? Or one of the Marys who come to Jesus' tomb on the day of resurrection? The Gospel mentions Matthew in 9:9 in a scene involving Jesus' call of a tax collector whom Mark, interestingly, identifies as Levi (Mark 2:14). Why this change of name? Does it indicate the Gospel's author? This is most unlikely since Matthew does not play any prominent part in the Gospel. He only appears in 9:9 and 10:3 (where he is eighth on the list of followers!), is not present in scenes that involve Jesus' inner circle such as the transfiguration (17:1), and, assuming he was a tax-collector-become-disciple, was probably dead by the 80s or 90s CE, when the Gospel was written.

Another explanation is that the name Matthew is associated with the Gospel because it sounds similar to the Greek word for "disciples" (*mathētai*). This noun is linked to the Greek verb translated "to learn," which appears in 9:13, just four verses after the call of Matthew in 9:9. Perhaps the name Matthew represents the model reader who reads and learns from Jesus as a disciple.

Another possibility is that the name Matthew is associated with the Gospel because it reflects a memory of a key role Matthew the disciple of Jesus played in initial teachings about Jesus. Perhaps he was a key teacher or leader in the community from which the Gospel later originated. Or perhaps this Matthew was the source of (some of) the teachings and stories about Jesus that subsequently became part of the Gospel.

What?

All this editorial and compositional activity creates a different yet similar Gospel. Why is it necessary to have another telling of the story of Jesus? Or in other words, why does "Matthew" (whoever Matthew might be) go to the trouble of creating this new account?

Matthew's reworking or redaction of Mark to form a new Gospel particularly involves changes in the presentation of Jesus, in the presentation of disciples, and in the presentation of the Jerusalem leaders. In the subsequent section, "Why?," I will suggest that these three changes in presentation and the new story they create address situations that Matthew's readers were experiencing and that Mark's Gospel did not particularly address. That is, we might think of Matthew's new version of the story of Jesus as a story-sermon that scratches the particular itches of Matthew's readers. Matthew's new story-sermon is a word-on-target that does pastoral work in reassuring and instructing its readers on how to be faithful followers in their challenging situations.

A New Presentation of Jesus

As we observed in the last chapter, Matthew's Gospel begins in a way that differs significantly from Mark's Gospel. Unparalleled in Mark's Gospel, Matthew's opening narrative block presents an account of Jesus' conception and birth (chapters 1–2) before expanding Mark's scenes involving John the Baptizer, Jesus' baptism, and Jesus' temptation (3:1—4:17). This opening section is crucial in framing the whole Gospel story. For example, the scene announcing Mary's conception of Jesus (1:18-25), unparalleled in Mark, establishes Jesus' God-given identity and authority. An "angel of the Lord"—an authorized and authoritative figure—names the baby Jesus and explains the name: "for he will save his people from their sins" (1:21). The name Jesus, which is the Greek form of the name Joshua and means "God saves," is, in other words, a commission or statement of his life's work of saving. Then a citation of Scripture (Isa. 7:14) provides a second name and statement of Jesus' identity, "and they shall name him Emmanuel, which means 'God is with us'" (1:23). Taken together, the angel and the Scripture name the Gospel's perspective on Jesus as the agent of God in manifesting God's saving presence (1:21-23). This is his mission and life's work, the framework that interprets all of the subsequent story.

This opening section does not, however, explain *how* Jesus is to carry out this mission. How is he to save from sins? Subsequently, the Gospel provides an answer. It does so by making some small but important editings or redaction of Mark's Gospel to link Jesus and saving from sins. The word translated "forgiveness," which literally means "release" from sins, is important here. Matthew removes from Mark's Gospel a reference to John preaching a baptism of repentance "for the forgiveness of sins" (3:1; Mark 1:4). Matthew associates repentance

(3:2) and confession (3:6) with John, but not forgiveness. Matthew's Gospel restricts forgiveness of sins to Jesus, as we can see in the following ways.

- That link between Jesus, his numerous healings, and forgiveness is expressed in the account of Jesus healing the paralyzed man that Matthew takes over from Mark and abbreviates (Mark 2:1-12; Matt. 9:1-8). In this scene, saving from sins involves both speaking the word of forgiveness and healing the disease. Healing is a "release" from sins. Diseases were often understood as the consequence of personal sin. But they also came about from unhealthy living conditions and nutritional deficiencies and so were the consequences of sinful imperial practices and structures that ensured the elite had plenty to eat while nonelites lived near subsistence levels. Inadequate diet means being susceptible to diseases of deficiency and contagion. Healings (and exorcisms that deliver people from the devil's power) save from all these types of sin. This scene in 9:1-8 shows us how to read the other healing scenes. The ultimate saving or release from sins will take place at Jesus' return, when he establishes God's empire in full, creating a world marked by physical wholeness and fertility (24:27-31).
- In the Last Supper scene, Matthew's Jesus gives thanks for the cup as "my blood of the covenant, which is poured out for many *for the forgiveness of sins*" (Matt. 26:28). The words in italics are added to Mark's scene (Mark 14:24), underscoring the link between forgiveness and Jesus' death. The alliance of the Jerusalem-based elite that crucifies Jesus sinfully rejects Jesus as God's messenger. His resurrection, though, accomplished through God's power, overcomes their sinful rejection and the worst that it accomplishes (Jesus' death).
- Matthew also adds several verses that link forgiveness by God with the responsibility of people forgiving people (5:23-24; 6:12, 14-15; 18:23-35). None of these passages has any parallel in Mark.

Linked to Jesus' commission to express God's forgiveness (1:21) is the commission to manifest God's presence (1:23). This mission is expressed initially in relation to Jesus' conception and associated with a name, Emmanuel, so that it frames the whole Gospel story. The Gospel underscores this aspect of Jesus' mission in the context of community gathered for worship (18:20), in the tasks of expressing practical mercy among the dispossessed (25:31-46), and in its teaching and preaching mission (28:18-20). The Gospel ends with the promise, "I am with you always." Recall that most of this material is not in Mark, indicating the importance of this emphasis for Matthew's telling of the story of Jesus.

The Gospel positions this emphasis on Jesus' God-given mission to manifest God's saving presence up front, in its opening chapter, underscoring its importance. It uses the "primacy effect," the notion that the material that the reader first encounters in the Gospel story sets up key perspectives on Jesus and on reading the whole Gospel narrative. Repetition of these themes throughout the Gospel keeps them before the readers. And the Gospel's closing scene emphasizes divine presence.

The Gospel employs other means to construct Jesus' distinctive identity as God's commissioned agent. The genealogy—unparalleled in Mark—sets Jesus the Messiah in the context of God's purposes from the call of Abraham to bless all the nations of the earth (Gen. 12:1-3); to the use of kings in the line of David to manifest God's life-giving rule (2 Samuel 7; Psalm 72); to the disaster of the Babylonian exile, when all of God's promises seem to have been defeated (2 Kings 24–25); to God's use of Cyrus the Persian to restore the people to the land and a new future (Isa. 44:28—45:13; Matt. 1:1-17). Like Mark, Matthew's opening verse identifies Jesus as Christ (Greek, *christos*), meaning messiah (from the Hebrew, *māšîaḥ*), literally "the anointed one," God's commissioned agent or representative. Anointing signifies a person is set apart for a particular role in God's purposes.[4]

4. Anointed figures commissioned to carry out God's purposes include kings (Ps. 2:2), prophets (1 Kgs. 19:16), priests (Lev. 4:3-5), and even the gentile Persian ruler Cyrus (Isa. 44:28—45:1). In

Matthew repeats the term *Christ* ("Messiah") regularly to emphasize Jesus' identity as commissioned by God. Three times at the end of the genealogy, the Gospel refers to Jesus as Christ (1:16, 17, 18) and again in 2:4. After these initial five references, Matthew includes eleven more designations of Jesus as God's anointed one. Sixteen times, then, in twenty-eight chapters, Matthew keeps Jesus' identity and authority as Messiah in front of the reader.[5]

Similarly, Matthew introduces another key term that denotes Jesus' identity as God's agent, "Son" (2:15) or "Son of God" (3:17). Matthew adds the term in the expanded temptation story with Satan, twice introducing temptations for Jesus with the conditional clause, "If you are the Son of God . . ." (4:3, 6). The issue is one of authority and obedience. Will Jesus be the agent of God's purposes, or will he betray this identity and obey the devil? Jesus' threefold rejection of the devil's commands underscores his identity as God's Son or agent.

Matthew differs from Mark in a major way in the subsequent uses of "Son of God" throughout the Gospel. For Mark, no human being can discern Jesus' identity as God's agent and Son only in terms of power. So for Mark, it is not until the cross, the site of Jesus' suffering and weakness, that the first human being, a centurion, names Jesus as Son of God (Mark 15:39). Only demons identify Jesus in relation to his power in exorcisms (Mark 3:11; 5:7). But for Matthew, disciples identify Jesus as Son of God long before the cross in relation to acts of power. They use this term to confess Jesus' identity when Jesus calms a storm at sea (added in 14:33 to Mark 6:51-52) and in response to Jesus' question about his identity (16:16, added to Mark 8:29). The term also appears in relation to weakness and suffering. Matthew adds "Son of God" in the passion narrative in 27:40, 43 (cf. Mark 15:30, 32) and retains it in 27:54 at the cross (Mark 15:39).

Matthew also gives Jesus something of a makeover in upgrading

Psalms of Solomon 17, a king from the line of David is called the Messiah. He will send the Romans out of Jerusalem nonviolently.

5. Check it out: Matthew matches Mark's references to Jesus as Messiah in 16:16 (Mark 8:29), 22:42 (Mark 12:35), 24:23 (Mark 13:21); 26:63 (Mark 14:61). He adds references in 1:1, 16, 17, 18; 2:4; 11:2; 16:20 (Mark 8:30); 23:10; 26:68 (Mark 14:65); 27:17, 22 (Mark 15:9, 12). Matthew omits two references from Mark 9:41 in Matt. 10:42, and Mark 15:32 in Matt. 27:42.

his image as God's agent. So Matthew omits from Mark instances in which Jesus does not know something,[6] or is limited in his movement or activity.[7] Matthew also removes references to Jesus' emotions that seem to him inappropriate.[8] The cumulative effect of these often small changes is to heighten Jesus' authority and identity as God's agent.

Another strategy that Matthew uses to underline Jesus' sanctioned place in God's purposes occurs in Matthew's citation of Scripture. Four times in chapter 2 (unparalleled in Mark), Matthew stops the action involving Herod, the magi, and Jesus' flight to Egypt with Joseph to use citations from the Hebrew Bible to interpret the action. The Gospel uses Scripture to identify the birthplace of the Messiah (Micah 5:2 in Matt. 2:5-6) and to interpret the flight to Egypt (Hos. 11:1 in Matt. 2:15), Herod's murder of the baby boys around Bethlehem (Jer. 31:15 in Matt. 2:17-18), and Jesus' move to Nazareth (Matt. 2:23). Interestingly, in this last instance, no one has identified a verse that says, "He will be called a Nazorean," though several suggestions have been made about possible references. In Matt. 3:3, another Scripture (Isa. 40:3) interprets John's role in preparing for Jesus' coming, and in 4:15-16 Jesus' move to Capernaum is interpreted in terms of a text that originally described Assyria's control of the land (Isa. 9:1-2). All of these references underscore God's purposes being accomplished in Jesus.

Matthew adds more of these Scripture citations through the Gospel. In 8:17, a citation from Isa. 53:4 interprets Jesus' healings and exorcisms. In 12:17-21, another text from Isaiah (Isa. 42:1-4) presents Jesus as God's chosen and beloved with whom God is well pleased (compare the baptism, 3:17, and transfiguration, 17:5). It interprets Jesus' ministry in terms of life-giving mercy and justice for all, including gentiles. The addition of a Scripture citation from Zechariah

6. Compare Mark 5:9 and Matt. 8:32 (not knowing the demon's name); Mark 5:30 and Matt. 9:21-22 (not knowing who touched his garment); Mark 9:16, 33 and Matt. 17:14; 18:1 (not knowing what the disciples are discussing); Mark 9:21 and Matt. 17:17-18 (not knowing how long the child has been sick).

7. Compare Mark 1:45 and Matt. 8:4 (limited movement); Mark 6:5-6 and Matt. 13:58 (limited acts of power). Matthew omits Mark's account of Jesus' double efforts to heal the blind man (Mark 8:22-26; cf. Matt. 16:12-13).

8. Compare Mark 3:5 and Matt. 12:12 (anger); Mark 3:21 and Matt. 12:21-22 (out of his mind); Mark 8:12 and Matt. 12:39; 16:2 (sighing deeply).

9–14 (9:9) to the scene of Jesus entering Jerusalem (Matt. 21:4-5) highlights his identity as a humble king who manifests God's rule over all. In 27:9, in a scene only in Matthew, the suicide of Judas is interpreted with a citation ascribed to Jeremiah, though in fact it also comes from Zechariah (Zech. 11:12-13). Most of these scriptural references are not present in Mark.

6.1 Jesus enters Jerusalem riding "an ass and the foal of an ass" (Matt. 21:7) in this painting by Pietro Lorenzetti; Lower Basilica, Assisi. Commons.wikimedia.org

In their original scriptural contexts, these texts referred to particular situations of their own time, and none of them referred to Jesus. But Matthew reads the Scriptures through his "Jesus glasses" and sees references to Jesus where others have not. The Gospel does so in order to present and interpret God's working through the whole of Jesus' life as well as his death.

One final aspect of the presentation of Jesus concerns his role as teacher or revealer of God's will. Mark frequently mentions Jesus actively teaching people (Mark 1:21-22; 2:13; 6:2), but only occasionally does the Gospel give any extensive account of the content of Jesus' teaching (4:1; ch. 13). Matthew's Gospel makes up for this lack by creating five blocks of extensive teaching—chapters 5–7, 10, 13, 18, 24–25.

Two of these blocks—in chapters 13 and 24–25—expand material in Mark. Matthew 13 expands Mark's collection of parables (Mark 4) by adding parables such as the weeds and the wheat, the yeast, the treasure, the pearl, and the net. All of these parables come from M material except for the parable of the yeast, which is from Q. Matthew 24–25 expands Mark 13, concerning the last days and the return of Jesus the Son of Man. Much of the expansion follows the end of Mark 13, as Matthew adds Q material after 24:36 concerning the coming of the Son of Man (Matt. 24:37-44; par. Luke 17:26-36), and parables concerning the wicked servant (Matt. 24:45-51; par. Luke 12:41-46) and the talents (Matt. 25:14-30; par. Luke 19:11-27). Matthew also adds M material, the ten bridesmaids (Matt. 25:1-13) and the judgment on the nations as sheep and goats (25:31-46).

The other three blocks of Jesus' teaching material have no explicit parallels in Mark's Gospel as blocks of teaching, though they include in places some material that is in Mark. So the Sermon on the Mount appears in Matthew 5–7, largely created from Q and M material. Matthew 10 concerns the mission activity of Jesus' followers. Matthew 18, known as the community discourse, instructs readers in community relations among disciples so as to provide support for one another. The chapter includes some Q material (the parable of the lost sheep: Matt. 18:10-14; Luke 15:3-7) and some M material that emphasizes important themes in Matthew's Gospel such as God's presence manifested in Jesus (Matt. 18:19-20), and the parable of (un)forgiveness (18:23-35).

Some interpreters of the Gospel have seen the presence of these five teaching blocks as an attempt to parallel Moses' teaching in the five books of the Pentateuch. One thing is for certain. They heighten the presentation of Jesus as a teacher and revealer of God's will—as part of his commission to manifest God's saving presence.

A New Presentation of the Disciples

It is not surprising that a presentation of Jesus that emphasizes, among other things, Jesus' teaching should be matched by a positive presentation of his disciples. A good teacher has good students. Consistently, Matthew upgrades Mark's fairly negative presentation of the disciples as nonunderstanding and fearful.

For example, Matthew omits Mark's description of the disciples as not understanding the parables (Mark 4:13; Matt. 13:16-17). Similarly Matthew omits Mark's reference to their not understanding his instruction about the loaves (Mark 6:52; Matt. 14:33). In the latter instance, Matthew not only removes the reference to their not understanding but also adds a reference that shows the disciples as understanding Jesus and insightfully confessing, "Truly you are the Son of God" (14:33). Two chapters later, Jesus' instruction about the "leaven of the Pharisees and of Herod" leads to nonunderstanding for Mark's disciples. Matthew changes their nonunderstanding into understanding of Jesus' teaching (Mark 8:21; Matt. 16:11-12). Likewise in Mark 9, Mark's disciples do not understand Jesus' teaching about resurrection (they were questioning "what this rising from the dead could mean"; Mark 9:10). Matthew omits this expression of ignorance (Matt. 17:8). Mark's disciples respond to Jesus' second instruction about going to Jerusalem to die by not understanding. Matthew upgrades their response to being "greatly distressed" (Mark 9:32; Matt. 17:23). The effect of Matthew's presentation of the disciples as often (though not always) understanding Jesus reinforces the presentation of Jesus as the authorized revealer and teacher of God's purposes.

Mark's disciples regularly choose fear rather than exercise faith. Matthew upgrades this presentation of disciples, presenting them as having "little faith" rather than no faith (Mark 4:40; Matt. 8:26). Matthew uses the same term, "little faith," three more times for the disciples, twice in M material (Matt. 6:30; 14:31; cf. Mark 6:50-51) and once in adding it to Mark material to emphasize the presence of some faith (Matt. 16:8; Mark 8:17). On the mount of transfiguration, Mark's disciples fear. Again Matthew omits the reference (Mark 9:6; Matt. 17:4) and transforms their role. After God identifies Jesus as "my beloved Son" in the next verse, Mark's disciples do or say nothing. Matthew changes the scene by adding a description of the disciples appropriately falling on their faces and being "filled with awe" (Mark 9:7; Matt. 17:6). Mark's disciples do not understand Jesus' second instruction about going to Jerusalem to die, but they are afraid to ask Jesus for elaboration. Matthew omits the references to their not understanding and to their fear, describing them instead as "greatly distressed" (Mark 9:32; Matt. 17:23). This upgraded presentation of the disciples in terms of faith rather than fear also underscores the effectiveness of Jesus' teaching as well as exhibiting important dimensions of being a disciple.

Matthew also eliminates and transforms inappropriate actions that Mark's disciples perform. In the storm-calming scene, Mark's disciples accuse Jesus of not caring if they perish. Matthew changes their accusation into a faithful prayer for Jesus' assistance ("Lord, save us!," Mark 4:38; Matt. 8:25). In Mark, two of the disciples, James and John, ask Jesus to grant them the preeminent positions at his right and left hand "in your glory." Matthew retains the scene but removes the question that expresses inappropriate ambition from the two disciples. Instead, Matthew has *the mother* of these two disciples ask Jesus for the places of prominence (Mark 10:35-37; Matt. 20:20-21).

This makeover for the disciples, of course, does not remove every blemish from their presentation in Matthew's Gospel (cf. Mark 8:32-33; Matt. 16:22-23). But Matthew's re-presentation of them elevates faith over fear, understanding over nonunderstanding, and appropriate following over inappropriate responses. These changes not only improve the presentation of the disciples but also contribute to the presentation of Jesus as a teacher who effectively manifests God's saving presence and will.

A New Presentation of the Jerusalem Leaders

Matthew's Gospel creates a sustained negative presentation of the Jewish leaders and the synagogue. It is crucial to remember that these leaders are not primarily religious figures like contemporary clergy, for example. Rather, while they of course have religious roles, they are also societal leaders. Religion and politics are not separated entities. Together these leaders form, as the Jewish historian Josephus comments, the ruling elite of Judea who exercise rule in tensive alliance with the Romans (*Ant.* 20.249).

Matthew's Gospel employs five techniques of editing or redaction to increase their negative presentation.

1. Matthew's Gospel maintains Mark's negative presentation of Jerusalem's leaders. These leaders comprise a shifting coalition of Pharisees, scribes, Sadducees, chief priests, and elders. They are opponents of Jesus who are responsible for his death (Matt. 16:21; Mark 8:31; Matt. 26:2-4; Mark 14:1). Jesus condemns them in a series of parables for not doing God's will in their leadership, for not producing the "fruit" that God wants, and for rejecting Jesus as God's agent (21:28—22:14). Two Matthean redactions in 21:43 (Mark 12:11) and 22:7 (Q, Luke 14:21) express divine judgment on the leaders.

Their rejection of Jesus is intensified by Matthew's presentation of Jesus as commissioned by God as God's agent to manifest God's saving presence. They first appear in 2:3-6 (unparalleled in Mark) in response to King Herod's question about where the Messiah is to be born. In quoting Micah's reference to Bethlehem, they know the right answer. But they don't know to interpret the Scriptures in relation to Jesus, and they do not act on the basis of what they know. They do not go to Bethlehem to pay homage to Jesus, as do the magi (the visitors from the East). This M material provides the first introduction to these characters in the story, and it is negative.

6.2 *Woe Unto You, Scribes and Pharisees*, by James Tissot (between 1886 and 1894); Brooklyn Museum.

The second reference to these leaders maintains the negative perspective. The Gospel adds Q material to Mark's account about John the Baptizer (Matt. 3:7-10; Mark 1:4-8). This material also portrays the leaders negatively. Matthew replaces Q's reference to "multitudes" coming to John for baptism (Luke 3:7-9) with a reference to "the Pharisees and Sadducees" coming to John. Whereas Luke describes these *multitudes* as a "brood of vipers," Matthew's redaction associates this negative term only with the Pharisees and Sadducees, who are rebuked by John for their lack of repentance.

Matthew's Gospel regularly condemns them for hypocrisy, for not faithfully living out God's purposes in their leadership. The Gospel keeps Mark's single description of the "Pharisees and scribes . . . from Jerusalem" as "hypocrites" for voiding God's commands concerning care for elderly parents (Mark 7:1, 6; Matt. 15:1, 7). But Matthew elaborates this feature by adding the polemical description "hypocrites" eight more times—to a Markan scene (Mark 12:15; Matt. 22:18), to a Q scene concerning their final or eschatological condemnation (Matt. 24:51; Luke 12:46), as well as in the M material of chapter 23, with its sixfold cursing of the leaders (Pharisees and scribes) as "hypocrites" for various shortcomings, including the neglect of "justice and mercy and faith" and the killing of Jesus (23:13, 15, 23, 25, 27, 29). In addition, chapter 23 consistently identifies them as "blind." Since "seeing" designates disciples who understand Jesus and his teaching, the adjective emphasizes that they are opponents, not followers, of Jesus (Matt. 13:10-17).

2. The Gospel associates the leaders with the devil. The key point of connection is that just as the devil opposes Jesus' mission and identity, so too do the leaders. Thus Matthew names the devil as "the tempter" or "tester" (4:3) in the lengthened temptation scene as the devil tries to overthrow Jesus' identity as God's agent or Son (4:1-11). The Gospel then uses this same language to describe the leaders. Twice Matthew keeps Mark's language of the leaders "testing" or opposing Jesus, but of course the association of the word with the devil established by 4:3 adds a whole new level of (nasty) meaning (Matt. 19:3 and Mark 10:2; Matt. 22:18 and Mark 12:15). Twice, Matthew's Gospel adds the word to give a negative spin to the leaders' interaction with Jesus. In 16:1, the Gospel presents the Pharisees and Sadducees' question as "testing" Jesus, an addition to Mark 8:11. And similarly in Matt. 22:35, the Pharisee who asks Jesus about the greatest commandment is presented as "testing" Jesus, an addition to Mark 12:28.

Matthew's Gospel also names the devil as the "evil one" (6:13; 13:38). The Gospel then uses the same word, "evil," for the leaders, again identifying them with the devil. Jesus asks why the scribes think evil in their hearts, an addition to Mark's scene (Matt. 9:4; Mark 2:8). In 12:34, in an unparalleled passage, Matthew's Jesus identifies the leaders directly as evil, an identification he repeats in 16:4, an addition to Mark 8:12. In the unparalleled 13:38, Jesus declares that the evil one has children who do not belong to God's kingdom/empire and are destined for condemnation in the final judgment. These "children" are the leaders.

3. Scribes are particular targets of criticism. In addition to the attack

on them as blind and hypocrites in chapter 23, Matthew's Gospel maintains Mark's negative references to them, especially their involvement in the death of Jesus as God's agent commissioned to manifest God's saving presence.[9] But the Gospel also increases the hostile references to scribes. In their initial reference, the scribes cannot interpret Scripture or pay homage to Jesus (M material, 2:4). In Q material, Matthew changes the *person* who volunteers to follow Jesus into a scribe whom Jesus rejects (Matt. 8:19-20; Luke 9:57-58). In Mark material, Matthew maintains Mark's contrast between Jesus' teaching authority and the lack of authority of the scribes' teaching but heightens distance from them by referring to "*their* scribes" rather than "*the* scribes" (Matt. 7:29; Mark 1:22). In Mark's scene concerning the greatest commandment, Mark presents the questioner as a scribe and Jesus commends him as being "not far from the kingdom of God" (Mark 12:28-34). Matthew, though, is not happy with such a positive presentation. Matthew's scene turns the questioner into a Pharisee, removes the scribe's commendation of Jesus for his answer, and removes Jesus' commendation of the scribe's answer (Matt. 22:34-40).

4. Two more terms are involved in the polemic against the leaders. "Rabbi" as a term of address appears three times in Mark. In the transfiguration, Mark's Peter addresses the transfigured Jesus as "rabbi" (Mark 9:5). Matthew removes the term and replaces it with the more respectful term that disciples commonly use, "Lord" (Matt. 17:4). Mark's Peter again addresses Jesus as "rabbi" in the scene concerning the fig tree (Mark 11:21). Matthew removes the term but does not replace it with another term of address (Matt. 21:20). Its third use in Mark comes in the scene in which Judas betrays Jesus with a kiss. Judas greets Jesus as "rabbi" (Mark 14:45). This time, Matthew retains the term (Matt. 26:49). Interestingly, this is the second time Matthew's Judas calls Jesus "rabbi." Some twenty verses previously, Jesus predicts one of the disciples will betray him. One after another, disciples ask

9. Opposing Jesus' pronouncing of forgiveness as blasphemy (Matt. 9:3; Mark 2:6-7); voiding the word of God concerning care for parents (Matt. 15:1; Mark 7:1); putting Jesus to death (Matt. 16:21; Mark 8:31; Matt. 20:18; Mark 10:33; Matt. 26:57; Mark 14:53; Matt. 27:41; Mark 15:31); failing to recognize Jesus as Elijah (Matt. 17:10-12; Mark 9:11-12).

Jesus, "Is it I?" (Mark 14:17-19). Matthew redacts the disciples' question by adding the term of address used by disciples, "Is it I, Lord?" (Matt. 26:22). But Matthew also adds a verse at the end of the scene that is not in Mark in which Judas asks Jesus, "Surely not I, Rabbi?" (Matt. 26:25). The term "rabbi," then, for Matthew is not a term that disciples use—they use "Lord" for Jesus—but a term of betrayal and faithlessness.

When it was evening, he came with the twelve. And when they had taken their places and were eating, Jesus said, "Truly I tell you, one of you will betray me, one who is eating with me." They began to be distressed and to say to him one after another, "Surely, not I?" He said to them, "It is one of the twelve, one who is dipping bread into the bowl with me. For the Son of Man goes as it is written of him, but woe to that one by whom the Son of Man is betrayed! It would have been better for that one not to have been born." (Mark 14:17-21)	When it was evening, he took his place with the twelve; and while they were eating, he said, "Truly I tell you, one of you will betray me." And they became greatly distressed and began to say to him one after another, "Surely not I, *Lord*?" He answered, "The one who has dipped his hand into the bowl with me will betray me. The Son of Man goes as it is written of him, but woe to that one by whom the Son of Man is betrayed! It would have been better for that one not to have been born." Judas, who betrayed him, said, "Surely not I, *Rabbi*?" He replied, "You have said so." (Matt. 26:20-25)

This negative view of the term is confirmed by Matthew's two remaining uses of it in 23:7-8. Here Jesus condemns the leaders who love the glory of being called "rabbi" in synagogues and marketplaces. Then he explicitly forbids its use among his disciples. The use and nonuse of the term "rabbi" function to reinforce a division between disciples and leaders.

A similar distancing is accomplished by another term of address, namely "teacher," though the evidence is a little more mixed.[10] Matthew retains Mark's use of it when the leaders and other disciples address Jesus as "teacher."[11] In fact, Matthew increases the association

10. Jesus refers to himself as teacher in Matt. 10:24, 25; 23:8; 26:8.

11. Matt. 22:16 retains Mark 12:14's address by the Pharisees and Herodians; Matt. 22:24 retains the Sadducees' address (Mark 12:19); Matt. 19:16 retains Mark 10:17, the rich man's address to Jesus as teacher.

of this term with the leaders by adding "teacher" several times to the language of the Pharisees and scribes in addressing or referring to Jesus (Matt. 9:11 added to Mark 2:16; Matt. 12:38 added to Mark 8:11; Matt. 22:36 added to Mark 12:28).

The Pharisees came and began to argue with him, asking him for a sign from heaven, to test him. (Mark 8:11)	Then some of the scribes and Pharisees said to him, "*Teacher*, we wish to see a sign from you." (Matt. 12:38)

In Q material, Matt. 8:19 adds "teacher" for the scribe who addresses Jesus as "teacher"; Jesus then rejects him (cf. Luke 9:57-62). Matthew omits the address "teacher" when Mark's disciples use it (Matt. 24:1 and Mark 13:1). Matthew also upgrades the term when Mark's disciples use it. So in the storm scene, Mark's frightened disciples call out to Jesus as "teacher" while Matthew's disciples address Jesus as "Lord" (Mark 4:38; Matt. 8:25).

But he was in the stern, asleep on the cushion; and they woke him up and said to him, "*Teacher*, do you not care that we are perishing?" (Mark 4:38)	A windstorm arose on the sea, so great that the boat was being swamped by the waves; but he was asleep. And they went and woke him up, saying, "*Lord*, save us! We are perishing!" (Matt. 8:24-25)

Likewise the father of the demon-possessed boy who seeks Jesus' help addresses him as "teacher" in Mark 9:17 but as "Lord" in Matt. 17:15.

Someone from the crowd answered him, "*Teacher*, I brought you my son; he has a spirit that makes him unable to speak." (Mark 9:17)	When they came to the crowd, a man came to him, knelt before him, and said, "*Lord*, have mercy on my son, for he is an epileptic and he suffers terribly." (Matt. 17:14-15)

The address "teacher," then, seems to be especially associated with the leaders. Why does the Gospel tag them with this term? Their use of it is ironic because consistently they do not want to learn from Jesus or welcome him. They are not his disciples. They are not open to his manifestation of God's saving presence and will in his actions and teaching. By repeatedly using it, they define themselves in this way and condemn themselves with its use.

5. The places with whom these leaders are associated also receive

increased negative press in Matthew's Gospel. The center of their power in Jerusalem is the temple. Matthew's first reference to the temple associates it with the devil. In Matthew's expanded temptation scene, the devil takes Jesus to the pinnacle of the temple and instructs him to throw himself off so that God's angels might rescue him (Matt. 4:5-6; added to Mark 1:12-13). The verse does not say the temple is allied with the devil, but it does link the two. Subsequently, Matthew repeats and emphasizes Mark's presentation of the temple as under God's judgment. So Jesus enters Jerusalem, visits the temple, and condemns it for failing to be a house of prayer (Matt. 21:11-13; Mark 11:15-17). Matthew adds to this scene Jesus healing the bind and lame in the temple, upsetting the leaders, and conflicting with them (Matt. 21:14-16). The temple is then the setting for their continuing conflict in chapters 21–22. In chapter 24, he announces the destruction of the temple, the end of the basis of the leader's power and rule.

The other location associated with these leaders' is the synagogue, and Matthew constructs this location negatively. While Mark refers to "their synagogues" once (Mark 1:39; Matt. 4:23), Matthew adds the phrase four times (9:35; 10:17; 12:9; 13:54) and "your synagogues" once (23:34) to underline distance between Jesus, his disciples, and "their/your" synagogues. Several of these additions construct synagogues negatively as hostile toward disciples (10:17, flogging disciples), and as rejecting Jesus (13:54-58). Other references to synagogues present their various failings as hypocrisy in almsgiving and prayer (6:2, 5) and leaders who love places of honor (23:6), in contrast to the practices of Jesus' disciples.

6.3 Remains of the Talmudic-era synagogue at Katzrin, Golan Heights. Commons.wikimedia.org.

Significantly, Matthew's Gospel removes positive references to synagogues from both Mark and Q sources. Mark presents a positive description of Jairus, who seeks Jesus' help to heal his daughter and, when news of her death arrives, chooses to believe Jesus' words rather than fear (Mark 5:21-43). Mark refers three times to Jairus as a "leader of the synagogue" (Mark 5:22, 36, 38). Matthew, though, omits these three references, leaving out any reference to a synagogue and describing Jairus as "a leader" but without stipulating what or who he leads (Matt. 9:18, 23). Strangely, the NRSV translation, probably under the influence of Mark, supplies the phrase "leader of the synagogue" in Matt. 9:18, with a note saying that the Greek lacks the phrase "of the synagogue"!

Matthew makes a similar omission from a Q story. The story of the healing of the believing centurion's servant introduces the centurion as one who loves the Jewish people and "it is he who built our synagogue for us" (Luke 7:5). Matthew maintains the emphasis on the centurion's faith in Jesus but completely removes from the Q source the description of his benefaction to the synagogue (Matt. 8:6-7).

A centurion there had a slave whom he valued highly, and who was ill and close to death. When he heard about Jesus, he sent some Jewish elders to him, asking him to come and heal his slave. When they came to Jesus, they appealed to him earnestly, saying, "He is worthy of having you do this for him, for he loves our people, and it is he who built our synagogue for us." And Jesus went with them, but when he was not far from the house. . . . (Luke 7:2-6)	When he entered Capernaum, a centurion came to him, appealing to him and saying, "*Lord*, my servant is lying at home paralyzed, in terrible distress." And he said to him, "I will come and cure him." (Matt. 8:5-7)

Taken together, these consistent and often detailed changes throughout the Gospel emphasize a negative presentation of the alliance of Jewish leaders.

Why? Redacting the Story of Jesus to Address Circumstances of Crisis

In this last section, I have suggested that Matthew's reworking or redaction of Mark to form a new Gospel particularly involves changes in the presentation of Jesus, in the presentation of disciples, and in the presentation of the Jerusalem leaders. I have shown that Matthew's Gospel heightens the presentation of the God-given authority of Jesus as the commissioned agent of God's saving presence, rule, and will. As a corollary, the Gospel presents Jesus' disciples quite positively (though not universally so) in terms of their understanding of Jesus and faithful commitment to Jesus. As a further corollary, the Gospel presents the Jerusalem leaders and their related institutions in increasingly negative light, as opposed to Jesus, and allied with the devil.

Why does the Gospel make these changes? I suggest that these three changes in presentations and the new story they create address situations that Matthew's readers were experiencing and that Mark's Gospel did not particularly address. What were these circumstances? And how does the new story of Jesus that Matthew's Gospel tells address them?

We might think that the changes to Mark's story of Jesus are of no particular significance. We might think that they are inconsequential changes. But we have seen in the material documented above that the changes are not random. They are pervasive and consistent throughout the Gospel.

It might be more useful in making sense of the changes to explore circumstances from around the time of the Gospel's writing in the late first century. What circumstances did Matthew's Gospel address?

A major event occurred in the year 70 CE that had far-reaching consequences. In that year, as we noted in discussing Mark, the Romans ended a four-year revolt in Judea and a siege of Jerusalem by its legions. They broke into the city of Jerusalem and destroyed the city and its temple by fire. This was a catastrophic event for first-century Judaism. It had profound implications not only for Judaism, which needed to be reconstructed after 70, but also for followers of Jesus. How were disciples of Jesus, crucified by Rome but raised by God, to make their way in relation to emerging Judaism and to this fresh and violent assertion of Roman power?

Matthew's Gospel seems to refer to this event in Matt. 22:7 in a verse inserted into the parable of the wedding feast found in Q material. The parable in Q (Luke 14:16-24) narrates an important person sending out his slaves to invite guests to dinner, but the guests dishonor him by refusing the invitation. In Matthew's version, the parable refers implicitly to Jesus. The dinner is now a wedding banquet that a king (God) gives in honor of his son (Jesus). The king sends out slaves to invite guests, but they dishonor him by refusing the invitation and by doing violence to his slaves.

The following table shows how both versions of the parable continue.

Luke 14:21-24	Matthew 22:6-10
21 So the slave returned and reported this to his master. Then the owner of the house became angry and said to his slave, "Go out at once into the streets and lanes of the town and bring in the poor, the crippled, the blind, and the lame."	6 while the rest seized his slaves, mistreated them, and killed them.
And the slave said, "Sir, what you ordered has been done, and there is still room."	7 The king was enraged. He sent his troops, destroyed those murderers, and burned their city.
Then the master said to the slave, "Go out into the roads and lanes, and compel people to come in, so that my house may be filled.	Then he said to his slaves, "The wedding is ready, but those invited were not worthy.
For I tell you, none of those who were invited will taste my dinner."	Go therefore into the main streets, and invite everyone you find to the wedding banquet."
	Those slaves went out into the streets and gathered all whom they found, both good and bad; so the wedding hall was filled with guests.

Notice what happens in Q/Luke 14:21. The slave reports the refusals to the owner. The owner becomes angry at the refusals but channels his anger into sending the slave to invite "the poor, the crippled, the blind, the lame" to the dinner. Compare Matthew's edited version. At verse 6, the slaves do not report back but are murdered. In verse 7, the king responds with anger and channels it into a violent action. Killing leads to killing. He sends troops, kills those who murdered his slaves, and burns their city as retaliation or punishment.

These events, especially the burning of the city, evoke Rome's burning of Jerusalem in 70 CE. The parable portrays these events in the context of God the king's punishing actions. God punishes the city, the base of the leader's power, for rejecting his Son and refusing to join in the marriage feast. The parable offers an explanation for the recent destruction of Jerusalem and the temple.

The destruction—punishment—of the temple raises other questions that need to be answered. The temple was a place where God's forgiveness of sin was especially, though not exclusively, encountered and celebrated. With the temple destroyed along with its liturgical life that celebrated festivals such as the Day of Atonement, where was forgiveness now to be encountered? The temple was a place where God's presence was especially, but by no means exclusively, encountered. With the temple now destroyed, how was God's presence to be especially known? The temple was a place where the Scriptures were read and the will of God made known. With the temple now destroyed, how was God's will to be proclaimed and heard? With the destruction of the temple and many priests, first-century Judaism lost a crucial center. Its reconstruction without Jerusalem and it temple was a major post-70 task.

6.4 Depiction of Rome's Destruction of the Temple at Jerusalem in 70 CE; by Francesco Hayez; Gallerie dell'Accademia, Venice. Commons.wikimedia.org.

In the midst of the post-70 laments and debates, Matthew's Gospel offers a way ahead. As we have seen, the Gospel especially promotes Jesus as the one who saves from sin, who manifests God's presence (Emmanuel), and who, in the interpretation of Scripture and in five major teaching blocks, reveals God's will. The changes made to the presentation of Jesus that we have noted in Matthew's Gospel address this situation.

So too does the presentation of the leaders in intensified negative terms. Linked with Jerusalem and synagogues, these leaders—presented as unfaithful, fruitless, and hypocritical—are shown in the Gospel's perspective to be part of the reason for Jerusalem's punishment. Worse, they are shown to reject Jesus, God's commissioned agent. By discrediting them, the Gospel shows that they can't be relied on to offer a legitimate way forward.

In the meantime, Jesus instructs disciples on God's will for the way ahead. While there is no denying Rome's power, the Gospel affirms that Rome's power is not ultimate. Jesus announces God's kingdom or empire and declares that it will one day be ultimate, and that Rome's empire will pass away. The limits of Rome's power are shown in that they can't keep Jesus dead and he will return. Disciples are to follow Jesus and his teaching (chs. 5–7, 10, 13, 18, 24–25), not only in finding a way ahead in relation to reconstructing Judaism but also in relation to a fresh assertion of Roman power that the Gospel contextualizes in relation to God's purposes. Ironically, the Gospel often imitates the language of Rome's empire to present God's greater, more encompassing, and ultimately victorious empire.

Matthew's new version of the story of Jesus is a story-sermon that scratches the itches of Matthew's readers living in challenging and difficult circumstances. Matthew's new story-sermon is a word-on-target that does pastoral work in offering an explanation for what has happened, in presenting commitment to Jesus as the way ahead, and in reassuring and instructing its readers on how to be faithful followers in these complex and multifaceted situations.

Questions for Review and Reflection

1. What explanation does the chapter offer to account for the similarities and differences among the three Synoptic Gospels, Mark, Matthew, and Luke?

2. Design a diagram that shows the interrelationships among the three Gospels that the chapter suggests.
3. Know your abbreviations: Explain Q and M. Also explain the term *redaction*.
4. The chapter describes the "new presentation of Jesus" in Matthew's Gospel. What are the features of this presentation of Jesus? How does the Gospel create this presentation of Jesus?
5. The chapter then describes the upgraded presentation of disciples in Matthew's Gospel. What are the features of this presentation of disciples? How does the Gospel create this presentation of disciples?
6. The chapter then describes the presentation of the Jerusalem leaders in Matthew's Gospel. What are the features of this presentation of the Jerusalem leaders? How does the Gospel create this presentation of the Jerusalem leaders?
7. This new Gospel story is created to address new circumstances. What are those circumstances, and how does Matthew's Gospel address them?
8. The chapter demonstrates that traditions about Jesus were fluid among Jesus-followers and not fixed in the late first century, when the Gospels were written. How does this awareness affect your reading of the Gospel according to Matthew?

7

The Tale Luke Tells

The TV game show *Jeopardy!* has been running in various formats since 1964. For those who have never seen it and can't hum or whistle the music (Google it!), the show's basic requirement is that contestants choose a category ("Fruity Loops"), are shown "answers" ("Jazz; Fuji") and are required to frame an appropriate question ("What are varieties of apples?"). Correct questions are rewarded with cash amounts.

To be clear, there's no cash available in this chapter, but I think a *Jeopardy!* approach to Luke's Gospel is helpful. In a moment, I'll identify some of the answers the Gospel seems to provide and identify some of the questions these answers seem to be addressing. But first I will address the category of Luke-Acts.

Luke-Acts designates a two-part work, the first part of which is the Gospel of Luke. Luke's Gospel is the only one of the four Gospels in the New Testament with a sequel. Even though the two works are separated in the New Testament by the Gospel of John, they essentially form a unified two-part work, with the Gospel telling the story of Jesus and Acts narrating the successive beginnings of the church. Significant overlaps between the end of Luke's Gospel and beginning of Acts are one of the ways the two works are joined. So the book of Acts begins:

> In the first book, Theophilus, I wrote about all that Jesus did and taught from the beginning until the day when he was taken up to heaven, after giving instructions through the Holy Spirit to the apostles whom he had chosen. After his suffering he presented himself alive to them by many convincing proofs, appearing to them during forty days and speaking about the kingdom of God. While staying with them, he ordered them not to leave Jerusalem, but to wait there for the promise of the Father. (Acts 1:1-4)

A quick comparison with Luke's Gospel shows that it too is addressed to Theophilus (Luke 1:3), that it described Jesus' ministry (Luke 4–24), that it ends with Jesus being taken up into heaven (Luke 24:50-51)—where Acts begins (Acts 1:9-11). In Luke, Jesus ascends after he has given his disciples last-minute instructions (24:44-49) and ordered them to stay in Jerusalem to receive the gift promised by the Father (the Holy Spirit; Luke 24:49), an instruction repeated in Acts 1:4, 8.

The two volumes of Luke and Acts constitute, then, a fifty-two-chapter narrative. Reading this large amount of narrative gives us good clues to the two works' emphases and concerns. Or, in terms of the *Jeopardy!* approach, in Luke-Acts we read answers to questions that aren't explicitly articulated but that we can formulate on the basis of what we read. Identifying these central questions helps us make sense of the significance of what we are reading.

Discussing fifty-two chapters is too much for this one chapter. So I will focus on the Gospel, though Acts will figure occasionally. Before outlining some of the questions and issues I think the Gospel is addressing, I want to highlight a big clue to the Gospel's central perspective, which is signaled in 1:4. The writer says he is writing "so that you [Theophilus and all who read the Gospel] may know the *truth*." The word translated "truth" is not a very accurate translation. A better translation for the word (*asphaleia* in Greek) would be "security," or "certainty," or "assurance." The Gospel is written to provide its readers with security, certainty, assurance.

But security, assurance, certainty about what? By paying attention to the Gospel narrative and especially to its redaction of Mark, the source scholars identify as "Q" (material common to both Matthew and Luke but not in Mark), and "L" material (material unique to Luke), we can build a picture of the sorts of questions the Gospel seems to be addressing to provide readers with assurance or security. Assuming such detailed analysis, we can articulate some of the likely questions:

- Is God trustworthy and reliable?
- What is God doing among human beings, if anything?
- How and where is God's salvation, God's kingdom or empire, encountered? What difference does it make, if any, in relation to pervasive everyday issues of the Roman Empire like sickness and food insecurity?

- Who are included in God's people: Jews and gentiles? Men and women? Rich and poor?
- Has God been faithful to Israel, or has God finished with Israel and replaced it with gentiles?
- How are followers of Jesus to live in the present? Is life in the present of any consequence, or is it a time of disappointed waiting?

- Is Jesus trustworthy when he says that he, the Son of Man, will return?
- How do we make sense of Jesus' death? If he is God's anointed one, the Messiah, why did he die on a cross?

I've grouped the questions into three divisions. The first division comprises three questions about God. The second division comprises three questions about the church and ethics. The third division comprises two questions about Jesus, or Christology. I am suggesting that the Gospel narrative seeks to provide security or certainty or assurance about God's purposes and power, about who is included in God's people and how they are to live, and about Jesus' roles and teaching.

In this chapter, we work through the Gospel narrative, staying attentive to the Gospel's certainties and assurances concerning these matters. Keeping these questions in mind will help us understand the force of Luke's "answers." We observe the flow of the narrative as well as some of the ways the Gospel redacts its sources of Mark and Q.

7.1 Reading Luke

As with the preceding chapters, read along in your Bible at the same time.

Prologue, Luke 1:1-4

The Gospel has a very distinctive beginning, not matched by the other Gospels. It employs a literary convention called a prologue, which was typical of ancient historical, medical, and scientific writings.[1] In it, the author sets the Gospel in relation to other accounts of Jesus; explains his way of working, which draws on eyewitnesses, sources, and the author's own research; and states the purpose of his work: "that you might have security/confidence/assurance."

The prologue has a clear historicizing flavor, with its references to eyewitnesses and sources. But it also has theological and pastoral concerns, which show the Gospel not to be a disinterested or "objective" report about Jesus but an "invested" or "committed" theological and pastoral account that functions as the means of assuring or providing confidence to the readers about God's being and purposes. We see this in the following ways:

- In verse 1, the writer refers to what has been "fulfilled among us." The passive form of the verb is a way of referring to what God has done. In Luke's Gospel, the verb "fulfilled" frequently denotes God

1. Lucian of Samosata, *How to Write History* 23; Josephus, *Ant.* 1.1–17.

keeping God's promises and acting in Jesus' actions according to God's previously declared commitments (so Luke 4:21; 9:31; 24:44).

- These divine actions have been accomplished "among us," and accounts of them have been passed on to "us" (1:1, 2). To whom does the "us" refer? All human beings? Or those who have discerned God at work and become participants in that work? The latter option is more convincing. This "us" language is confessional. It denotes a particular group—to whom the author belongs—that discerns and narrates God's actions.
- In verse 2, the narrating of God's actions is summed up in the term "the word" (the same term in 1:4 is translated "the things"). Throughout the Gospel, the words of God and Jesus will be presented as efficacious and trustworthy in accomplishing God's purposes.
- As I've already noted, the purpose of this account is to ensure that Theophilus gains security or assurance or certainty in the matters about which he has been "instructed" (1:4). This last verb is the Greek form of our English word "catechized." The word refers to religious instruction (see Acts 18:25). Theophilus has received previous instruction about God's actions and about Jesus, but he is not yet assured or secure or certain in that instruction. The Gospel has this purpose of providing assurance in relation to the sorts of questions I identified above.
- Who is "most excellent Theophilus"? Usually in a prologue, this would represent the person to whom the work was dedicated. The dedication would normally acknowledge this person as the patron or sponsor of the work, the one who probably contributed financially to the writer's support while writing the Gospel and to the costs of its production. So Theophilus may well be this sort of wealthy patron. But there is a wrinkle that prevents us being certain. The name Theophilus comprises two Greek words meaning "one who loves God." Jesus will subsequently teach that loving God is the foremost definition of being a human being (Luke 10:27). The name Theophilus, then, encapsulates the central claim of Jesus' teaching.

Is this a happy coincidence, or does it suggest that "Theophilus" is an ideal reader, the sort of reader the Gospel requires to fully understand it and to experience the assurance and certainty it offers about God, the church, and Jesus?

7.2 Who Is the Author of Luke's Gospel?

As with the other Gospels, we do not know who "Luke" was, or why his name came to be linked with this Gospel late in the second century. The traditional identification of this "Luke" as Paul's "fellow worker" (Philem. 24) and as the "beloved physician" (Col. 4:14; cf. 2 Tim. 4:11) originates in the second century. For example, the Muratorian Canon, traditionally dated to the 170s CE or so, claims "Luke the physician" wrote the Gospel "in his own name." Irenaeus, writing around the 180s, identifies Luke a companion of Paul as the writer (*Against Heresies* 3.1.1; 3.14.1). However, there is no evidence that the writer of the Gospel was a physician. The Gospel shows no more specialized medical language than other writings for which no one claims a physician as author, such as the Septuagint or the works of Josephus.

Though we do not know who this author is, I will continue to call the writing by its familiar name, Luke's Gospel.

Conception and Birth (1:5—2:52)

Like Matthew's Gospel but unlike Mark's, Luke's Gospel commences with a conception and birth story. But compared with Matthew, Luke's account has three major differences.

First, Luke's opening two chapters intertwine *two* conception-and-birth accounts, one concerning Jesus and one concerning John the Baptist. John did not figure in Matthew's birth story at all. In Luke, the two story lines parallel one another first with conception accounts,

1:5-25 Elizabeth's Conception of John

1:26-45 Mary's Conception of Jesus

and then with birth accounts,

1:57-80 Birth of John

2:1-21 Birth of Jesus.

Second, Luke's account includes expressions of praise that celebrate and interpret the significance of these events as God's actions. Four hymns pause the action and highlight that God is at work and what God is doing. First, Mary sets her conception in the context of God's previous faithful, merciful, and powerful actions. Her song of praise (commonly called the Magnificat[2]) praises God as a warrior who delivers the people and mercifully acts to reverse the current imperial structures by bringing down the powerful and wealthy and blessing the lowly and hungry (1:46-56). Then at John's birth, his father Zechariah celebrates God's actions in similar terms in the Benedictus (1:67-80). God is faithful to the covenant and redeems or saves the people. In this context, he announces John's role in God's plan as going before Jesus and preparing his way. At Jesus' birth, angels praise God for God's favor and the gift of peace (2:14). When the infant Jesus is presented in the temple, the aged Simeon celebrates the scope of God's action that embraces all people, "a light for revelation to the Gentiles and for the glory of your people Israel" (2:29-32, known as the Nunc dimittis). These hymns function not only to express praise but also to interpret and proclaim what God is doing.

Third, these two chapters are structured in such a way as to provide assurance or security about the effectiveness and reliability of God's word. So an angel makes the surprising declaration to Zechariah that the postmenopausal Elizabeth will conceive (1:13-17). Zechariah doubts these words because he and Elizabeth are elderly. The angel Gabriel silences him (1:18-20, 64). But the angel's announcement of God's purposes proves to be efficacious. Elizabeth becomes pregnant (1:24, 35, 41) and gives birth to John (1:57). God's word proves to be powerful, effective, and trustworthy despite the obstacles.

A similar dynamic is at work in the account of Jesus' conception and birth. The angel Gabriel appears to Mary and announces that she will conceive (1:28-33). Mary raises the objection that she is a virgin (1:34). The angel repeats the message and offers the now pregnant Elizabeth

2. These names derive from Latin translations of the opening words: Mary's hymn, 1:47-55, *Magnificat* (the Latin verb for "magnifies"); Zechariah's hymn, 1:68-79, *Benedictus* (translated "Blessed"); the angels' hymn, 2:14, *Gloria* (translated "Glory"); and Simeon's hymn, 2:29-32, the *Nunc dimittis* (translated "Now you are dismissing").

as a "visual aid" of the power and reliability of God's word (1:35-37). Subsequently, the angel's announcement is shown to be accurate when Mary becomes pregnant (1:42) and bears her son Jesus (2:7). In addition to this demonstration of the effectiveness and trustworthiness of God's word, both Mary (1:38) and Elizabeth (1:45) explicitly draw attention to the reliability of God's word. The same dynamic of declaring God's plans and then narrating their accomplishment is repeated in the accounts of the shepherds (2:8-12, 15-18, 20) and the circumstances of Simeon (2:29). Both accounts explicitly highlight the reliability of God's word (2:17-18, 21, 29).

7.1 *The Adoration by the Shepherds*, by Peter-Paul Rubens (1608). In contrast to Matthew's narrative, Luke portrays shepherds as the first to learn of the Messiah's birth. Hermitage Museum, St. Petersburg; Commons.wikimedia.org.

These two opening chapters have set about providing Theophilus—and all readers of the Gospel—with assurance, security, certainty, concerning God's actions and purposes. They have shown God to be at work, declaring God's plans ahead of time and then reliably accomplishing them. God's word is trustworthy. Moreover, the angel's declarations (1:32-33, 35; 2:11-12) and the hymns, especially that of the aged Simeon in the Jerusalem temple in 2:29-32, identify God's trustworthy plans to be accomplished through Jesus. Jesus is God's agent or Son or Messiah, commissioned to exhibit God's reign in the line of David (1:32-35; 2:26). He is the Savior (2:11), a light for gentiles and for Israel (2:32; 2:33-52).

7.3 Mark and Matthew Watch

If we look back over the beginnings of these three Gospels, we notice some significant differences. Mark presents no material related to Jesus' conception or birth. For Mark, the adult Jesus is in action already in 1:14. Both Matthew and Luke devote two chapters to Jesus' conception and to events related to Jesus' birth. But significantly, the two accounts are quite different, with different actions and personnel (John the Baptizer, for example, is more prominent in Luke 1). What other differences do you observe? And what aspects are shared between the two accounts?

Preparation for Jesus' Ministry (3:1—4:13)

Between the end of chapter 2 and the beginning of chapter 3, the narrative skips ahead an unspecified number of years to present John's ministry (3:1-20). The opening verses set him in the context of the Roman emperor Tiberius; the Rome-appointed governor Pilate; Rome-sanctioned client kings Herod, Philip, and Lysanias; and the Jerusalem-based but Rome-sanctioned high priests Annas and his successor Caiaphas. This parade of powerful figures suggests a date for John's activity around perhaps 28–29 CE. More significantly, it sketches some key figures in the imperial world in which John and Jesus (and through them, God) will be active. And verse 2b makes clear that these powerful figures do not define or control the world no matter what their collective display of power suggests. In prophetic style (Jer. 1:2), "the word of God came to John" (3:2b). This word, as we have seen from chapters 1–2, is effective, reliable, powerful in conducting God's purposes even in difficult circumstances. The account provides assurance and security.

John carries out the role declared for him from his conception by the angel (1:16-17). Again God's word and purposes are seen to be effective and reliable. John preaches "a baptism of repentance for the forgiveness of sins" (3:3). He declares God's salvation for all people (3:6). He challenges people to live lives marked by repentance and good deeds (3:7-9) such as sharing possessions and food, just actions, and actions free of threats and false accusations (3:10-14). He exhorts crowds to repent and especially speaks against the misuse of power by tax collectors and soldiers, agents of Roman power. And he witnesses to Jesus, whose ministry is about to begin (3:15-17).

John's activity comes to an end, however, in a collision with the powerful Herod. John has criticized Herod's relationship with his brother's wife Herodias, so Herod imprisons him (3:19-20). The Gospel continues to signal an uneasy relationship with ruling power (cf. 1:51-53).

Three successive scenes turn the attention to Jesus. First, Jesus is baptized (3:21-22). The scene reflects important themes in Luke's narrative, notably the importance of prayer and of the presence of the Holy Spirit empowering Jesus' activity as the Spirit will empower the church in Acts 2 at Pentecost. And the scene functions to provide assurance about the identity of Jesus. God speaks, declaring Jesus to be God's agent or Son, beloved by God, who is well-pleased with him (3:21-22; cf. 2:52). If Jesus has God's seal of approval, Theophilus and all readers can be assured and secure in what Jesus' teaching and actions disclose of God's purposes.

Second, the Gospel provides a genealogy for Jesus that differs significantly from Matthew's (Luke 3:23-38). Whereas Matthew begins with Abraham (Matt. 1:1-17), Luke's genealogy begins with Adam, the son of God. This starting point reinforces the emerging theme of Jesus' significance for all people, both Jews and gentiles (2:32; 3:6).

And third, Jesus' identity as God's Son or agent is reinforced in the temptation scene (4:1-13). Jesus, full of the Holy Spirit, is confronted three times by the devil. The heart of the scene is that it is the devil who tries to direct Jesus' action instead of God. The devil wants Jesus to turn stones into bread, to worship him, and throw himself off the temple so that angels can rescue him in a daring midair interception. Here's the rub. If Jesus obeys any of these temptations, he is no longer the Son or agent of God. He becomes the agent of the devil's will. But by using Scripture, Jesus rejects each temptation, drives the devil away, and remains faithful to his identity (1:32, 35; 2:49; 3:23).

This scene that displays Jesus' steadfast faithfulness to his identity and calling as God's agent and Son frames the following account of his public activity, which begins in 4:14. Readers can be assured, confident, and secure in Jesus' display of and teaching about God's purposes that follow.

7.4 Mark and Matthew Watch

We are now on the edge of Jesus' public ministry in Luke's account. Recall that Mark has Jesus in action at 1:14-15, while Matthew, like Luke, also has a long buildup to Matt. 4:17, when Jesus begins his public activity. Note that Luke's genealogy (Luke 3:23-38) differs significantly in content, placement, and structure from Matthew's tightly organized genealogy (three × fourteen generations), which was prominently located at the very beginning of the Gospel. Mark does not offer a genealogy. Luke's account of the temptation is similar to Matthew's, both much more developed than Mark's short account.

Jesus' Ministry in Galilee (4:14–9:50)

With Jesus' identity and faithfulness to God established, Luke's account of Jesus' ministry in Galilee gets underway. It comprises five chapters, shorter than Mark's nine chapters and Matthew's fourteen chapters. Displays of God's beneficent power, teaching, and divisive responses to Jesus mark these chapters.

The opening scene in the synagogue at Nazareth has programmatic significance (4:14-30). First, the scene continues the emphasis of the opening chapters on Jesus' Jewish contexts. Synagogue, Sabbath, and the scroll of Isaiah indicate the scene's location, time, and cultural focus. Second, Jesus reads a passage that combines Isa. 58:6 and 61:1-2, is concerned with Israel's restoration, and draws on the Jubilee-year emphasis on release and divine favor for marginal folks such as the poor, the captives, the blind, and the oppressed (see Leviticus 25). Jesus interprets the passage in relation to himself and his forthcoming activity (4:21). He goes on to elaborate the poor and marginal with reference to the actions of two of Israel's prophets, Elijah and Elisha, in benefiting a gentile, sonless, woman, and a gentile leprous man (4:25-27). Gentiles belong to the sphere of God's blessing. Third, by citing Isaiah and evoking Elijah and Elisha, he places himself in the line of prophets who speak and act on behalf of God. He explicitly identifies himself as a prophet and acknowledges the rejection that often accompanies that role (4:24). Fourth, the quoted passage underscores the Spirit as the power at work in Jesus' activity (3:22). Fifth, the scene foregrounds response to Jesus' activity. No doubt some, especially the poor and marginalized, welcomed the announcement of God's favor. The scene, though, chooses to underscore an intensely negative response whereby some try to kill Jesus. This opening scene of Jesus' public ministry, which presents Jesus as a prophet, led by the Spirit, and acting in accord with God's will manifest in Scripture, provides assurance and security about the reliability of the Gospel's account concerning God and Jesus.

The following scenes display the power of the Spirit at work in Jesus' itinerant ministry. He effects transformative favor in the lives of suffering people. Jesus exorcizes a demon (4:31-37), heals a woman with a fever as well as numerous other sick and demon-possessed folks (4:38-41), preaches the "good news of the kingdom of God" (4:42-44), calls followers (5:1-11, 27-32), commands a big catch of fish (5:4-7), and heals and forgives a paralyzed man (5:17-26). With this last scene, opposition comes to the fore, led by the Pharisees and scribes. In the following scenes, they oppose Jesus' claim to forgive sin (5:17-26), his association with undesirable folks like tax collectors and sinners (5:27-32), his neglect of fasting (5:33-39), and his use of the Sabbath to benefit people (6:1-11).

In the context of prayer, Jesus calls twelve followers (6:12-16), heals and exorcizes (6:17-19), and teaches disciples in the Sermon on the Plain (6:20-49). This sermon, much shorter than Matthew's Sermon on the Mount (Matthew 5–7), sets out key aspects of Jesus' teaching, beginning with blessings or beatitudes on the poor, hungry, the mourning, and the hated—echoing Jesus' sermon in Nazareth (6:20-23). Four "woes" or condemnations follow, which denounce the rich and socially powerful, evoking the condemnations of Mary's song in 1:46-56 (6:24-26). Thereafter, Luke's Jesus exhorts love for enemies and haters (6:27-36), forbids judging others (6:37-42), and urges lives of action based on Jesus' teaching.

In 7:1—9:51, Jesus continues to elaborate God's favor or salvation in transforming works of power. He heals a slave (7:1-10), raises a widow's son (7:11-17), forgives a woman (7:36-50), heals and exorcizes some women (8:1-3), teaches in parables (8:4-18), rescues his disciples from a stormy sea by calming wind and sea (8:22-25), heals a demoniac (8:26-39), heals a hemorrhaging woman (8:43-48), restores a girl to life (8:49-56), feeds a crowd of five thousand (9:10-17), and heals a demon-possessed boy (9:37-43). Jesus' work as the agent of God's favor-full purposes is recognized, supported and elaborated by an alliance of various characters; the witness of John the Baptizer (7:18-35), the financial and material resources of some women followers (8:1-3), those who hear and do God's word (8:19-21), his twelve followers whom he sends out in mission (9:1-6) and who confess his identity (9:18-20), and an exorcist (9:49-50).

A new emphasis emerges. Jesus the prophet and agent of God's work declares that he will be crucified by the Jerusalem-based power elite (9:21-27, 43b-45). Immediately, God confirms the reliability of Jesus' predictive word in Jesus' transfiguration that foreshadows his resurrection glory. Repeating the declaration from Jesus' baptism, God announces Jesus' identity as God's agent or Son (9:35).

This five-chapter account of Jesus' activity in Galilee elaborates the reading from Isaiah with which the section began (4:18-19). The narrative shows Jesus to be acting consistently with the vision he articulated at the outset. His word is both efficacious and trustworthy in conveying God's favor and reign, engendering security and confidence in God's purposes.

Jesus Travels to Jerusalem (9:51—19:27)

Having twice predicted that he must go to Jerusalem and die (9:21-27, 43b-45), Jesus now sets out from Galilee to do precisely that (9:51). Again the Gospel underscores that he is reliable and trustworthy in keeping his word and in being faithful to God's purposes. Throughout the ten chapters, the Gospel reminds its readers regularly that Jesus is traveling to Jerusalem (13:22; 17:11). Jesus reiterates his destiny of being killed as a rejected prophet there (13:33-34) and instructs his disciples that while he will be rejected by this ruling elite and by gentiles, God will reverse this human rejection and raise him from the dead (18:31-33). The narrator articulates Jesus' destiny beyond resurrection, namely, his ascension into heaven to be with God. The narrator describes this destiny as Jesus' "departure" (lit. his "exodus," 9:31) and his being "taken up" in the ascension (9:51; see 24:50-52; Acts 1:9-11).

7.5 Mark and Matthew Watch

In Mark's Gospel, Jesus' journey to Jerusalem takes one chapter (Mark 10). In Matthew, it takes two chapters (Matthew 19–20). Here in Luke, the journey takes ten chapters, from 9:51 until 19:11 or 28 or 41.

While this lengthy ten-chapter journey presents Jesus on the way to a confrontation with the power elite in Jerusalem, his death on the cross, and God's vindication of him, it provides the framework for a significant amount of Jesus' teaching. Since the Gospel begins by referring to previous accounts about Jesus that the author has consulted (1:1-2), we might wonder about the sources from which this teaching derives. We can identify three sources for this material that comprise Luke's travel narrative.

One source provides very little material, namely, Mark's Gospel. Some of these passages include the following:

- The two commandments: Luke 10:25-28 and Mark 12:28-31
- Exorcisms and Beelzebul: Luke 11:14-23 and Mark 3:22-27
- The parable of the mustard seed: Luke 13:18-19 and Mark 4:30-32
- Teaching about divorce and remarriage: Luke 16:18 and Mark 10:11-12

Much more material comprising the travel narrative comes from Q.

- The Lord's Prayer: Luke 11:1-4 and Matt. 6:9-13
- Teaching about prayer: Luke 11:9-13 and Matt. 7:7-11
- Teaching concerning light: Luke 11:33 and Matt. 5:15
- Teaching concerning a sound eye: Luke 11:34-36 and Matt. 6:22-23
- Woes against the Pharisees: Luke 11:39-12:1 and Matt. 23:4, 6-7, 13, 23, 25-26, 27-28, 29-32, 34-36
- Teaching that exhorts faithful confession: Luke 12:2-12 and Matt. 10:26-33
- Teaching against anxiety concerning material things: Luke 12:22-32 and Matt. 6:25-34
- Teaching about treasures in heaven: Luke 12:33-34 and Matt. 6:19-21
- Teaching about being watchful and faithful: Luke 12:39-46 and Matt. 24:43-51
- Teaching about divisions in households: Luke 12:51-53 and Matt. 10:34-36
- Teaching on how to interpret the times: Luke 12:54-56 and Matt. 16:2-3
- Teaching on settling with an accuser: Luke 12:57-59 and Matt. 5:25-26
- The parable of the yeast: Luke 13:20-21 and Matt. 13:33

- Teaching on being excluded from God's reign: Luke 13:22-30 and Matt. 7:13-14, 22-23; 8:11-12; 19:30
- Lament over Jerusalem's rejection of prophets: Luke 13:34-35 and Matt. 23:37-39
- The parable of the guests and great dinner: Luke 14:15-24 and Matt. 22:1-10
- Teaching on the cost of being Jesus' disciple: Luke 14:25-27 and Matt. 10:37-38
- The parable of the lost sheep: Luke 15:1-7 and Matt. 18:12-14
- Teaching on not serving two masters, God and Mammon: Luke 16:13 and Matt. 6:24
- Teaching on the permanence of the law: Luke 16:16-17 and Matt. 11:12-13; 5:18
- Teaching about forgiveness: Luke 17:3b-4 and Matt. 18:15, 21-22
- Teaching about the return of Jesus as Son of Man: Luke 17:24-30 and Matt. 24:27, 37-39

Much of this teaching material concerns practical matters of being a disciple of Jesus. It addresses prayer, use of possessions, being faithful disciples, the divisive impact of following Jesus, competing loyalties, forgiveness, interpreting the signs of the times, and anticipating Jesus' return. Several passages attack Jerusalem, Jesus' destination, and the failed leadership of its leaders.

In addition to this material from Q, another source provides material for Luke's travel narrative. This is the source known as L comparing material unique to Luke's Gospel. Chapters 1–2 (the conception and birth stories) are examples of L material. There is much L material in chapters 9–19. This material includes three healing stories:

- The crippled woman, Luke 13:10-17
- The man with dropsy, Luke 14:1-6

- The ten lepers, Luke 17:11-19

And there are several scenes involving models of discipleship (Mary and Martha, 10:38-42; Zacchaeus, Luke 19:1-10, who divests his ill-gotten wealth) as well as attacks on powerful figures (a warning about Herod, 13:31-33; reproof for the Pharisees and their love of money, 16:14-15). But a significant amount of the L material includes eleven parables that Jesus tells:

- The good Samaritan, Luke 10:29-37
- The persistent friend at midnight, Luke 11:5-8
- The rich fool, Luke 12:13-21
- The barren fig tree, Luke 13:6-9
- The parable about places of honor at a banquet, Luke 14:7-14
- The lost coin, Luke 15:8-10
- The prodigal son, his brother, and their father, Luke 15:11-32
- The dishonest manager, Luke 16:1-9
- The rich man and Lazarus, Luke 16:19-31
- The widow and the unjust judge, Luke 18:1-8
- The Pharisee and the tax collector, Luke 18:9-14

Among other things, these parables, found only in Luke, offer teaching on showing mercy, prayer, the dangers of possessions, the need for compassion, and God's searching and patient love.

The long section of teaching in chapters 9–19 as Jesus travels to Jerusalem presents a vision of discipleship. Jesus faithfully carries out the task God has given him as God's Son or agent in going to Jerusalem while also instructing disciples on how to live out God's purposes. The teaching is reliable and trustworthy because its teacher is reliable and trustworthy. Theophilus and other Gospel readers can know security and assurance.

Jesus in Jerusalem (19:28—23:56)

Jesus arrives in Jerusalem. This section comprises Jesus' final days in Jerusalem, in conflict with the alliance of the Jerusalem elite and the Roman governor Pilate that leads to Jesus' death. Jesus continues to be faithful to his prophetic identity, including his recognition that rejection and death at the hands of the powerful is the prophets' frequent fate.

Jesus enters Jerusalem on a colt that he has ordered his disciples to procure (19:28-40). Again, this scene uses the pattern of prediction and accomplishment that shows Jesus' word to be reliable. He tells his disciples where to find the colt and what to say (19:30-31), and the scene plays out reliably "as he had told them" (19:32-35). The crowds greet him by praising God for the "deeds of power they had seen" even as some of the Pharisees protest the praise session.

Jesus speaks words of destruction and judgment on the city in predicting its military destruction (19:41-44). Of course, when the Gospel was written late in the first century, Jerusalem had already been destroyed and its temple burned by the Romans in 70 CE. The Gospel readers' knowledge of this event frames Jesus' words as "prediction" (a *vaticinium ex eventu*) and as reliable and trustworthy. In effect, his words function as a post-70 explanation for the Roman victory that has already been accomplished. Jerusalem was overcome, according to this interpretation, as an act of divine judgment for not recognizing "the time of your visitation from God."

The term "visitation" refers to God bringing salvation in the person of Jesus (so 1:68; 7:16 "looked favorably" = "visited"). But when the intended salvation is rejected, judgment takes effect. Jesus follows up this announcement with an action that enacts judgment on the temple, the center of the Jerusalem leaders' power (19:45-46). Further teaching enhances his popularity with the people even while he attacks the Jerusalem elite for their faithlessness. They challenge his authority and increase their efforts to kill him (19:47—20:19; esp. 19:47-48; 20:19).

The conflicts continue through several verbal exchanges motivated by the elite's desire to "trap" Jesus (20:20, 26). Jesus silences them (20:40) and denounces the scribes for their love of social prestige and economic exploitation of the vulnerable (20:45-47). In chapter 21, Jesus escalates the conflict by announcing both the end of the temple, the base of the elite's power, and of the imperial world in which they are embedded as allies of Rome. In 21:5-8, Jesus predicts the temple's imminent destruction but refuses to specify a time for it. He then sets out a threefold progression of events that lead to the eschatological, or end-time, accomplishment of God's goal of establishing God's reign: social chaos, persecution, and witness (21:9-19); the destruction of Jerusalem and "the times of the Gentiles" (21:20-24); and the cosmic signs and earthly distresses that lead to the return of Jesus as Son of Man and establishment of God's empire (21:25-28).

The chapter concludes with exhortations to his followers to discern the signs and meanings of the time, to be alert and watchful (21:29-38). The inclusion of the (already accomplished) destruction of Jerusalem in this progression validates Jesus' words. If he is accurate in this dimension, he is trustworthy in the rest of the progression. There is security and assurance for Theophilus and all hearers of the Gospel that the world's destiny is in God's good hands.

Luke's Passion Narrative (Chapters 22–23)

The movement from the eschatological vision of God's coming triumph and establishment of God's reign in chapter 21 to the narrative of Jesus' crucifixion in chapters 22–23 is starkly contrastive. Through these chapters, Jesus continues in his faithfulness to his prophetic role even as the elite effect his death and his followers prove fickle. The first forty-six verses lead to Jesus' arrest by offering a variety of perspectives on and motivations for this upcoming death.

7.6 Certainty about Jesus' Return to Establish God's Reign

The vision of Jesus' return as Son of Man in 21:25-28 is not unique in Luke's Gospel, but attention to Luke's use of his sources suggests it gets extra emphasis in this Gospel. Perhaps this was one of the issues about which Theophilus needed assurance in the light of the fact that Jesus had not returned. Is Jesus reliable? Is God powerful enough to accomplish the establishment of God's reign?

We may compare Luke's use of Q material in Luke 12:35-48 with Matt. 24:42-51. There is significant similarity between Luke 12:39-46 and Matt. 24:43-51 (the householder who would not have left his house if he had known when the thief was coming; the "faithful and wise" slave, who attends to the master's business when the master is absent, in contrast to the unfaithful slave who misrules the master's business). But significantly, Luke adds material both immediately before and after this scene. In 12:35-38, Luke uses the image of slaves ready for their master's return to emphasize readiness for an unknown return. In 12:47-48, Luke adds two verses that again make the same point of faithful readiness. These additions emphasize the certainty, but not the immediacy, of Jesus' return and the need for active discipleship in the meantime.

Similar emphases occur in Luke 19:11-27 (par. Matt. 25:14-30), the parable of the pounds or talents. Luke adds an introduction in verse 11 that explains why Jesus tells the parable, to correct the notion that "the kingdom of God was to appear immediately," thus emphasizing that the delay in Jesus' return is not a matter of Jesus' unfaithfulness or powerlessness. Rather it is within God's purview.

One more change can be noted. In Mark 14:62, Jesus says, "You will see the Son of Man seated at the right hand of Power, and *coming with the clouds of heaven.*" Luke 22:69 has Jesus say the first part, but the italicized words are omitted. The effect is to emphasize Jesus' present elevated status as one to be obeyed in the present, thereby diminishing attention to his return.

The overall effect is an emphasis that Jesus will return, but not soon, and that disciples are to be active and faithful in the meantime.

- 22:2: The chief priests and scribes want Jesus dead, but are hindered by the people who "would get up early in the morning to listen to him [teaching] in the temple" (21:38). Jesus' societal vision and influence trouble the elite leadership.
- 22:3-6: "Satan entered into Judas called Iscariot, who was one of the twelve." This verse frames Judas's betrayal of Jesus as the devil's work. Judas allies with the temple leaders to betray Jesus to them for a price. This act allies Judas, the temple leaders, and the devil as opponents of God's purposes.
- 22:7-30: Jesus acknowledges his imminent suffering as an agent or prophet of God's purposes (22:15, 22). He is not a victim, not taken by surprise, not defeated in being put to death. Again the dynamic of prediction or foresight-and-accomplishment underscores his

reliable word as he makes arrangements for the Passover (22:8-13). He interprets his imminent death in terms of the Passover meal, as an anticipation of the coming kingdom (22:16-18, 28-30), and of a new covenant sealed by Jesus' self-giving in giving his life and blood.

- 22:31-34: Peter boasts that he will remain loyal to Jesus even to death. Jesus predicts Peter will deny him three times. Peter does so, again showing Jesus' words to be reliable and trustworthy (22:54-62).
- 22:39-46: Jesus prays for God to remove this "cup," a metaphor for Jesus' suffering and death. But through prayer, he comes to accept the inevitable destiny of being a prophet who challenged the powerful status quo (19:28—22:38). He remains faithful to his identity. His (unnamed) disciples, though, sleep "because of grief" (22:45).

Yet while Jesus is faithful, the Jerusalem elite (the chief priests, temple police, and elders, 22:52) are determined to put him to death. Judas's betrayal of Jesus with a kiss ensures his arrest (22:47-53). They torture Jesus with beatings and verbal insults (22:63-65). They interrogate him about his identity (the Messiah? 22:66-71). Echoing the enthronement of God's anointed in Pss. 2:6-7 and 110, Jesus asserts his imminent exaltation to the right hand of God, a place of great honor and recognition of his identity as God's agent or Son. The term "Son of Man" evokes Daniel 7, where this heavenly figure overcomes the empires of the world and enacts God's rule. The rulers seem to have some insight into Jesus' identity as God's dangerous agent or representative (Messiah, Son of God), but it does not lead to confession. Consistent with their opposition, they use Jesus' declaration of his God-given identity as a reason to condemn him (22:71). It is important to recognize that Jesus' statements are not just religious doctrine. They are political claims that assert power to threaten Rome's ordering of the world.

The Jerusalem leaders take Jesus to their ally Pilate, the Roman governor (23:1). Both the Jerusalem leaders and Pilate need each other to exercise their power. They exist in a tensive relationship with a shared interest in maintaining the hierarchical status quo, which benefits them at the expense of nonelites. They bring Jesus to Pilate because he holds the power of capital punishment. They need his decision to execute Jesus. But if he consents too readily, he cedes power to them. Hence through the scene, the two groups struggle with each other to gain the upper hand. There is no doubt that Jesus will be crucified, but not before a power struggle among these allies has been played out (23:1-25).

The Jerusalem leaders accuse Jesus of "perverting our people" and stirring them up, forbidding payment of taxes to the emperor, and making himself king or Messiah (23:2, 5, 14). These are serious political charges that center on disrupting Roman control. Refusal to pay taxes was viewed as rebellion, as was claiming to be a king without Rome's permission. Any of these three charges alone merited death.

Why, then, does Pilate maintain that Jesus has done nothing to deserve death (23:4, 14-16, 22)? Is he genuine in this assertion, or is this a ruse to provoke the Jerusalem leaders to beg more forcefully and become more dependent on Pilate's greater power? The second option seems more likely. Pilate is ready to flog Jesus (23:17, 22), an action that makes no sense if he thinks Jesus is harmless. But more importantly, Pilate knows that if his allies charge Jesus with three capital offenses, this man is dangerous, and for the sake of the ruling alliance, Jesus must be crucified. Why then does he delay? Verses 21 and 23 show Pilate's plan at work. The more Pilate hesitates, the more Jesus' accusers demand his execution, placing themselves in greater dependence on Pilate. Pilate can then condemn Jesus and grant their demand, having gained greater power in the alliance.

Jesus' crucifixion affects a range of characters (23:26-43). In an act of colonial subjugation, Simon of Cyrene is pressed into carrying Jesus' cross (23:26). Jesus addresses the weeping women, warning them of impending distress, a reference to Jerusalem's imminent destruction (23:27-31). Luke thus links the leaders' rejection of Jesus to Jerusalem's defeat and destruction by the Romans in 70 CE. This latter act is interpreted as an act of judgment for the crucifixion of Jesus. This link continues the condemnation of the city stated previously in 13:33-34; 19:41-44; and 21:20-24. Two other criminals, or "brigands," are crucified with Jesus. Jesus assures one of them of his place in paradise (23:32-33, 39-43). The leaders and soldiers mock Jesus' claim to exercise God's rule as a king (unsanctioned by Rome, 23:35-38). Throughout, Jesus actively issues a warning about Jerusalem's judgment (23:26-31), prays on behalf of his opponents (23:34), and assures one of the criminals of God's salvation (23:43).

7.2 Women of Jerusalem weep for Jesus (Luke 23:27-31); Eighth Station of the Cross, Calvary of the Sick, Lourdes, France. Commons.wikimedia.org.

Jesus dies just as he predicted he would (cf. 9:22, 44; 13:33-34; 18:31-34). Again, his word is shown to be reliable and trustworthy. He dies in darkness, suggesting the "triumph" of the destructive, even devilish, power of the alliance of Jerusalem and Roman elites (23:44; cf. 22:3, 53). The curtain torn in the temple suggests judgment on this center of the elite's power (23:45). Jesus cries out as he dies. This is not a cry of abandonment by God, as in Matthew and Mark (citing Ps. 22:1). Rather, it is a cry of trust in God's triumphant purposes that echoes Ps. 31:5, a psalm of deliverance from enemies. A centurion confesses that Jesus was "righteous," or one faithful to God (23:47). Women followers from Galilee (who had used their resources to support Jesus' activity, so 8:1-3) are present (23:49). They delay their washing and anointing of Jesus' body because of the Sabbath, showing them to be faithful Jewish women (23:55-56). And one of the Jewish leadership alliance, Joseph from Arimathea, who was waiting for God's kingdom, exhibits faithful piety and an act of charity in burying Jesus' body (cf. Tob. 1:16-20).

7.7 Mark and Matthew Watch

Mark's passion narrative spans chapters 14–15, Luke's narrative occupies chapters 22–23, and Matthew's narrative spans chapters 26–27. Compare their quite different resurrection accounts: Mark's very short eight verses (16:1-8), Matthew's neatly structured account (28:1-20) comprising three scenes (28:1-10, the empty tomb; vv. 11-15, the alternative story; vv. 16-20, the commission to disciples), and Luke's fifty-three verses covering the empty tomb (24:1-12), the Emmaus journey (24:13-35), appearance to the disciples (24:36-49), and his ascension (24:50-53). Neither Mark nor Matthew references an ascension.

Jesus' Resurrection and Ascension (Luke 24)

Jesus has predicted not only his death but also that he would be raised on the third day (9:22; 18:33). Just as his word was accurate and reliable in relation to his death, so also it is accurate and trustworthy in relation to resurrection.

At the empty tomb, the women who have come to anoint Jesus' body encounter two angels (24:1-12). The angels remind them of Jesus' declaration that he would rise on the third day, thereby drawing attention to Jesus' reliable and trustworthy words. The women report the angels' words to the eleven male apostles who do not believe. Peter, though, runs to the tomb and finds it empty of Jesus' body.

In the meantime, verses 13-35 tell the story of two followers of

Jesus. Returning from Jerusalem to their village of Emmaus, they have been discussing Jesus' crucifixion, naming their disappointed hope that he might redeem Israel, and the reports (that they did not believe) that he is alive. Jesus joins them, but they do not recognize him. He explains to them how the events that have taken place are in accord with the Scriptures. When they reach Emmaus, they invite the still unrecognized Jesus to stay with them. During the evening meal, he breaks bread, and they recognize Jesus. He disappears, and the two followers return to Jerusalem, proclaiming, "The Lord has risen indeed."

7.3 Jesus (wearing a hat) is revealed to two disciples as he breaks bread: Supper at Emmaus, anonymous, late 17th century. Museo Nacional de Belas Artes, Rio de Janeiro; Commons.wikimedia.org.

The story encapsulates the security that the Gospel offers to Theophilus and other hearers. The scene begins with despair and disappointment but moves to proclamation of good news and certainty. It begins with nonrecognition and blindness but ends with recognition and insight. It develops from uncertainty about God and Jesus to certainty and security. It shows that the present, the time between Jesus' resurrection and his awaited return, is not a time of disappointed waiting and uncertainty but a time of proclamation and faithful discipleship in living according to Jesus' teaching. Again, Jesus' words are seen to be certain, secure, trustworthy, and reliable.

Jesus appears to the male disciples, who struggle to believe even when Jesus displays his hands and feet, and eats a piece of fish (24:36-43). He elaborates the Scriptures to show that his death and resurrection enact God's purposes (24:44-49). He declares them to be witnesses, hints at a subsequent mission beginning in Jerusalem and extending to all nations, promises them power for this task, and identifies their immediate task to wait for God-given empowering.

The Gospel closes with Jesus blessing the disciples, who return to Jerusalem and the temple to wait. Jesus is then lifted up into heaven. He had predicted his ascension in 22:69 before the Jerusalem leaders. With its description here, the Gospel ends with another demonstration of the reliability and trustworthiness of Jesus' word. Theophilus and other hearers of the Gospel can have security, certainty, assurance concerning Jesus' teaching and activity as the agent of God. His mission continues in the book of Acts through his followers.

But how does that happen? Has Jesus abandoned his followers and left them to it? Does the church carry out this mission without his presence or any assistance? Will God deliver on the promise to "clothe them with power from on high" (24:49)? Is Jesus' word reliable and efficacious?

The book of Acts sets about providing security and assurance about these matters. The Holy Spirit comes to the fore, coming upon the gathered followers in the event of Pentecost in Acts 2. Thereafter, the Spirit leads and empowers and nudges these Jesus-followers to carry out the task the risen Jesus gives to them: "You will be my witnesses in Jerusalem, in all Judea and Samaria, and to the ends of the earth" (Acts 1:8). Acts offers the assurance that the present is not a time of failed promises or disappointed waiting for Jesus' return. It is a time of witness and opportunity.

Questions for Review and Reflection

1. What is the evidence that the Gospel according to Luke has a sequel, the book of Acts?
2. The chapter suggests Luke 1:4 is very important. On what basis? Assurance or security about what?
3. What does the Gospel's prologue (1:1-4) contribute?
4. What are the significant emphases of Luke's conception and birth story (1:5—2:52)? How does Luke's story compare with Matthew's?
5. And the contribution of 3:1—4:13, and the account of Jesus' public ministry in Galilee (4:14—9:50)?
6. The travel narrative takes Jesus from Galilee to Jerusalem (9:51—19:27). What are some of its features and sources?
7. How does the Gospel provide certainty or security about Jesus' return? Check the redaction by comparing Matthew's Gospel.
8. How do chapters 22–24 present Jesus' crucifixion and resurrection? Compare Luke 24 with Mark 16:1-8 and Matthew 28.

8

Luke: The Kingdom of God

After beginning his public ministry, Luke's Jesus declares: "I must proclaim the good news of the kingdom of God to the other cities also; for I was sent for this purpose" (Luke 4:43). In this declaration, Luke's Gospel identifies a central matter about which its hearers/reader can have certainty, security, assurance. Jesus' mission and compulsion are to proclaim the good news of the kingdom of God.

First in this chapter, I ask, what is this "kingdom"? How does the Gospel construct its purpose, scope, nature, presence, impact, and future as part of the security or assurance that the Gospel offers Theophilus and other Gospel readers (1:3)? Then, I consider the communal dimensions of the kingdom's impact, especially concerning ethnicity, the roles of women, and the relationship between God's kingdom and the most powerful kingdom in the Gospel's world, the Roman Empire. Finally, I ask how the Gospel constructs interactions between the kingdom of God and the nonhuman world. I examine connections within the Gospel narrative as well as intertextualities between the Gospel narrative and external societal and environmental realities.

8.1 Intertextuality

The term *intertextuality* has a range of meanings. Some users understand it in a very restricted sense, referring only to a relationship between two texts on the basis of one text quoting another. This use would refer to a New Testament text citing or evoking a Hebrew Bible text. In the chapter on Mark, I discussed the intertextuality between Mark's passion narrative and Psalm 22. This is an author-centered approach, where the author of a text is understood to control it through interaction with a specified text. But the term can have a much broader or more open meaning. It might refer to the intertextuality created between the text and any other media (text, visual, etc.) in existence in its time of origin, whether the author signals it or not. Or even broader still, it can refer to the intertextualities or interactions between any two texts that a reader or viewer puts into conversation with each other. This is a reader-centered approach, which understands readers to have an active role in making meanings from texts. My use of the term here is more reader-oriented in choosing to put the "kingdom" or "empire" of God into conversation with the empire of Rome.

Intratextuality refers to making meaning by connecting various elements that occur within the same text.

The Kingdom of God

Luke's Jesus declares his mission and commission to center on the kingdom of God (4:43). What is this kingdom? What difference does it make in the world and in the lives of people? How does one recognize or encounter the presence of this kingdom? How might Gospel readers be assured of its presence?

One starting point for thinking about these questions is to consider the phrase "the kingdom of God" (Greek *hē basileia tou theou*). The first issue is one of translation. The Greek word translated "kingdom" can also be translated as "reign" or "rule" or "empire." Each word brings a different nuance of understanding. The word *kingdom* denotes more a space where God's dominion or kingship is established and into which people enter and live (13:28-29). Kingdoms always have kings, so the phrase also evokes God as the king who rules this domain, especially through his agent, Jesus, who is also identified as a king (23:2-3, 38). Yet for many contemporary readers, the word *kingdom* has outdated associations with castles, dragons, knights on white horses, and long-haired, fair-haired damsels in distress! The words *reign* and *rule* denote more an activity than a space, namely, God's activity in ruling as king. Instead of *kingdom*, some have suggested using the term *kin-dom*, which evokes transformed relationship—a family marked by love—created among those who encounter God's reign in following Jesus. The word *empire* draws together the sphere and activity of God's rule, but also calls to mind the empire of Rome, in which daily life in the first century took place and in the midst of which God's ruling activity took place, according to Luke (3:1-3). We might think, then, of "kingdom of God" as denoting the assertion of God's rule or sovereignty in the midst of Rome's imperial world, an assertion that makes a difference for the better.

The little word *of* in the phrase *kingdom of God* is worth thinking about also. Its function is to link the two entities "kingdom" and "God." It can suggest several relationships between the two entities. One relationship that "of" signifies is possession. For example, in the phrase "the owner of the dog," the word *of* indicates that the owner possesses the dog. So the phrase *kingdom of God* indicates that God possesses or owns the kingdom. It is *God's* activity or rule. What role is there for humans? How can God's activity be the center of Jesus' activity? Another relationship that *of* signifies concerns "origin." The "kingdom" comes from God. Humans do not create it. It denotes God's activity in the world.

We might also gain more understanding through an intertextual approach that utilizes understandings of God's kingship and kingdom in the Hebrew Bible. Luke's Gospel knows and utilizes the Hebrew Bible, usually in its Greek translation (known as the Septuagint), so these writings may inform its presentations of God's ruling activity. These presentations divide into three categories. (1) God is king of all the world because God is its creator (Pss. 47:2, 7-8; 103:19); (2) God is the king of the covenant people of Israel (Exod. 15:18; 1 Chron. 28:5; 2 Chron. 13:8); (3) God's rule, while active in the present, is yet to be established in full forever (Ps. 145:11-13; Dan. 7:9-14, 23-27; Zech. 14:9, "And the Lord will become king over all the earth"). The Gospel's use of the phrase "God's kingdom," then, may well draw on these Hebrew Bible traditions that denote God's ruling activity that is both present and future, particular to Israel yet universal, present partially now while awaiting fullness. The phrase denotes the space and scope of God's ruling activity and presence among human beings.

Attention, then, to the language and traditions associated with the phrase "the kingdom of God" provides some understanding of this entity. Moving to an intratextual approach, the use of the phrase within Luke's Gospel, we can notice the particular nuances of Luke's presentation of God's ruling activity, the kingdom of God. The phrase, or its shortened form "the kingdom," occurs nearly forty times.

As is appropriate for any discourse about God, the Gospel recognizes that mystery surrounds the presence of God's ruling activity. Where is it to be found? How is it recognized? (17:21). Jesus provides reassurance that to some, namely, Jesus' disciples, "it has been given to know the secrets of the kingdom of God, but to others" the kingdom's presence remains invisible and incomprehensible (8:10). Subsequently, Jesus emphasizes the mysterious presence of God's activity by telling a parable that compares the kingdom to a small mustard seed that is invisible under the ground. Nevertheless, it grows and becomes a tree. A small seed, hidden from sight, has a big and very visible impact (13:18-19). Or again, Jesus compares the kingdom to yeast that a woman mixes into a batch of dough. The yeast is invisible, yet its impact on the whole batch is evident in transforming its size (13:20-21). These images suggest mystery and elusiveness in discerning God's ruling activity and presence at work in the world—even while they confidently attest the kingdom's presence and effect. These parables provide assurance that God's reign is active in the world, though elusive.

If God's activity in the present is elusive and mysterious, perhaps the future manifestation of God's activity will be more clearly discerned. Yet Jesus corrects those who expect only a future kingdom, thinking that they will recognize its self-evident signs and find it in particular places ("here it is . . . there it is"). Jesus directs their attention away from such expectations. He declares that it is already present in their midst in his activity (17:20-21). Its presence in his activity and person is the secret of God's reign that his disciples discern (8:10).

That presence, though, has further paradoxical dimensions. The kingdom, or God's ruling activity, is appropriately identified as a gift from God. So God gives the gift of God's ruling presence to Jesus and to Jesus' followers concerned with how they live their lives and what they might wear or eat (12:32; 22:28-29). The gift has the impact of creating among them a lifestyle free of anxiety and fear. It is a gift, yet this gift is also a mandate. Jesus urges its recipients to resemble his activity in living a life centered on God's ruling activity or presence (12:31).

So while God's reign is God's gift and activity, God designates Jesus as its agent, as God's Son (1:32, 35) and anointed one (*christos*, that is, "Messiah," 2:11) who manifests it in his activity. It defines Jesus and directs his life; to proclaim God's ruling presence is Jesus' mission and compulsion (4:43). This declaration of Jesus' mission in terms of manifesting God's ruling activity and presence at the outset of Jesus' activity frames all the rest of his life.

So Jesus uses *words* to announce "the good news" of God's reign (4:43; 8:1; 16:16). Along with his words, all Jesus' *actions* demonstrate God's reign in the midst of human beings. So, for example, God's ruling presence disrupts daily life, priorities, and commitments when it claims human loyalty and priorities in the calling of disciples. The fishermen Peter, James, and John, partners in their small fishing business, are so seized by God's rule manifested in Jesus' summons that they leave their boats, contracts, and employees to live a life of a new purpose and commitment in following Jesus (5:1–11). Levi the tax collector experiences a similar thing, much to the surprise of some Pharisees and scribes (5:27–32), as do at least nine others named in 6:12–16, numerous women including Mary, Joanna, and Susanna (8:1–3), and seventy more in 10:1–12. Jesus conveys the gift of God's ruling activity to them, thereby giving them a new purpose and mission in manifesting God's rule among humans. He gives his followers "power and authority over all demons and to cure diseases, and he sends them out to proclaim the kingdom of God and to heal" (9:2). They are to "cure the sick . . . and say to them, 'the kingdom of God has come near to you'" (10:9–11). In this way, the work of manifesting God's ruling activity among humans spreads further.

Doing this work faithfully now means participation in the future fullness of God's reign (22:29).

Jesus' *healings* manifest God's ruling presence. Jesus asserts God's rule over disease, repairing bodily damage, and restoring people to human communities: a leper (5:12–16), a paralyzed man (5:17–26), a man with a withered hand, fatal in a society where manual work was the primary means of support (6:6–11). The narrative explicitly links Jesus' proclamation of the kingdom with healings (9:11) and with *exorcisms* that manifest the presence of God's rule over demons (11:20) and over the kingdom of Satan (11:18–20). Such actions of healing and liberation transform human lives and communities.

The Gospel affirms the presence of God's ruling activity especially among the poor. Jesus announces a blessing on the poor, "for yours is the kingdom of God" (6:20; also 14:15). Who are these people identified as the poor? One immediate clue comes from the following verses (6:20-26). The poor are associated with the hungry, those who weep, and those who are hated and reviled. They are contrasted with the rich, the full, the laughing, and those who speak well of others. The contrast, especially between the economically poor and the rich, reflects a key socioeconomic divide in the ancient world that marked social position and power. The ancient world comprised, as we have seen, a small percentage of very wealthy people on one hand and the vast majority of the population who comprised a gradation of poor folks on the other. This gradation spanned the very destitute, to those who lived precariously around subsistence levels, to those who experienced some stability slightly above subsistence levels.[1] Such folks experienced significant vulnerability, a lack of power and privilege, personal and structural brokenness, limited resources that frequently resulted in poor nutrition and diseases of deprivation and contagion, social disdain, and marginalization. To be poor, then, meant to be vulnerable to regular food crises and their often fatal consequences; exclusion from various forms of social and political participation; and personal

1. Steven Friesen, "Poverty in Pauline Studies: Beyond the So-Called New Consensus," *JSNT* 26 (2004): 323–61.

and social shame, indignity, and envy in the desperation of not being able to generate "enough"—whether clothing, food, shelter, or social respectability.[2] Jesus declares that among these poor folks is the ruling activity of God.[3]

8.1 This seventeenth-century Russian Orthodox icon presents a fairly literal rendering of Mary's Magnificat (Luke 1:46-56). Commons.wikimedia.org.

2. Neville Morley, "The Poor in the City of Rome," in *Poverty in the Roman World*, ed. Margaret Atkins and Robin Osborne (Cambridge: Cambridge University Press, 2006), 21–39, esp. 33–36.
3. This emphasis on the poor raises the question of the place of the wealthy. See further below. A number of passages warn the rich to change their way of life, avoiding greed (the parable of the rich fool, 12:13-21), selling possessions and giving alms (13:33), inviting "the poor, the crippled, the lame, and the blind" to banquets (14:12-14), making friends with "dishonest wealth" (16:1-9), sharing food with the poor (the rich man and Lazarus, 16:19-31), selling all and redistributing it to the poor in order to follow Jesus (18:18-30), and divesting wealth to the poor and compensating those who have been defrauded fourfold (Zacchaeus, 19:1-10).

What does the blessing of the presence of God's ruling activity among such folks accomplish? In part, the Gospel demonstrates something of the new life that results for the poor and vulnerable when Jesus manifests God's rule (so 1:46-56; 4:18-19): The sick are healed, the demonized set free, the socially despised (e.g., tax collectors) gain community (5:27-29), "sinners" (a polemical term naming anybody someone did not like) encounter God's forgiveness and human community (5:30-32), enemies and slaves are blessed (7:1-10), women as well as men benefit (8:40-56), the hungry are fed (9:10-17; 14:13-14, 21), powerless and vulnerable children are included (18:16-17), disabled beggars are healed and their lives transformed (18:35-43), a crucified criminal considered unacceptable by elite-ruled society is accepted into God's presence (23:39-43).

But what is good news for the poor seems to be bad news for the rich. The valuing and blessing of poor folks by God's ruling presence are part of a larger transformation that God's reign accomplishes. God's ruling presence is envisaged as upsetting societal expectations, values, and structures. It is the rich, powerful, and successful that are usually assumed to be blessed and whose lifestyle supposedly displays divine sanction. By these standards, to be poor and powerless, vulnerable and valueless, denotes apparent failure, misery, curse, and rejection by God. Yet Luke's Jesus reverses this verdict and offers a vision of a different valuing, a world upside down, an alternative social vision where the wealthy do not have an automatic and privileged place (18:24-25), where the powerful are brought down and the lowly lifted up and the rich are sent away and the hungry are filled (1:52-53; 16:19-31), and where God's ruling presence is found especially among the poor, the vulnerable, and the socially excluded and shamed (6:20-23). Jesus does not declare poverty and social hierarchy to be ended, but his transforming actions point to a different way God is at work among humans in anticipation of a new world in which that transformation will be completed.

God's kingdom, then, is not completely realized in the present. It awaits a future completion (22:16, 18, 29-30). Jesus is to accomplish that future in-breaking and establishment when he returns in power and glory (9:26; 17:24). His appearing will surprise some (17:22-37). Its impact will be worldwide, overwhelming, sudden, and inescapable. In 13:28-30, the rule he establishes is imaged as a place that people enter, a grand feast that echoes the vision of Isa. 25:6-10a, in which God's reign appears as an extravagant banquet for all nations, both Jews scattered in the Diaspora as well as the gentile peoples of the world.

But though disciples are to pray for the full and future coming of God's reign (11:2), Luke's Jesus seems clear that the kingdom's completion is not imminent. He tells a parable because some disciples "supposed that the kingdom of God was to appear immediately" (19:11). His parable tells the story of a nobleman, a wealthy man with much land, who leaves his estate to go to another country. He gives ten "minas" to each of ten slaves to use wisely in his absence. This term "mina" is often translated "pounds," as though it were English money! A mina was worth about three or four month's wages for a laborer, so these are significant amounts of money, the equivalent of about two and a half years' pay for a laborer. The man then returns and holds them accountable for how they have used the wealth in his absence. The emphasis falls on faithful discipleship in the time of Jesus' absence so as to be ready for his eventual but certain return (19:11-27).

A similar point is presented in 12:35-48. The center point seems to be a parable in 12:42-46, which concerns a master who goes away but entrusts a slave to manage the other slaves in his absence. The parable contrasts two sets of behavior by the slave: In the first, the slave faithfully attends to the task, and in the second, the slave beats and abuses the other slaves. When the master suddenly returns, he blesses the behavior that is faithful to the task but punishes the unfaithful and abusive behavior (12:41-46). Interestingly, the verses immediately preceding (12:35-40) and following (12:47-48) the parable also use contrast to repeat the same exhortation to be found faithful when Jesus returns unexpectedly.

8.2 Luke and Matthew on Expectation of the Kingdom Compare how Luke has used, and added to, material from Q (also in Matthew) to convey his message about expectation of the kingdom of God.	
Luke 12	**Matthew 24**
Verses 35-38 ("L" material) has no parallel in Matt. 24:40-42.	
Be dressed for action and have your lamps lit; be like those who are waiting for their master to return from the wedding banquet, so that they may open the door for him as soon as he comes and knocks. Blessed are those slaves whom the master finds alert when he comes; truly I tell you, he will fasten his belt and have them sit down to eat, and he will come and serve them. If he comes during the middle of the night, or near dawn, and finds them so, blessed are those slaves.	Then two will be in the field; one will be taken and one will be left. Two women will be grinding meal together; one will be taken and one will be left. Keep awake therefore, for you do not know on what day your Lord is coming.
Q Material (or double tradition) follows.	
"But know this: if the owner of the house had known at what hour the thief was coming, he would not have let his house be broken into. You also must be ready, for the Son of Man is coming at an unexpected hour." Peter said, "Lord, are you telling this parable for us or for everyone?" And the Lord said, "Who then is the faithful and prudent manager whom his master will put in charge of his slaves, to give them their allowance of food at the proper time?	"But understand this: if the owner of the house had known in what part of the night the thief was coming, he would have stayed awake and would not have let his house be broken into. Therefore you also must be ready, for the Son of Man is coming at an unexpected hour. Who then is the faithful and wise slave, whom his master has put in charge of his household, to give the other slaves their allowance of food at the proper time?

"Blessed is that slave whom his master will find at work when he arrives. Truly I tell you, he will put that one in charge of all his possessions. But if that slave says to himself, 'My master is delayed in coming,' and if he begins to beat the other slaves, men and women, and to eat and drink and get drunk, the master of that slave will come on a day when he does not expect him and at an hour that he does not know, and will cut him in pieces, and put him with the unfaithful."	"Blessed is that slave whom his master will find at work when he arrives. Truly I tell you, he will put that one in charge of all his possessions. But if that wicked slave says to himself, 'My master is delayed,' and he begins to beat his fellow slaves, and eats and drinks with drunkards, the master of that slave will come on a day when he does not expect him and at an hour that he does not know. He will cut him in pieces and put him with the hypocrites, where there will be weeping and gnashing of teeth."
Further material in Luke 12:47-48 has no parallel in Matthew 24:	*Matthew 24 ends here; Matthew 25 begins the parable of the bridesmaids.*
That slave who knew what his master wanted, but did not prepare himself or do what was wanted, will receive a severe beating. But the one who did not know and did what deserved a beating will receive a light beating. From everyone to whom much has been given, much will be required; and from the one to whom much has been entrusted, even more will be demanded.	

This emphasis on faithful living in the time until Jesus' return negates any uncertainty or insecurity that God's reign is ineffective or invisible in the present and merely a promise of future "pie in the sky when you die." For Luke's Gospel, the present is not a time of disappointed waiting or divine impotence. In the present, God's ruling presence is creating an alternative community through Jesus' followers who are actively engaged in embodying God's ruling presence. They are to perform not only their mission tasks of proclaiming, healing, and exorcising (9:1-2, 6; 10:1-12) but also social interactions marked by acts that share limited resources so as to sustain the survival of others:

> Love your enemies, do good to those who hate you, bless those who curse you, pray for those who abuse you. . . . Give to everyone who begs from you; and if anyone takes away your goods, do not ask for them again. Do to others as you would have them do to you.

> . . . If you lend to those from whom you hope to receive, what credit is that to you? . . . But love your enemies, do good, and lend, expecting nothing in return. . . . Be merciful, just as your Father is merciful.
>
> Do not judge, and you will not be judged; do not condemn, and you will not be condemned. Forgive, and you will be forgiven. (Luke 6:27-37, selections)

Even the rich are given an opportunity to change their ways and use their wealth compassionately and justly in the meantime. Jesus instructs them to "be on your guard against all kinds of greed; for one's life does not consist in the abundance of possessions" (12:15). He follows the warning with a parable about a "rich fool" beset with material acquisitiveness who is "not rich toward God" (12:16-21). Subsequently, he warns the rich against associating only with "friends . . . or your relatives or rich neighbors" and instructs them to extend hospitality to "the poor, the crippled, the lame, and the blind" and include them in their banquets (14:13). He then tells a parable about a wealthy, high-status elite person whose elite allies and clients do not reciprocate the honor of a dinner invitation, so the wealthy person does precisely what Jesus instructs and invites "the poor, the crippled, the blind, and the lame" to his dinner (14:15-24). The parable of a rich man and a poor man named Lazarus depicts the fate of a rich man who is grossly insensitive to and utterly lacking in compassion for the hungry poor (16:19-31). For the wealthy among Luke's readers, the scenarios provide instruction and imaginatively reframe their societal practices and structures so as to benefit the poor.

8.2 A graphic depiction of the story of the rich man and Lazarus (Luke 16: 19-31), from the Eadwine Psalter (ca. 1150). Upper panel: a rich man feasts while the poor man begs at his door; an angel retrieves the soul of the poor man at his death. Lower panel: a demon seizes the soul of the rich man; the poor man resides "in the bosom of Abraham" in heaven while demons torture the damned in hell. Morgan Library and Museum; Commons.wikimedia.org.

But with all this emphasis on the transforming presence of God's reign in Jesus' activity in the present, and exhortations to Jesus' followers to faithful living that continues the assertion of God's reign, why does evil exercise such a continuing hold in human society? Is God's reign unable to accomplish God's purposes? Several factors account for the ongoing presence of evil.

One factor is the incompleteness of God's purposes. As we have noted, God's reign or empire is at work in Jesus' activity and in that of his followers. But it is not yet established in full. That will take place in the future when Jesus returns (9:26; 17:22-37).

A second factor concerns the continuing role of the devil or Satan as an opponent of God's purposes. In the temptation scene in chapter 4, the devil seeks to turn Jesus aside from his identity and work as God's Son or agent of God's reign (4:1-13). Three times, the devil tries to gain Jesus' allegiance and direct his efforts away from doing God's purposes. Instead of the kingdom or empire of God, the devil offers Jesus "all the kingdoms or empires of the world" for the price of worshiping not God but the devil. This is an extraordinary claim that constructs the devil as the power behind the dominant Roman Empire (4:5-7).

The devil's oppositional efforts are varied. He employs agents called demons to take over human lives with devastating effects (11:26), causing strange public behavior (4:31-37), sickness and physical disabilities (4:41; 8:2), social isolation and personal torment (8:26-39), seizures (9:37-43), and crippling of limbs (13:10-17). The devil opposes the proclamation of the message about God's reign (8:12) and turns disciples away from loyalty to Jesus. He succeeds with Judas (22:3) but fails with Simon Peter (22:31).

Jesus' exorcisms overcome demons and repair the damage they have inflicted (7:21). Luke presents these exorcisms as an assertion of the kingdom of God (11:20). Similarly, he authorizes and empowers his followers, both the Twelve and the Seventy, to cast out demons (9:1; 10:17). These efforts counter the effects of the devil's work, but not until the full and final establishment of God's reign will the devil finally be overcome.

Third, the Gospel recognizes that humans do evil things. There is an indication that all humans are evil (11:13), but also a recognition that some with good hearts do good things, while some with evil hearts do or say evil things (6:45). Their evil actions include those who "hate . . . exclude . . . revile . . . defame" Jesus' followers (6:22). Elites particularly do evil things as societal leaders. King Herod is rebuked by John the Baptizer not only "because of Herodias, his brother's wife," but also "because of all the evil things that Herod had done" (3:19). The "evil things" that Herod as a powerful, wealthy ruler has done are not specified, though exploitative rule that harms the poor is an obvious guess (3:18-20). Likewise, the poor man Lazarus has experienced "evil things" including at the hands of the wealthy and powerful "rich man" (16:19-30). These "evil things" involve being deprived of adequate nutrition because the rich man did not share his largesse, including abundant food, as well as suffering from sickness that "covered [him] with sores" (16:20-21). Beyond these instances, perhaps the worst evil that the ruling elites commit as part of this "evil generation" is to reject Jesus and not receive him as God's agent who manifests God's reign (11:29-32). The alliance of Jerusalem leaders and the Roman governor will express their rejection of Jesus by crucifying him.

Community

This community, created by God's ruling presence in the Gospel narrative, particularly privileges the poor, as we have seen. But along with attention to social structures, what about factors of gender and ethnicity? How does the kingdom of God involve and/or affect men and women, Jews and gentiles?

Ethnicity

With respect to ethnicity, much of the Gospel's attention predictably concerns Galileans and Judeans, since Jesus' ministry is conducted initially in Galilee and then in Judea and Jerusalem. The opening hymns of Mary and Zechariah place God's initiative with Jesus in the context of God's covenant relationship with "his servant Israel, in remembrance of his mercy according to the promise he made to our ancestors, to Abraham and his descendants forever" (1:54-55; cf. 1:68-79). The missions of John (3:4-5) and Jesus (4:18-19) are defined in relation to and by Hebrew Scriptures, constructing both figures in the context of God's purposes for Israel. The Gospel encloses the destruction of Jerusalem and the temple by the Romans in 70 CE in this same context. Luke's Jesus laments Jerusalem's fall. The event is presented as punishment for not recognizing "the time of your visitation from God" (19:44; also 13:33-35; 21:20-24), which refers to

God's ruling presence manifested in Jesus' activity. The lament is directed, like most of Jesus' conflict in chapters 19–22, not toward all Judeans nor toward all Jerusalemites, but especially toward the elites who will, in alliance with the Romans, crucify Jesus. Punishment, though, does not mean the end of God's covenant with Israel. God has not abandoned Israel or broken covenant. The opening hymns of chapter 1 frame all these events in the context of God's continuing covenant faithfulness.

Yet the Gospel also presents a thread to be developed much further in the book of Acts, the inclusion of gentiles as beneficiaries of God's ruling presence. Mary's song celebrates God's action according to the promise made to Abraham (1:55), a promise that concerned God's blessing not only to Israel but also to "all the families of the earth" (Gen. 12:3). Her celebration that God's ruling presence "has scattered the proud . . . brought down the powerful from their thrones . . . [and] filled the hungry with good things" (1:52-53) concerns, then, God's action not only among Israel but also in the whole world. The angels maintain an emphasis on the worldwide scope of God's ruling activity by announcing to the lowly shepherds that Jesus' birth signifies not peace in Judea but "peace on earth" (2:14). Simeon greets the infant Jesus in terms of the universal impact of his "salvation . . . a light for revelation to the Gentiles and for glory to your people Israel" (2:32). John the Baptizer's ministry is one in which "all flesh shall see the salvation of God" (3:6). Jesus adds to the theme of gentile inclusion by aligning himself with Elijah being sent to heal a non-Jewish widow's son and Elisha being sent to heal Naaman the Syrian (4:25-27). This alignment shows Jesus' prophetic ministry to the poor (4:18) to include gentiles, the desperate, women, and men. Jesus then demonstrates this gentile inclusion by showing love to one of Israel's enemies (see 6:27, 35), a centurion of Rome's army concerned for his sick slave (7:1-10). At the close of the Gospel, Jesus speaks twice of mission among the gentiles. After judgment is expressed on Israel's elite in the destruction of Jerusalem, a time of particular focus on gentile inclusion opens up (21:24). And the risen Jesus sends his followers "to all nations beginning from Jerusalem" to proclaim the good news of "repentance and forgiveness . . . in his name" (24:47). God's reigning presence extends to and includes Jews and gentiles. Acts will tell this story by various means, framing it as the commission of the risen Jesus (Acts 1:8), telling the story of Cornelius and Peter to show numerous ways of divine intervention that sanctioned this extension and inclusion (Acts 10:1-11:18), and narrating the approval of a church council in Jerusalem (Acts 15).

Gender

The gender question is more complicated and much debated.[4] Luke's Gospel has often been regarded as a Gospel that treats women positively, even enhancing the status of women.[5] The Gospel can certainly be read in these positive terms.

The opening two chapters, for example, feature three very important women. One, Mary, is greeted by an angel as having "found favor with God" and as performing a key place in the divine purposes (1:26-38). She declares herself to be one who serves God, just as Jesus declares himself to be one who serves God (22:27). Two women, Mary and Elizabeth, bear sons, John and Jesus, who play key roles in God's purposes. These two women, along with Anna, discern God's activity in their lives and respond with obedience and praise (Elizabeth, 1:25, 39-45; Mary, 1:46-56; Anna, 2:36-38). Mary offers a hymn of praise that constructs her as a prophetic preacher proclaiming God's liberating action on behalf of the powerless and oppressed, announcing personal and societal deliverance from the systemic injustice of the Roman Empire (1:46-56).

Women experience Jesus' healing power: in individual scenes (Simon's mother-in-law, 4:38-39; the hemorrhaging woman, 8:43-48),

4. Amy-Jill Levine (introduction to *A Feminist Companion to Luke*, ed. Amy-Jill Levine with Marianne Blickenstaff [London: Sheffield Academic, 2002], 3) observes that "the gospel has been such a storm center concerning the question of women's roles." The selections in this volume identify the contours of the debate.

5. For example, Robert Karris, "Women and Discipleship in Luke," in Levine, *Feminist Companion*, 23–43.

in scenes paired with males,[6] as well as in summary scenes as part of the crowds whom Jesus heals (4:40). Women also experience Jesus' preaching and teaching, in crowds (6:17-49; 7:24; 8:42-43) and individually (10:39), learning among other things that Jesus will go to Jerusalem to be crucified (9:21-22; 18:31-33; 24:6-7). Women exhibit features associated with being disciples of Jesus. Mary depicts herself as "the servant of the Lord" who commits herself to God's will and word, declaring, "Let it be with me according to your word" (1:38; 2:19), an emphasis consistent with Jesus' commendation for those "who hear the word of God and obey it" (11:28). Anna waits faithfully for Jesus' birth and then "speaks about the child to all" (2:36-38). In contrast to Simon, an inhospitable Pharisee, a woman washes Jesus' feet, dries them with her hair, kisses his feet, and anoints him with oil in an act of devotion (7:38, 44-46). Jesus commends her faith and her behavior, which illustrates that those who are forgiven much love Jesus much (7:47-48, 50). Jesus praises the hemorrhaging woman for her faith (8:48), commends Mary for listening to his teaching (10:39-42), and hails the healed, formerly crippled woman as a "daughter of Abraham," thereby affirming her place in God's purpose (13:16). The actions of women, like those of men, exhibit features of God's ruling presence and actions: while a man plants a mustard seed, a woman mixes yeast in a batch of dough (13:18-21); while a man searches for a lost sheep, a woman searches for a lost coin (15:3-10). In these scenarios, women represent God's activity just as men do.

Women with some resources and of some status travel with Jesus and use their resources either as benefactors to support Jesus (and the disciples) or "in going on mission for him"[7] (8:1-3). Though the text is not explicit, perhaps women are among the seventy whom Jesus sends out in a healing and preaching mission (10:1-12). Women remain loyal to Jesus through his crucifixion (23:49), burial (23:55-56), and resurrection, where the women receive an angelic appearance and are

6. So Jesus raises the widow's only son and Jairus's daughter (7:11-17; 8:40-42, 49-56), and on Sabbaths he heals a crippled woman (13:10-17) and a man with dropsy (excessive fluid or edema, 14:1-6).
7. This is the alternative translation of Karris, "Women and Discipleship in Luke," 31.

the first to hear the resurrection gospel. Without being told, they take the initiative to proclaim the resurrection gospel to the rest of the (unbelieving) male apostles (24:3-7). Subsequently, as "companions" of the Eleven, they hear the testimony of the two who had encountered the risen Jesus on the road to Emmaus; Jesus appears to them (24:33-49), and they along with the men are commissioned to a mission of proclamation "to all nations" in the power of the Spirit (24:47-49).

In this positive reading, women shape and support Jesus' ministry, benefit from it, and participate in its extension.

But other interpreters are not persuaded by this reading, arguing that the positive picture is possible only if inconvenient negative factors are ignored.[8] They find the construction of women to be at least ambiguous, if not consistently restrictive, with the Gospel reinscribing common patriarchal cultural roles that domesticate and subordinate women, thereby excluding them from Jesus' inner group and its tasks. This analysis can take various forms.

One approach attends to the numbers. By one count, the Gospel names a total of 133 men but only ten women.[9] Men speak hundreds of times, with Jesus' voice dominant, while women speak only fifteen times, including five times when their words are not given. While men are spoken to many, many times, women are explicitly spoken to fifteen times, nine of which are by Jesus. One of these includes Mary, the sister of Martha, who listens to Jesus in complete silence without asking any questions or making any observations on the teaching (10:39). By the numbers, the Gospel is relentlessly androcentric, with women marginalized and silenced.

8. Mary Rose D'Angelo, "Women in Luke-Acts: a Redactional View," *JBL* 109 (1990): 441–61; Jane Schaberg, "Luke," in *Women's Bible Commentary: Expanded Edition with Apocrypha*, ed. Carol Newsom and Sharon Ringe (Louisville: Westminster John Knox, 1998), 363–80.
9. Schaberg, "Luke," 368.

8.3 Mary Magdalene announces the resurrection of Jesus to the male apostles (Luke 24:8-10); illumination from the St. Albans Psalter (1120s), St. Godehard's Church, Hildesheim. Commons.wikimedia.org.

Another matter concerns the interpretation of the women's roles in chapters 1–2. The positive reading of Mary's conception sees her as a model disciple believing the word of God and consenting to God's will. The negative reading finds troubling aspects in the scene. Mary, a virgin, is informed by an angel that she will conceive (1:31). Her question, "How can this be?" remains unanswered (1:34). Her consent is not sought. She has no option but to agree, which she does in terms of the socially despised and marginalized institution of slavery, calling herself God's slave (1:38). She is passive and submissive. As a pregnant single woman, a violated virgin to all public appearances, she has to live with shame and social misunderstanding (cf. Sir. 23:22-26; Wisd. of Sol. 3:16-19; 4:6). And while her role in giving birth to Jesus is crucial, the angel (and the narrative) pay much more attention to her son than to her.

At the end of chapter 2, Anna a prophet appears. She is paired with another character in the temple, the male Simeon. Three times (2:25, 26, 27) the Spirit is linked with Simeon, who greets Jesus and then praises God directly in a four-verse hymn (2:29-32). The Simeon scene takes ten verses. Anna's scene takes three verses. There is no reference to the Spirit, and though the narrative says she is a prophet and reports that she praises God, she is given no direct voice, speech, or hymn.

A further matter concerns the presentation of disciples in the Gospel. While there are call stories involving male disciples (5:1-11, 27-28), no such scenes involve women. Twelve male apostles are named as Jesus' inner group, but no women are included (6:12-16). Discipleship seems to be restricted to men. Disciples leave wives—but not husbands—indicating male gender as the norm for discipleship (18:29; an addition to Luke's source, Mark 10:28-30). Male disciples are given power to exorcize, preach, and heal (9:1-6), but no scene explicitly commissions women to do so. No woman confesses Jesus' identity in the way Peter, for example, does (9:20). Women accompany Jesus, but they are not called disciples (8:1-3). These women have resources, but there is debate about their rọle. The less positive view sees them as playing a subordinate role in serving Jesus and his male disciples by financing their mission, thereby obeying Jesus' teaching in using their possessions to give alms (12:33; also 4:38-39). Or, more positively, do these women "go on mission for him" that involves preaching and healing?[10] Similarly, there is debate about whom the risen Jesus commissions in 24:36-49 to mission among the nations: Only the male disciples, or the male disciples *and* women followers, who are referred to as "their companions" (24:33)?

This second perspective reads the Gospel much more negatively in

10. Karris, "Women and Discipleship in Luke," 31.

its construction of women. It concludes that women are not included among Jesus' disciples. They are not equal participants in his movement. They are passive and subordinated.

There are, then, two quite different interpretations of the roles of women in the Gospel. Which is more convincing? While both positions enjoy "exegetical advocacy,"[11] the truth, perhaps, lies somewhere in between.

Ambiguities mark a number of the scenes, as we have noted, whereby positive *and* negative features are evident. Mary is submissive and slavish, yet also a feisty and powerful preacher (1:38, 46-56). The seventy sent out in a mission that extends Jesus' mission may or may not include women (10:1-12). Also ambiguous is the woman who has been forgiven much and loves much and anoints Jesus (7:36-50). Some note that this anointing occurs so early in Jesus' activity that the narrative depoliticizes her anointing, so that it has nothing to do with Jesus' death but expresses only her gratefulness. But on the other hand, the scene is positioned just before Jesus sets off on his journey to Jerusalem to die (9:51). Her actions, including drying his feet with her hair (7:38), can be understood as expressing not only appreciation but also prophetic[12] understanding of Jesus' significance and destiny even before he has named it (which he will do in 9:22). The scene provokes a final question that focuses on Jesus' identity ("Who is this?," 7:49), a question to be answered through the journey to the cross, resurrection, and ascension.

11. Levine, "Introduction," 2.
12. Women with unbound hair are identified as prophets in 1 Cor. 11:5-6.

8.4 A woman weeps on Jesus' feet and dries them with her hair in Peter Paul Rubens' Feast of Simon the Pharisee (between 1618 and 1620). The woman's bare shoulder is an iconographic feature of representations of Mary Magdalene, with whom this woman has long been confused. Hermitage Museum, St. Petersburg; Commons.wikimedia.org.

Certainly women were included in and benefited from God's ruling activity manifested by Jesus. Readers of the Gospel, though, continue to debate the extent of that inclusion and the roles that women perform in the community created by God's ruling activity.

8.3 Mary Magdalene?

In Luke 7:36-50, while Jesus eats with Simon the Pharisee, an unnamed woman "who was a sinner" washes his feet with her tears, dries them with her hair, and anoints them. The woman's name is not given, and Jesus commends her for showing great love. Since the fourth century, some have identified her as Mary Magdalene and understood her to be a repentant prostitute. This identification was made popular in a sermon preached by Pope Gregory in 591. He (mis)identified the woman as Mary Magdalene, who is mentioned in the next section of the Gospel in Luke 8:2. There she is described as one "from whom seven demons had gone out." Gregory not only confuses Mary with the unnamed woman of 7:36-50 but also interprets the woman's sin as sexual when neither passage explicitly says so.

The Roman Empire

How does God's ruling presence, God's kingdom or empire manifested in Jesus' words and actions, interact with the dominant kingdom or empire of the Gospel world, the Roman Empire?[13]

Luke's Gospel was written under the rule of and in the context of the Roman Empire. The Gospel explicitly sets Jesus' ministry in the time and structures of the Roman emperor Tiberius and the governor of Judea, Pilate, along with Rome-appointed client kings Herod, Philip, and Lysanias, as well as the Rome-appointed high priests of Jerusalem, Annas, and Caiaphas (3:1-2a). These power structures are typical of the ways Rome ruled. Instead of creating a huge civil service to administer the empire, Rome appointed governors of provinces, sanctioned local kings as client rulers, and appointed local leaders like the Jerusalem chief priests as dependent allies with political as well as religious power.

We know from various studies, especially those known as postcolonial studies, that colonized peoples negotiate ruling imperial power with multiple and diverse strategies. These strategies can simultaneously span accommodation and cooperation, dissembling and ambivalence, competition and mimicry, opposition and resistance. In such contexts, hybrid identities commonly emerge, combining aspects of both the dominant and the dominated peoples. Not surprisingly, Luke's Gospel does not negotiate Roman power with just one approach; it does so with multiple and simultaneous strategies.

Such ambiguity is evident in the scene concerning paying taxes. Paying taxes was regarded as a sign of loyalty; failure to pay was rebellious and treasonous. In response to the loaded query about whether paying tax to Rome was lawful, Jesus offers a very ambiguous

13. On imperial-critical and postcolonial studies investigating the New Testament and Luke's Gospel in relation to Rome's empire, see Warren Carter, *The Roman Empire and the New Testament: An Essential Guide* (Nashville: Abingdon, 2006); Carter, "Postcolonial Biblical Criticism," in *New Meanings for Ancient Texts: Recent Approaches to Biblical Criticisms and Their Applications*, ed. Steven McKenzie and John Kaltner (Louisville: Westminster John Knox, 2013), 97–116; David Rhoads, David Esterline, and Jae Won Lee, eds., *Luke-Acts and Empire*, Princeton Theological Monograph Series (Eugene, OR: Pickwick, 2010).

response: "Then give to the emperor the things that are the emperor's, and to God the things that are God's" (Luke 20:25). What exactly does Jesus instruct? How do the two clauses about the emperor and God relate to each other? Does he say not to pay the tax because everything belongs to God (so Ps. 24:1)? Or does he say to pay the tax because it is due to the emperor but ultimate loyalty belongs to God? By paying attention to the relative weighting of both clauses, we might understand that he simultaneously advocates relative cooperation and compliance in paying the tax, while exercising some self-protective and disguised protest in rendering acknowledgment of God's greater sovereignty.

The same sort of ambivalence is evident in the discussion of the kingdom or ruling presence of God that the Gospel recognizes as both the present and future establishment of God's reign. For starters, the language of God's "reign" or "kingdom" or "empire" imitates and reinscribes the language of Rome's empire, even as it asserts a quite different and antithetical reality. Or further, the Gospel expects Jesus to return and establish God's reign in supremacy over everything (21:25-28). This expectation means the end of the present world as it currently exists and its transformation into a very different world. That, of course, means the end of Rome's hierarchical empire. This expectation, then, of the future establishment of God's reign seems at first glance to be an act of resistance. God's kingdom or empire overcomes and destroys Rome's empire.

But the matter is more complex. Also at work is mimicry or imitation. Just as Rome asserts its power over all, including overcoming those who rebel or resist its reign, so also God's empire will prevail over all, overcoming and punishing any and all opposition (10:13-16; 12:8-9; 21:34-36). God is presented as behaving like Rome. God reinscribes Rome's ways. God out-Romes Rome. Resistance and imitation go hand in hand.

But in the meantime, Rome's empire does not go away, so negotiating its presence is necessary. The Gospel sets out another dynamic, combining both antithesis and a transforming alternative.

This dynamic is evident in the Gospel's visions of the societal order created by God's ruling presence. The Roman world was hierarchical and patriarchal, with social structures favoring the minority ruling elite. This elite controlled political power and offices, the military, land ownership as the basis of the ancient economy, cheap slave labor, taxes and rents, trade, the legal system, patron-client relations, and material benefits (food, clothing, housing), often to the harm of nonelites. The temptation scene constructs the empire and these structures as being in the hands of the devil. The devil has in his control "all the empires of the world," and he offers them to Jesus if Jesus will worship him (4:5-8).

Such a view of the Roman world as being in the hands of the devil might suggest there is no hope for the world. But Jesus' activity outlined in the discussion above shows that instead of giving up on the world, Jesus sets about instigating another reality in its midst and even transforming it. Mary's hymnic vision of God bringing down the powerful from their thrones and sending the rich away while elevating the lowly and filling the hungry articulates the "large picture" of God's ruling activity in this devil-controlled world in seeking both to end and transform Rome's rule (1:52-53). Jesus' reading from Isa. 61:1-2 in Luke 4:18-19 also envisages a different societal order that evokes and is shaped by Israel's Jubilee traditions. These traditions posit that every fifty years, people are released from debt and slavery, and land is returned to households (Leviticus 25). The Jubilee year was a socioeconomic mechanism that, if enacted, would prevent wealth and power continuing to accumulate in the hands of a few wealthy elites. It would also prevent the formation of a permanent class of the poor deprived of access to necessary resources. The gloomy analysis of Rome's devilish world coexists with visions of God's transforming work in its midst.

The story line of Jesus' crucifixion is crucial to the Gospel. Crucifixion was a Roman means of execution, a death penalty Rome used for those low-level nonelites like runaway slaves or political rebels who were considered threats to Roman rule and its societal order. That Jesus is crucified constructs him as a rebel or enemy of Roman rule.

The power to crucify in Judea belonged to the Roman governor, Pontius Pilate. Central to understanding Luke's story is the interaction between the Roman governor Pilate and the Jerusalem leaders comprising the chief priests, scribes, and elders of the people (22:66). As I noted above in a brief discussion of 3:1-2a, Rome ruled distant territory through alliances with local leadership that it sanctioned. The Jerusalem leaders were not solely religious leaders (like contemporary clergy). In the ancient world, there was no division of politics and religion in the way we understand there to be. Rather, the chief priests, scribes, and elders were the local rulers of Judea exercising political, social, economic, and religious rule.[14] The Romans permitted them to maintain their position as local leaders as long as they remained loyal allies with Rome. Both groups—the Jerusalem leaders and the Roman governor—needed each other to maintain not only their own dominant positions but also to uphold the whole societal structure from which they as leaders benefited considerably. Yet the alliance of governor and local leaders was contestive, with both parties constantly struggling with each other to gain the upper hand. This tense alliance plays out in the account of Jesus' crucifixion.

The Jerusalem leaders bring Jesus to Pilate for crucifixion, accusing him of "perverting our nation, forbidding us to pay taxes to the emperor, and saying that he himself is the Messiah, a king" (23:2). There are several treasonous charges here. As we saw above, payment of taxes was a test of loyalty to Rome; refusal to pay taxes was understood to be rebellion. Rome appointed local rulers as kings (like Herod and Philip named in 3:1), but to claim to be a king without Rome's sanction was also deemed to be rebellion. Jesus is not a Rome-sanctioned king. To claim to be God's appointed king in the line of David was treason (1:32-33). These charges, then, present Jesus as very opposed to Roman rule. The charges also present the Jerusalem leaders

14. Josephus (*Ant.* 20.251) describes the chief priests as the rulers of Judea.

as very loyal to their Roman allies and masters in turning in Jesus as a rebel.

Pilate, having the power to execute, asks Jesus about his kingship. Jesus does not deny it (23:3). Jesus is guilty as charged, yet very strangely, Pilate immediately declares, "I find no basis for an accusation against this man" (23:4). This is an incredible statement given Pilate's task as governor to maintain Roman rule and given Jesus' lack of a denial. And Pilate continues to resist the demand of Jesus' accusers to crucify him (23:6-7, 13-16, 20, 22-25). How do we account for Pilate's strange behavior?

Usually interpreters claim that Pilate knows Jesus is not guilty and does not want to put him to death. But this claim is not convincing and ignores Jesus' nondenial (23:3). It also ignores Pilate's job to maintain order against any treasonous threat. A better explanation is found in recalling the conflictual alliance between Pilate and the Jerusalem leaders.[15] Pilate knows that if his allies want to end Jesus' influence by executing him, he needs to take their concern seriously, since Pilate and the Jerusalem leaders share common interests in maintaining the status quo against any imagined threat. But if Pilate quickly and readily agrees to their demand for Jesus' crucifixion, he would place himself under their control and make himself subject to their desires and power. He would become a "yes man" and concede power to them. Pilate refuses to put himself in this weak position, and so asserts his independence and power by denying their requests. His repeated denials have the effect of making the Jerusalem leaders plead more energetically for Jesus' crucifixion (23:5, 18, 21, 23). Pilate's tactic works. The more he refuses, the more they plead. The more they plead, the more they make themselves dependent on Pilate. Pilate's power increases until he finally grants their demand (23:24-25).

Jesus' crucifixion seems to foreground both Jesus' opposition to the empire and his defeat at the hands of the ruling elite. But again, it is more complex. The Gospel presents Jesus' death as exposing the

15. Warren Carter, *Pontius Pilate: Portraits of a Roman Governor* (Collegeville, MN: Liturgical, 2003), 101–25.

opposition of the alliance of the Jerusalem leadership and the Roman governor Pilate to God's anointed one (22:69-71; 23:35-38). And his death also exposes the limits of their power. They cannot keep Jesus dead. After his crucifixion comes his resurrection (ch. 24). On the third day, God raises him just as Jesus had predicted. Jesus will return to displace them in establishing God's empire or ruling presence in full.

Clearly, the interaction between God's ruling presence or kingdom and Rome's empire is complex. Even the use of the word *empire* or *kingdom* as the way of imaging or talking about God's activity in the world shows how deeply embedded in and imitative of imperial structures is the Gospel's construction of God. God's coming triumph maintains the same imperial worldview of domination, yet the Gospel is also able to envision and enact a transformed world of very different structures and interactions.

The Human and Nonhuman Worlds?

Does God's reign, God's empire, involve only humans and their imperial structures? Or does Luke's presentation also recognize the interrelationship between humans and the nonhuman world? In order to answer these questions, Michael Trainor sets out three interrelated interpretive principles that frame his reading of Luke's Gospel:[16]

- A suspicion of readings that are exclusively anthropocentric and blind to earth's presence;
- A commitment to identify the presence of the earth and its ecosystems especially when they are not to the fore in the Gospel narrative; and
- A commitment to retrieve the Gospel's environmental story and ecological presence.

These approaches embody three hermeneutical principles that recognize

16. Michael Trainor, *About Earth's Child: An Ecological Listening to the Gospel of Luke*, Earth Bible Commentary Series 2 (Sheffield: Sheffield Phoenix, 2012), 5–6.

- The intrinsic worth of creation and the wider nonhuman community contributing to human identity but also independent of it;
- Earth as an interconnected web of relationships inclusive of human and nonhuman; and
- Voice that allows the silenced or unnoticed earth to be heard.

Trainor translates these principles into two specific questions concerning Luke's Gospel:

- Does Luke's Gospel reinforce a destructive and utilitarian attitude in subjugating creation for human purposes?
- Can Luke's Gospel contribute to an ecological theology that encourages a respectful attitude to the earth as an integral part of contemporary discipleship?[17]

Trainor recognizes that Luke's Gospel offers a range of answers to these questions. We will briefly consider three examples.

By way of a first example, Trainor notes the very positive embracing of all creation in the account of Jesus' birth in chapter 2. In 2:14, a multitude of angels, identified as a "heavenly host," interprets Jesus' birth as a gift of God's favor or blessing of peace on the earth, the realm of humans and nonhumans. The angels' words bring together both heaven and earth as the realm of God's favor. All of creation, human and nonhuman, is embraced by God's favor, which comprises "peace." This peace is not the same as Rome's peace, which is built on military power to defeat and dominate. "God's act in Jesus' birth transforms Earth from a place of rivalry, violence, and rapaciousness, to an abode of total earthly communion inclusive of the human and non-human household."[18] This is a vision of all creation, human and nonhuman, under the reign of God. This reign "expresses God's liberating presence to release humanity and creation from evil and bring about healing and reconciliation."[19]

17. Ibid., 10.
18. Ibid., 89.

In a second example, Trainor is ambivalent about Luke's use of Isaiah 40 to frame the baptizing ministry of John the Baptizer.

> As it is written in the book of the words of the prophet Isaiah, "The voice of one crying out in the wilderness: 'Prepare the way of the Lord, make his paths straight. Every valley shall be filled, and every mountain and hill shall be made low, and the crooked shall be made straight, and the rough ways made smooth; and all flesh shall see the salvation of God.'" (Luke 3:4-6)

On one hand, Trainor declares the text has "the potential to be a text of 'Earth terror,'" in which much violence is done to the earth. He notices that the images of filling valleys, flattening mountains, and smoothing rough places are "ecologically violent," bringing pain to the earth, whose voice is not heard.[20] But on the other hand, Trainor also observes that what happens to the earth is not pointless violence. It serves the purpose of issuing to humans "a call to conversion and forgiveness." The earth mediates a call to "all flesh," all humans, to conversion.[21] This is the earth's ministry; allied with John the Baptizer, the earth furthers God's reign.

As a third example, Trainor finds in Jesus' teaching about possessions and in his parables about meals some central affirmations concerning human interaction with the earth in God's reign.[22] Jesus warns against greed or ecological irresponsibility, the *excessive* and/or exploitative accumulation of earth's resources (12:13-34). Luke's Jesus also warns against people who exhibit their status at meals. He declares, "For all who exalt themselves will be humbled, and those who humble themselves will be exalted" (14:11). Trainor finds here "a central truth in Luke's gospel. The source of everything is God."[23] The recognition of God as the originator of all things requires a fundamental human posture of humility or modesty. This humility is expressed in relationships with other humans as well as in embracing

19. Ibid., 129.
20. Ibid., 99–100.
21. Ibid., 100–101.
22. Ibid., 183–90.
23. Ibid., 206.

an "Earth relatedness." In Jesus' next parable, concerning invitations to "the poor, the crippled, the blind, and the lame" to a dinner, humility means a recognition of the inclusion of all as recipients of divine favor in human community (14:21). And "Earth-relatedness" means recognizing that all such folks are sustained by and enjoy the abundant fruits of the earth in the food of the festive banquet.[24]

8.5 In Matthew (21:18-19) and Mark (11:12-14), Jesus curses a fig tree that bears no fruit, and it withers. Luke omits the event, but has Jesus tell a parable of a landowner who demands that an unproductive fig tree be cut down; his gardener persuades him to give the tree another chance. In all three Gospels the fig tree may be a symbol for the temple; nevertheless, Jesus' wrath against a tree has long provoked readers. Etching by Jan Luyken in the Bowyer Bible, Bolton, England. Photo by Harry Kossuth; Commons.wikimedia.org.

Trainor pursues his discussion across the whole of Luke's Gospel. These three examples are sufficient to indicate that the Gospel constructs

24. Ibid., 206–8.

complex interactions between the human and nonhuman worlds in relation to God's reign. These examples are also sufficient to show that Luke's Gospel does not reinforce a destructive and utilitarian attitude in subjugating creation, but encourages humility toward the earth as an integral part of contemporary discipleship.

In Luke's Gospel, God's reign is active among human beings in individual lives, in human community, in contesting and imitating imperial structures, and in interaction with both the human and nonhuman world.

Questions for Review and Reflection

1. The chapter outlines several ways by which we might gain some understanding of the central phrase "kingdom of God." What are they?
2. Thinking over the discussion of the phrase "kingdom of God" in the first section, write out your own informed explanation for what this phrase signifies.
3. The second section claims that the presence of God's kingdom creates a community. What are the contours of this community, according to Luke? Consider factors of social class, ethnicity, and gender as they are portrayed in the Gospel.
4. How does the chapter present the interactions between the kingdom of God and Rome's empire in Luke? What are some aspects of Luke that imply a positive relationship; what aspects suggest a negative relationship?
5. How does the chapter present the relationship of humans to the environment/the nonhuman world/the earth? Can you find other scenes in the Gospel where this issue comes to the fore?
6. Thinking about the discussion of this chapter, in a couple of sentences, write a paraphrase of Jesus' statement in 4:43: "I must proclaim the good news of the kingdom of God" to elaborate its meaning.
7. The "kingdom of God" is a way of talking about God's activity in the world. Does the Gospel's presentation help you to think

about how or what God might be doing in our world? Explain your response.

9

The Tale John Tells

Even a quick skim through John's Gospel indicates we have a very different telling of the story of Jesus.[1] In this chapter, we will first identify some of the features of the Gospel that make it so different: particular scenes, settings, characters, and language. Then we will put the pieces together to describe John's plot. In the next chapter, we will seek to explain why John's account is so distinctive in its presentation of the story of Jesus.

Distinctive Scenes

We will consider three types of distinctive scenes in the Gospel: the opening Prologue, quest stories, and sign scenes.

Prologue

The Gospel's opening eighteen verses are commonly called the Prologue. As the Gospel's opening unit, the Prologue, unparalleled in

1. For discussions of John's Gospel, Robert Kysar, *John: The Maverick Gospel*, rev. ed. (Louisville: Westminster John Knox, 1993); Warren Carter, *John: Storyteller, Interpreter, Evangelist* (Peabody, MA: Hendrickson, 2006).

the other Gospels, introduces the audience to four major elements that will be elaborated subsequently in the gospel story.

- Jesus' origin: Verses 1-5 locate the Word, "in the beginning . . . with God" (1:1-2), functioning with God as co-creator (1:3). The Gospel will constantly emphasize Jesus' origin with God as the guarantee of the reliability of his revelation of God and God's purposes (life and light, 1:4-5, 18), and as a major point of conflict between Jesus and his opponents.
- John the Baptizer: Verses 6-8 (also verse 15) introduce John the Baptizer, who bears witness to Jesus.
- Response to Jesus: Verses 9-16 sum up what happens when "the Word becomes flesh" to reveal God's purposes and life (1:14, 18). Some people receive Jesus, become God's children (1:12-13), and behold his glory (1:14), while others reject him (1:10-11). With verses 10-13 as a plot summary, the Gospel will elaborate accounts of his acceptance and rejection.
- Jesus' relation to Moses: Verses 17-18 distinguish and link Jesus and Moses. Both reveal God's purposes. The Gospel will debate which of them makes a definitive revelation of God's purposes and how people encounter this revelation. It asserts that Jesus' origin with and return to God guarantees the reliability of his making God known (1:18).

9.1 John the disciple supports Jesus' mother at the foot of Jesus' cross (see John 19:26-27); detail from Matthias Grünewald's painting of the crucifixion from the Isenheim altarpiece (1512–1516). Museum of Unterlinden, Colmar, France; Commons.wikimedia.org.

Quest Stories

Quest stories are a second distinctive feature in John's plot.[2] People frequently seek Jesus, sometimes positively, sometimes negatively, asking friendly or hostile questions about his identity, mission, and allies. Sometimes they fulfill their quest; sometimes they reject Jesus.

2. John Painter, *The Quest for the Messiah: The History, Literature, and Theology of the Johannine Community* (Nashville: Abingdon, 1993).

These quest stories elaborate the Prologue's claim that some received him while others rejected him (1:10-13). Here are the main examples:

- Agents sent by Jerusalem's ruling elite search for and interrogate John the Baptizer (1:19-28).
- Would-be disciples seek the Messiah, who calls them to discipleship (1:35-42, 43-51).
- Jesus' mother seeks his help at the Cana wedding when the wine runs out (2:1-12).
- Nicodemus seeks God's kingdom (3:1-15).
- The Samaritan woman quests for the Messiah and his water of life (4:1-42).
- The royal official seeks life for his son (4:46-54).
- The crowd looks for Jesus (6:1-40).
- Mary and Martha look for Jesus' help after Lazarus dies (ch. 11).
- Judeans seek to kill Jesus and Lazarus (11:7, 46-57; 12:9-11).
- Greeks seek Jesus (12:20-36).
- The *Ioudaioi* seek to arrest and kill Jesus (chs. 18–19).
- Women seek Jesus' body and find the risen Jesus (20:1-18).

Jesus is also on a quest, to find those who receive or believe him, seeking true worshipers (2:13-22; ch. 4) and disciples (1:35-51; 20:19-21:23). At times, Jesus is elusive, difficult to find (6:15, 25; 7:1, 10-11, 32-36; 8:59; 9:12; 11:21, 54; 12:36), and difficult to understand (3:3-9; 8:21-22; 11:23-25).

This game of hide-and-seek throughout the first twelve chapters underlines the significance of encounter with Jesus. While such encounters can be elusive, they nevertheless provide access to life for those who are open to God's purposes. Yet they can also provoke great hostility. Jesus' hiding from opponents who want to kill him reinforces the notion that despite their apparent power, he is in control, even of the timing of his death (7:8; 10:17-18). These quest scenes keep the Gospel's audience focused on who Jesus is, his revealing mission, and how characters respond to his revelation.

Sign Scenes

A third distinctive set of scenes concerns deeds of power that Jesus works.

- Jesus changes water into wine (2:1-11).
- Jesus heals the royal official's son (4:46-54).
- Jesus heals the crippled man (5:1-18).
- Jesus feeds the large crowd (6:1-14).
- Jesus walks on water (6:16-21).
- Jesus heals the man born blind (9:1-7).
- Jesus raises Lazarus from death (11:1-46).
- At the command of the risen Jesus, the disciples catch 153 fish (21:1-14).

While miracle stories, along with summary scenes indicating many such actions, are common in the Synoptics, in John they are not common. Among the eight scenes of power, there are only four healings and no exorcisms. Significantly, the Gospel does not identify these actions as "miracles" or "works of power." In fact, the word *dynamis*, used in the Synoptic Gospels for Jesus' miracles as works of power, does not appear in John. Rather, John's Gospel labels them "signs" (*sēmeia*).[3] Rather than emphasizing a display of power, the term "signs" indicates that these powerful actions point beyond themselves to reveal something of greater significance. They are signs in that they provide those who experience the miraculous action an opportunity to discern Jesus' identity as the definitive revealer of God's purposes, to

3. See 2:11, 18, 23; 3:2; 4:4, 54; 6:2, 14, 26, 30; 7:31; 9:16; 10:41; 11:47; 12:18, 37.

understand God's purposes of transforming life at work, and to commit themselves to Jesus.

It is significant that most of these miraculous signs concern giving life, especially in the form of healing (4:46-54; 5:1-18; 9:1-7; 11:1-46) and supplying nourishment (2:1-11; 6:1-14; 21:1-14). Both wholeness and nourishment were in short supply in Rome's imperial world, where the elite removed food supply and resources from much of the population through taxation and rents. The resultant inadequate diets, variable food supply, anxiety, overwork, and diseases of deprivation and contagion caused lives of vulnerability and short life-spans for many. These realities are reflected in the crowds' demand of John 6:34, "Give us this bread always." Prophetic (Isa. 25:6-10; 35:5-6) and apocalyptic traditions (2 Baruch 72–74) expected God to end such injustice and transform the world with a dramatic establishment of God's purposes. Jesus' actions of healing and supplying nourishment draw on and enact these visions of life as God intends it to be, thereby reversing daily realities of Rome's world. His actions are signs that God's purposes for human life comprise wholeness, fertility, and abundance. The Jerusalem-based, Rome-allied leadership with whom Jesus conflicts are not able to accomplish these purposes because they structure a hierarchical society for their own benefit and they resist Jesus' efforts and vision for a different society.

Settings

The use of geographical and temporal settings also contributes to the distinctiveness of John's Gospel.

In the Synoptic Gospels, Jesus carries out most of his ministry in Galilee. Then, toward the end of Mark and Matthew and the middle of Luke, he travels to Jerusalem for the last week of his life, which ends with crucifixion (Mark 10:1-11:1; Matt. 19:1-21:1; Luke 9:51-53; 19:28-40). John's plot, by contrast, has Jesus going back and forth between Galilee and Jerusalem throughout the narrative. He begins by conducting ministry in the villages and countryside of Judea (1:28-42) and in Galilee (1:43; 2:1, 12, Capernaum). Already in 2:13, Jesus makes his first journey to Jerusalem to the temple. In 3:22, he leaves Jerusalem for the Judean countryside and Samaria (ch. 4). But in 5:1, Jesus again travels from Galilee to Jerusalem, where he remains until chapter 6. In 7:1, Jesus is in Galilee. In 7:10, after saying he is not going to Jerusalem (7:8-9), he goes there "in private" and teaches (7:14). In 10:22-23, Jesus is still in Jerusalem but then leaves and spends time in the vicinity of Bethany (see 1:28; 11:1, 18; 12:1). Jesus reenters Jerusalem, where he raises Lazarus (12:12) and remains there for the rest of the story.

This distinctive back-and-forth movement functions to keep Jerusalem to the fore. Jerusalem is the center of power for the alliance of Israel's leaders centered on the temple (1:19). In his visit, Jesus attacks the Jerusalem temple, charging them with making "my Father's house a marketplace" (2:16; cf. 4:20-21). Jesus challenges their power, denouncing their exploitative economic-political leadership.

9.2 *Christ Expels the Money Changers*, by Caravaggio (1610). The Fourth Gospel is unique in placing the event at the beginning of the narrative (John 2). Gemäldegalerie, Berlin; Commons.wikimedia.org.

In Jesus' second excursion into Jerusalem, there is further conflict. The leaders plan to kill him because in claiming authority over observance of the Sabbath and claiming God as his Father, they think he makes "himself equal to God" (5:18). In 7:1, he is reluctant to go to Jerusalem because they want to arrest and kill him, motifs that continue throughout chapters 7–12. In chapters 18–19, in Jerusalem, these leaders, along with their ally, the Roman governor Pilate, accomplish their plan in crucifying Jesus. Jesus' back-and-forth movement between Jerusalem and Galilee throughout the Gospel keeps Jerusalem and its leaders consistently to the fore and presents them as life-and-death opponents of Jesus and his revelation of God's purposes. But their hostility will be thwarted in Jesus' resurrection.

A further distinctive element comprises the use of festivals to provide the temporal and cultural settings for Jesus' frequent journeys to Jerusalem. With others, he travels to Jerusalem to join in temple-led celebrations of "the mighty acts of God" and to anticipate the completion of God's saving purposes. Evoking festivals recalls key events in Israel's history with God and locates Jesus in relation to such divine acts. Here are the festivals mentioned in the Gospel:

- Twice Jesus is in Jerusalem for the Festival of Passover (2:13–25; 12:1, 12, 20; chs. 13–17). Another Passover is mentioned in 6:4 while Jesus is in Galilee. Passover celebrates liberation from slavery in Egypt as God's act of saving the people from the tyrannical Pharaoh (Exodus 11–15). This victory included the exodus journey to the promised land, during which God supplied the people with manna and water (Exodus 16–17) and revealed God's will in giving the Torah ("teaching"). Jesus' feeding of the five thousand, walking on water, and description of his identity and mission as "bread from heaven" recapitulates God's liberating and revealing work in chapter 6.
- In chapter 5, Jesus is in Jerusalem for an unnamed festival (5:1).
- In chapter 7, Jesus travels secretly to Jerusalem for Tabernacles or Booths (Sukkoth), an eight-day festival celebrated in September/

October. This festival provides the context for chapters 7–8, and possibly for 9:1–10:21. Originally an agricultural festival marking harvest, it also celebrated God's provision for the people during their sojourn in the wilderness (Lev. 23:42–43), and it anticipated the time when all the nations would journey to Jerusalem to honor Israel's God (Zechariah 14), not a good sign for Roman domination.

- In 10:22, in Jerusalem, Jesus celebrates the Festival of Dedication, or Hanukkah, which celebrated God's saving the people from the Seleucid tyrant Antiochus IV Epiphanes. Observed in November/December, it commemorates the Maccabean-led struggle against and defiance of Antiochus, and the rededication of the altar and temple in 164 BCE (see 1 and 2 Maccabees).
- The Sabbath occurs regularly (5:1–47; 7:14–24; 9:1–41), celebrating God's deliverance of the people from Egypt (Deut. 5:12–15), God's covenant with Israel (Exod. 31:16), and God's creative work and rest (Gen. 2:2–3). These events were extended to observance of Sabbath and Jubilee years, which emphasized God's justice in renewing the land, supplying the poor with food, canceling debt, returning land, and liberating slaves (Exod. 23:10–11; Deut. 15:1–18; Leviticus 25). In chapters 5 and 9, Jesus' healings on a Sabbath provoke conflict over how the Sabbath is to be honored.

The constant references to festivals locate Jesus' actions in the midst of Israel's life. The festivals carry the memory and social vision of a different and just way of life ordered by God. By associating Jesus' actions with these festivals, the Gospel interprets his actions and teaching as manifestations of God's ongoing work in saving the people from that which is contrary to God's purposes, including Rome's oppressive rule, and as anticipations of the completion of God's salvific work in giving people life.

Characters

As in the Synoptics, Jesus frequently interacts with common folks or nonelites, the 97 percent of first-century society (6:2, 5; 7:20, 40). These folks experience the scorn of the Jerusalem-based Pharisees, who view the despised Galilean "people of the land" as ignorant and accursed (7:49). These elites also dismiss the man born blind as incapable of teaching them anything (9:34).

The Powerful *Ioudaioi*

Distinctive in the Gospel, though, is the use of the term *Ioudaioi* to identify a specific group of elite characters. How to translate the term (used some seventy times) and identify its referents are much-debated issues.

The term has been commonly translated as "the Jews," but since most of the characters in the Gospel could be identified as "Jews" (as is Jesus in 4:9), this translation is not very helpful. Another suggestion translates it as "the Judeans" to refer to residents of Judea, but the text refers to feasts "of the *Ioudaioi*" (5:1; 6:4), suggesting a cultural-religious, not geographical, meaning. Further, while the term often designates negative responses toward Jesus, it can sometimes signify positive interactions (8:31; 11:31–33, 45). And translators have to be sensitive to not contributing further to a long line of hateful anti-Judaism associated with the Gospel. It seems better to leave the term untranslated, which requires us to think about its meaning each time it is used.

The most common referent for the term *Ioudaioi* involves the alliance of powerful leaders (chief priests, Pharisees, scribes) centered on the Jerusalem temple.[4] In 1:19, these leaders send agents to investigate John the Baptizer. In 2:18, 20, the leaders confront Jesus after his attack on their temple. Nicodemus belongs to this group (3:1), but he can't understand Jesus. In 5:16–18, after Jesus has healed on the Sabbath and made claims about his relationship with God, they want to kill him (5:16–18), a recurring motif throughout chapters 5–12. Jesus attacks them for not hearing God or loving him (5:37, 42), for

4. Note the interchangeable terms: 1:19, "the Jews," and 1:24, "the Pharisees"; 9:13, 16, "the Pharisees," and 9:18 "the Jews."

not believing in Jesus and receiving life from him (5:38–40), for not knowing how to interpret the Scriptures (5:39), and for having the devil as their father (8:44). They do not understand the Gospel's central claims—Jesus' origin from God (6:41-42), his destiny with God (7:35; 8:21–22), his identity as God's agent (8:22–27). The conflict is harsh and bitter; not surprisingly, the *Ioudaioi* figure prominently in chapters 18–19 in crucifying Jesus as allies of the Roman governor Pilate (18:28–19:16). This ruling elite is generally hostile to Jesus, though there are a few exceptions, such as the royal official in chapter 4 and Joseph of Arimathea, who seems to be a secret believer in Jesus, bravely providing a burial for Jesus (19:38; see 12:42–43).

Jesus

The discussion above of the Gospel's Prologue indicates something of the distinctive presentation of Jesus in this Gospel. The emphasis in John's Gospel on Jesus' origin with God in the beginning (1:1) is unmatched in the Synoptics. Jesus comes from God (3:2; 6:46), from the Father (8:38), from heaven (6:31–51). He "descends" (3:13), "comes down from heaven" (6:41–42), and "comes from" God (8:42). Repeatedly, Jesus is presented as *sent* by God: "My food is to do the will of him who sent me and to complete his work" (John 4:34; also 5:23–38; 6:35–58; 8:12–30). Jesus's unique relationship with God is the basis for his identity and mission of revealing God's life and purposes in coming among human beings (1:14, 18). The Word dwelt with God in the beginning (1:1–3). Jesus is the only one to see God (6:46). He is one with God in doing the will and work of God (4:34; 10:30). The Gospel closely identifies Jesus and God, claiming that Jesus does only God's will (6:38; 14:9; 14:24).

But the Gospel is also careful to emphasize that Jesus is not another God. Jesus' opponents accuse him of making himself God (5:18), but Jesus immediately asserts that he "can do nothing on his own" (5:19, 30). He thus subordinates himself to God. They again make this charge in 10:33, and again Jesus defines himself in subordinate terms as "sent" from God and as God's agent ("Son," 10:36). This subordination protects the fundamental affirmation of monotheism. Jesus consistently recognizes God's supreme authority (5:30; 8:28). God gives him roles to fulfill and a mission to accomplish (5:22–23, 26–27). Jesus does not do his own will but does the will of God and imitates what he sees God doing (5:19; 8:29). He does the works that God has given him to do (5:36). He speaks words that he has heard from God and that God tells him to speak (3:34; 8:28, 40; 12:50; 14:10, 24). As "the Word," he reveals or communicates God's words, works, and will. As the child or Son of God, he brings other children of God into existence (1:12–13) to know God and to share in God's life (17:3).

The pattern of Jesus descending from God to reveal God among humans is, then, distinctive to John's presentation of Jesus. This origin marks his identity as God's agent and his mission as the revealer of God. He then ascends to God by being "lifted up" through his crucifixion, resurrection, and ascension.

Jesus' Way of Talking

John's Jesus has a distinctive way of talking. Jesus' words manifest what the Word saw and heard from God (3:32, 34; 8:38a, 40). Response to Jesus' words reveals and divides disciples and opponents of God's purposes revealed in Jesus. We note five distinctive features of "Johnspeak."

For starters, the speech of John's Jesus is *self-referential*. Whereas in the Synoptics Jesus speaks about the "kingdom of God," this phrase rarely appears in John. Instead, in John Jesus frequently talks about himself. Jesus presents himself with a series of "I am" sayings, which describe aspects of his identity and mission (6:35, "I am the bread of life"; see also 8:12; 10:7, 9, 11, 14; 11:25; 14:6; 15:1, 5). As we have noted, he talks about his origin from God and mission to do God's will. Jesus also frequently calls people to entrust themselves to him, urging them to "believe in me/him/the Son" (3:16-18, 36; 6:35, 40).

Second, in the Synoptic Gospels, Jesus' speech often occurs in brief exchanges involving pithy one-liners or sound bites. In John, by contrast, Jesus frequently speaks in *lengthy monologues*. Chapter 3 begins with a brief dialogue between Jesus and Nicodemus (3:3-10), which is followed by ten continuous verses of Jesus talking. In chapter 4, involving his meeting with the Samaritan woman, Jesus talks for twelve of the first twenty-six verses. In chapter 5, after healing the paralyzed man, Jesus talks continuously from verse 19 to verse 47. In this section of the Gospel in which Jesus' conflict with the elite intensifies (chs. 5–10), further long monologues appear in chapters 6, 8, and 10, whose content contributes significantly to the unfolding conflict. The longest monologue appears in chapters 14–16 as Jesus instructs the disciples. He appears to stop in 14:31, but carries on for two more chapters before praying for all of chapter 17.

Third, Jesus' speech often involves ambiguities and misunderstandings as he moves *between literal and metaphorical language*. His listeners often miss these transitions and misunderstand him. So in 4:31-34, the ambiguity centers on meanings of "food." Jesus turns a literal reference to food into a reference to his mission ("I have food to eat that you do not know about"). His disciples, though, miss the metaphor and wonder about literal food that someone might have brought to Jesus (4:33). Jesus goes on to elaborate his "food" as doing God's work (4:34). In 6:52, Jesus' opponents, "the *Ioudaioi*" misinterpret Jesus' metaphor of "eating his flesh" (believing in him) and wonder how he can give his literal flesh for eating. In 8:22, they do not understand his reference to going away to his Father, God, where they cannot go, and they speculate (ironically!) that he means to kill himself. The move between literal and metaphorical language enables John's Jesus to reveal his mission; the misunderstandings of his hearers often expose them as those who are not receptive to this revelation.

Fourth, the speech of John's Jesus is also frequently *dualistic*. He employs pairings and contrasts to depict the fundamental dualism of the Gospel, the realm of God or that of the devil (8:42-44). This dualism is elaborated through a number of subsequent dualisms and distinctive vocabulary: light and darkness, above and below, truth and lies/falseness, heaven and earth, resurrection and judgment, love and hate, not of this world and of the world, believing and not believing. The language is soteriological in that it designates the origin, identity, and destiny of both Jesus and his followers, as well as ethical in that it shapes a way of living.

Fifth, John's language expresses what is called *realized eschatology.* In the Synoptic Gospels, Jesus' speech is often forward-looking in directing attention to the eschatological or end-time events of his return, judgment, and resurrection. In John's Gospel, Jesus' language directs attention to the present. His language makes available these future "end-time" or eschatological realities now in the present. So "eternal life," or life that belongs to the future new age and encounter with God, is available *now* in Jesus' words (3:16-18; 17:3). To not believe in Jesus is to experience the future condemnation *now* (3:18). To believe Jesus and God means *now* having eternal life, no judgment, and having already passed from death to life (5:24).

The Gospel thus presents Jesus' words or teaching as originating with God, who sent Jesus (7:16; 8:25-26; 14:10, 24). In speaking, he expresses God's authority and follows God's instruction (12:49). His words carry out God's purposes to reveal the world's evil (7:7; 15:22), to reveal life (6:63), to save from sin and death (5:34; 8:51), and to draw disciples into ongoing, obedient relation with Jesus (10:27) and loving relation with each other (13:34-35). Jesus' words have continuing value; the Spirit, the Paraclete whom Jesus has God send, is charged with the task of reminding disciples of Jesus' words when Jesus returns to God (14:26). By recalling Jesus' words, the Paraclete continues the work of revealing God's life-giving purposes.

John's Plot

How, then, does the Gospel's author combine these, and numerous other, distinctive features to form the Gospel's plot? Recalling the discussion of plot in chapter 5, on Matthew's Gospel, we will take our cues from the ancient literary theorist Aristotle, who argued that the end of the plot is the "necessary and/or usual" consequence of the previous events that form a unity of action that draws together the beginning and middle of the narrative.[5] Aristotle highlights the importance of recognition (movement from ignorance to discovery) and of reversal (changing from one state to another) in plots and endings. What, then, are the events that lead to the Gospel's surprising conclusion?

Beginning (1:1-18; 1:19-4:54)

The Gospel has a double beginning. The plot itself, comprising the events that lead through challenge and conflict to Jesus' death, resurrection, and ascension, begins at 1:19. The first eighteen verses, the Prologue, offer a big-picture narrative and thematic preview of the Gospel's general movement. The Word, who will become incarnate in Jesus, begins with God and is active in creation (1:1-5), is witnessed to by John (1:6-8), comes into the world especially to his own people, is received by some and rejected by others, and carries out the task of revealing God and God's purposes (1:9-18). These verses alert the Gospel's audience to important emphases in the story and frame all that follows.

But while the eighteen verses orient the reader, they also raise questions that require answers, make affirmations that require elaboration, and conceal what will require revelation. These eighteen verses name the main character, Jesus, only in verse 17. How does he do his revealing work? What does he reveal? What difference does it make and to whom? What is the "life," "light," "grace and truth" that he reveals? Why do some reject him? Who are these rejecting people? What interaction do they have with Jesus? What causes their rejection of him? How do they express it? Are they effective? Who receives him? How do some "see his glory"? How do "children of God" live? What happens to Jesus after he has made God known? These questions render the rest of the plot "necessary" in working out the consequences of these declarations. The only way of answering these questions is to read the Gospel's story.

The story takes as its starting point in 1:19-34 the development

5. Aristotle, "On the Art of Poetry," in *Classical Literary Criticism: Aristotle, Horace, Longinus*, ed. T. S. Dorsch (Baltimore: Penguin, 1965), 29–75.

of the role of John the Baptizer. Two scenes focus on John, first introduced in 1:6-8 and 15, as a witness to Jesus. In his first scene, John testifies that he is not the light (1:8a) but prepares the way for Jesus (1:19-28). In the second scene (1:29-34), John testifies to Jesus (1:8b) as the lamb who takes away the world's sin (1:29) and who bears the Spirit as God's agent or Son (1:32-34).

Equally important is the context in which John makes this testimony. His testimony is framed by an inquiry from the Jerusalem-based elite officials (*Ioudaioi*) into his identity (1:19, 21) and baptizing activity (1:25). The inquirers' lack of interest in joining John's movement casts their inquiries in a suspicious light. Why are they checking up on him? Who are they that John seems to threaten their control?

As John bears witness to Jesus (1:35-36), Jesus appears. In contrast to Matthew and Luke, here there is no account of his birth or upbringing. The Prologue has emphasized his origin with God and his mission to reveal God among humans. But now he appears as an adult. The plot narrates initial positive responses to his ministry (cf. 1:10). He begins to gather followers in Judea (Andrew, Simon Peter, 1:35-42) and Galilee (Philip, Nathanael, 1:43-51). In both instances, the first disciple bears witness to the second one. With a series of titles (Messiah, 1:41; Son of God, 1:49; king of Israel, 1:49), they recognize him as one commissioned by God to reveal and accomplish God's purposes.

Two incidents in chapter 2 reveal God's purposes. At the wedding in Cana in Galilee, the wine runs out (2:1-12). Jesus performs his first sign, changing water into abundant and high-quality wine. Both weddings and wine figure prominently in Israel's traditions about the future establishment of God's good and just purposes in which God blesses all people with abundant fertility (Isa. 25:6-10). The scene reveals God's purposes, which contrast with and reverse the exploitative, Roman-dominated world where many lack resources to sustain life. The disciples discern God's power and presence with Jesus (his "glory," 2:11) and commit themselves to him ("believe in" him, 2:11).

The next scene presents the revelation of God's purposes as a challenge to the ruling elite's way of structuring business as usual (2:13-23). Jesus attacks the Jerusalem temple, the power base for the Jerusalem leaders (*Ioudaioi*) who maintain and benefit from the present unjust structures. Observing the sale of animals to pilgrims in Jerusalem for Passover offerings, and the collection of the temple tax (2:14), Jesus denounces them for "making my Father's house a marketplace/house of trade" (2:16). His attack on this trade challenges an activity crucial for the administration of temple worship and for the wealth, political power, and status of the Jerusalem leaders.

Two Scripture citations interpret the action. The echoes of Zech. 14:21 in Jesus' denunciation of 2:16 locate Jesus' action in relation to God's anticipated future intervention on behalf of God's people to establish God's just and life-giving purposes over God's enemies. The echo presents the temple leadership as God's opponents, signals their inevitable downfall, and foreshadows the vindication of Jesus. The citation of Ps. 69:9 in verse 17 ("Zeal for your house will consume me") signals the inevitable outcome of Jesus' challenge. It is a fatal challenge; he will die at their hands. But as the Zechariah citation about God's triumph indicates, they will not have the last word.

The leaders respond to Jesus' action by confronting his authority to do such things (2:18). Jesus' response intensifies the hostility by charging them with destroying the temple (2:19a) and mysteriously claiming its replacement in his risen body (2:19b-22). The reference anticipates Jesus' death, links the temple leaders to it, and suggests an intensification of the conflict, which will develop through subsequent exchanges in the context of temple-based festivals. It also raises the question of how this death will come about while signaling that their attempts to remove him will not, finally, be successful, thwarted by resurrection. Moreover, it points to the end of the temple, with the risen Jesus the locus of God's presence.

This temple scene is thus of great importance for the plot (2:13-25). It introduces the conflict between Jesus and the Jerusalem authorities/*Ioudaioi*, which will intensify through the Gospel in Jesus' repeated trips to Jerusalem and the temple. With its reference to resurrection, it signals the limits of the leaders' power, the vindication of Jesus, the special relationship between Jesus and God, and the inevitable triumph of God's life-giving purposes. The scene introduces and anticipates these developments.

Jesus' relationship with these leaders deteriorates in 3:1-21 as Jesus exposes the limits of one of them. Nicodemus is unable to understand Jesus' explanation of God's working (3:1-10). Jesus' explanation centers on his role as the revealer of God. He descended from heaven (1:18, 51) and dies (3:13-14), the second reference to Jesus' death (after 2:18). Jesus also emphasizes God's love (3:16a), eternal life as the benefit of receiving him by believing or entrusting oneself to him and his revelation of God's purposes (3:16b-17), judgment (3:18), and the importance of how one lives (3:19-20). Two short scenes follow, restating John's significance as subordinate to but a witness to Jesus (3:22-30), and Jesus' significance as sent from God to reveal God's purposes (3:31-35).

This negative response among the power elite is offset by a contrasting response. The lengthy dialogue of chapter 4 introduces a Samaritan woman who contrasts with Nicodemus in significant ways:

- He is named; she is not.
- He is a man; she is a woman.
- He lives in the powerful city of Jerusalem; she lives in the small and powerless village of Sychar in Samaria.
- He is a Jew; she is a despised Samaritan (4:9). Jesus' mission includes Jews and gentiles.
- He is wealthy, powerful and of high societal status (3:1); she is poor, powerless, and of low societal status (4:7).
- He is unable to understand Jesus' theological talk (3:3-10); she persistently questions Jesus and gains understanding from him (4:11-12, 15).
- He recognizes Jesus as "a teacher who has come from God" (3:2,

though he can't learn from Jesus); she recognizes Jesus as a prophet (4:19, 29, 39). In response to her confession of waiting for a revealer-messiah (4:25), he identifies himself as such a figure (4:26). She receives his claims (4:29, 39).

- Nicodemus appears not to believe in chapter 3; the woman believes and, like a good disciple and missionary, bears witness to many others in her hometown who commit themselves to Jesus' revelation (4:39-42). They understand Jesus to be the Savior of the world, a title commonly claimed for Rome's emperors.

Jesus returns to Galilee, where he is welcomed (4:43-45; contrast Jerusalem, 2:13-23). Another positive interaction occurs. In the village of Cana (cf. 2:1-12), he heals the son of a royal official, one of the elite who is probably a retainer (and perhaps a gentile) in the service of Herod Antipas (4:46-54). Jesus' second sign enacts God's purposes for wholeness, repairing the damage of life lived in the Roman world. Health and wholeness demonstrate the establishment of God's reign (Isa. 35:5-6).

The plot has begun with Jesus carrying out his task of revealing God's purposes in gathering disciples, in his words, and in his actions. Some have received or entrusted themselves to his revelation and encountered God's purposes. But the plot has also put in play another response. Suspicion from the ruling elite attends John's task of bearing witness to Jesus. Jesus has directly challenged their center of power in the Jerusalem temple. Jesus has shown one of their leaders to be incapable of understanding God's purposes at work in him. Several references to Jesus' death indicate the high stakes involved in this negative response.

The Middle (5:1—17:26)

These negative, as well as positive, responses continue in the middle part of the Gospel story. Jesus' challenge to the elite necessarily intensifies as the plot moves toward his death at their hands (chs.

5–12); chapters 13–17 address those who have responded positively to Jesus' mission.

Jesus' challenge to the power group in chapters 2–3 inevitably leads to further conflict. In Jerusalem for an unidentified festival (5:1), Jesus again manifests God's purposes for physical wholeness and health by enabling a man paralyzed for thirty-eight years to walk again (5:1-15). But this action provokes a hostile response from the Jerusalem leaders/*Ioudaioi* because it violates their understanding of Sabbath as a day of rest, and because Jesus claims God as his Father and the authority to act on God's behalf and do God's will (5:18). They decide that such behavior is "high-handed" and an affront to God (Num. 15:30-31), in a word, blasphemy, which deserves death (Lev. 24:13-16). It is of course an affront to their authority also. Jesus interprets the Sabbath traditions to permit life-giving action that transforms the world they control. And he claims to be God's agent in declaring such purposes. They don't think he has any such right, or role.

Jesus elaborates these claims about his identity and authority in the long monologue that follows (5:19-47). His authority is based in his loving yet dependent relationship as Son with God his Father. Jesus carries out God's purposes in giving life (5:21-22) and passing judgment (5:26-27). But this relationship and these activities reveal not only his identity but also that of his hearers, either as those who by committing themselves to Jesus share in God's life (5:24-25, 28-29) or by rejecting him miss out on that life (5:29). In 5:31-47, he provides five witnesses to these claims: John the Baptizer (5:32-35), Jesus' works (5:36), God (5:37-38), the Scriptures (5:39-44), and Moses (5:45-47).

Jesus' discourse in chapter 5 has emphasized his authority and subordinate relationship to God, his role as agent of God's purposes in giving life and judging, and the consequences of belief and unbelief. Chapters 6–10 develop these same themes by employing essentially the same pattern as chapter 5. Jesus performs a sign, and dialogue follows that develops into a long discourse delivered by Jesus. Throughout, a few believe, while the opposition and hostility between Jesus and the

Jerusalem leadership intensifies. Their intentions to put Jesus to death figure prominently.

In chapter 6, in Galilee around Passover, Jesus further demonstrates his God-given authority by performing two signs that evoke the exodus story. He feeds five thousand people, and walks on water so as to ensure the disciples reach the shore safely (6:1-21). Both scenes employ Hebrew Bible themes to manifest God's life-giving purposes, power, and presence. The dialogue centers on the feeding story as a display of God's life-giving purposes (6:25-34). Jesus claims that he is the bread of life that has "come down from heaven" or been sent from God into the world to reveal these purposes (6:35-59). But the leaders find these claims difficult to understand, as do some disciples (6:60-71).

In chapter 7, Jesus avoids Jerusalem because of increasing danger but then elusively returns to Jerusalem for the Festival of Booths or Tabernacles (Sukkoth). He continues to assert his origin from God along with the life-giving benefit of accepting/believing and obeying his teaching. The leaders' threat to Jesus' life figures prominently, as do the people's divided responses to and speculation about Jesus' identity.

The same themes continue in chapter 8, as Jesus dominates a series of increasingly bitter dialogues with the elite/*Ioudaioi*. Jesus speaks about his own death and emphasizes the unacceptable identity and destructive consequences for those who reject his claims and revelation (8:12-30). He and the leaders debate what it means to be a descendent of Abraham and child of God (8:31-59) and the truth of Jesus' revelation (8:32, 45-47). Jesus charges the leaders with being false and descended from and loyal to the devil (8:42-45). They charge him with being a despised Samaritan and controlled by a demon (8:45-55), and try to stone him to death (8:59).

Despite the danger, Jesus continues his life-giving mission, restoring sight to a man born blind (9:1-7). The rest of the chapter focuses on responses to the man's healing from his neighbors (9:8-10), parents (9:18-23), the Jerusalem leaders (9:13-41), and the man himself. While the leaders continue their opposition and disparage Jesus as not from God but a sinner (9:16, 24), their hostile interrogations of the man who has gained his physical sight assist him in gaining insight into Jesus' identity. He identifies Jesus first as the man Jesus (9:11), then as a prophet (9:17), then as one from God (9:33), and finally as Son of Man and Lord (9:37-38).

The tension increases and the dialogue continues to unfold as a monologue in which Jesus condemns the leaders in contrast to himself as the true shepherd (10:1-18). The image signifies a leader or ruler, and one who represents God's rule and purposes (Psalm 23; Ezekiel 34). Jesus claims a close and caring relationship with the sheep, so much so that he is willing to lay down his life for them (10:11). By contrast, he attacks the Jerusalem leaders as "thieves and bandits" who steal resources from the people and threaten their well-being (10:1-21). Around the Festival of Dedication, Jesus further claims to be God's agent and one with God in doing God's will. These claims sound like blasphemy to the leaders (10: 22-38; cf. 5:16-18). They attempt to stone him and arrest him, but Jesus withdraws and many entrust themselves to him.

After the escalating animosity of chapters 5–10 and Jesus' intensifying challenge to the integrity, identity, legitimacy, authority and societal vision of the Jerusalem leaders, and his repeated claims to be the definitive revealer of God's purposes, only one outcome seems possible. Jesus' challenge cannot go unanswered. Jesus will die at their hands. Chapters 11–12 play out these consequences.

Jesus' raising of Lazarus from death provokes this action (11:1-44). Ironically, Jesus' act of giving life becomes the catalyst for the leaders' act of putting him to death. Fearing Jesus' popularity, their own loss of power, and Roman retaliation, the leaders plot to arrest and kill Jesus (11:45-57). The death theme increases as Mary, Lazarus's sister, lovingly anoints Jesus for burial (12:1-8), and some inhabitants of Jerusalem enthusiastically welcome Jesus (12:12-19), as do gentiles (12:12-22). Jesus speaks of the arrival of his "hour," the time of his death and departure to God. He rehearses his claims of God-given authority, his role as agent of God's purposes in giving life and judging, and the consequences of belief and unbelief (12:23-50).

9.3 The raising of Lazarus, an event unique to John's Gospel (John 11:43-44); sixth-century mosaic in the Basilica of Sant'Apollinare Nuovo, Classe; Commons.wikimedia.org.

While the movement to Jesus' inevitable death slows in chapters 13–17, the reality of his death pervades these chapters. Facing imminent death, Jesus gathers his disciples to prepare them for life in his absence. During a farewell meal, in an act of loving service as the host, Jesus washes their feet (ch. 13). He challenges them to lives marked by loving service (13:12-20, 31-35), and predicts that Judas and Peter will betray him as his own death approaches (13:21-30, 36-38). He then instructs them at length about their discipleship after his death (chs. 14–16). Repeated assurances of his continuing presence with them after his death, the necessity of his return to the Father so that he can send the Spirit to assist them until Jesus returns to earth, exhortations to continue in love, and the expectation of continuing opposition as they faithfully live out God's purposes in a rejecting world are all prominent in his teaching. Jesus ends his teaching with a lengthy prayer for God to display God's purposes in Jesus' death (17:1-8), in the community of disciples (17:9-19), and in the ongoing life of the church (17:20-26).

The End (Chaps. 18–21)

Chapters 18–19 narrate the "necessary and/or usual" consequences of what has happened in the beginning (chs. 1–4) and middle (chs. 5–17) sections of the plot. The movement to Jesus' death proceeds through betrayal by Judas, denial by Peter, and arrest by Roman soldiers and police from the Jerusalem leadership (18:1-18, 25-27). Jesus appears before the high priest (18:12-14, 19-24) and Pilate, who condemns him to be crucified as an unsanctioned king of the Jews (18:28—19:30). His death is confirmed (19:31-37), and Joseph and Nicodemus bury him (19:38-42). By the end of chapter 19, the story has finished as far as the elite/*Ioudaioi* are concerned. Jesus is dead, silencing his critique, claims, and challenge. The elite seem to have prevailed, reducing his claims to naught.

But to use Aristotle's terms, a surprising reversal takes place in the last two chapters, with a series of recognition scenes. Early on the morning of the third day, Jesus appears alive to Mary Magdalene (20:1-18). That evening, he passes through locked doors and appears to the disciples (20:19-23). A week later, he appears to Thomas and the disciples (20:24-29). Sometime thereafter, at the Sea of Tiberias or Galilee, Jesus appears again to the disciples (21:1-14). In the resulting breakfast (21:15-24), Jesus speaks to two of the disciples, Peter in 21:15-19 and the Beloved Disciple in 21:20-24, about their future roles as part of the church that continues Jesus' work. Peter faces persecution and martyrdom; the Beloved Disciple is entrusted with mission work.

9.4 *The Appearance of Jesus to Mary Magdalene after Resurrection* (John 20:11-18), by Alexander Ivanov (1835); Jesus' command that he not be touched is unique to John. Commons.wikimedia.org.

This last scene raises several interesting questions about the "end" of the Gospel plot. The plot of course ends in chapter 21; there is no chapter 22. But what happens to Jesus? Several earlier references indicate that he returns to God his Father (13:1; 3:14), though the Gospel does not narrate how this happens. The end of the Gospel and the departure of Jesus, though, do not mean the end of Jesus' mission. The final commissioning scene involving the two disciples elaborates Jesus' previous sending of the disciples (20:21b) to continue his task of manifesting God's life-giving purposes.

Conclusion

I have suggested that John's plot is best understood by attending to its end as the "necessary or usual consequence" of the preceding action.

John's story of Jesus centers on the assertion of Jesus' claim to be God's chosen agent, authorized by God to make a definitive revelation of God's life-giving purposes. In living out this claim in his words and works, Jesus conflicts with the Jerusalem elite and their Roman ally, Pilate, confronting and challenging their power over, and vision of, an unjust societal order that is contrary to God's life-giving purposes. The Jerusalem elite/*Ioudaioi* reject Jesus' claim and revelation of God's purposes of life, ultimately putting him to death. But surprisingly, his death is not the end. God raises him, thereby revealing the limit of their power. In the meantime, some people discern Jesus' origin, identity, and mission; commit themselves to his revelation; and form a countercommunity that, assisted by the Holy Spirit, continues Jesus' mission.

Questions for Review and Reflection

1. The initial discussion highlights distinctive features of John's Gospel's telling of the story of Jesus. Be clear on the contributions of the distinctive scenes (Prologue, quest stories, and sign scenes), the distinctive geographical and temporal settings, characters (*Ioudaioi*, Jesus), and Jesus' distinctive way of talking.
2. Outline the main scenes of chapters 1–4. What stands out to you?
3. Outline the main scenes of chapters 5–17. Why are chapters 13–17 distinctive among all the Gospels?
4. What do you notice about the narratives of Jesus' death and resurrection in chapters 18–21? How does it contrast with the narrative in the Synoptics?

10

John's Gospel: The Presentation of Jesus as Wisdom

As I emphasized in the last chapter, the presentation of Jesus in John's Gospel differs significantly from that of the three Synoptic Gospels. How did this very different presentation come about?

Scholars have suggested a number of factors that might have contributed to this distinctive shaping of the presentation of Jesus.

One approach highlights the contribution of the Gospel's author(s). As with the other Gospels, we don't know who the Gospel's author was. The name John is not associated with the Gospel until later in the second century. Nevertheless, there is no doubt that a key figure—or several key figures—contributed significant creative insight to the Gospel's presentation of Jesus. The challenge is to identify what traditions or circumstances might have influenced this unknown figure or figures.

10.1 How Many Authors Does It Take to Write A Gospel?

Readers of the Gospel have noticed some unusual sequences in the Gospel. At the end of chapter 14, for example, Jesus seems to come to an end of his teaching by saying, "Rise, let us be on our way." But then he talks for two more chapters and prays for another one after that (chs. 15–17). In chapter 20, the Gospel seems to draw to an end with the final reflection in 20:30-31. But then another whole chapter follows. In some verses in the Gospel, we read that by believing in Jesus now, a person already has eternal life (literally, "life of the age," 3:16; 5:24), yet in other places, the emphasis moves from the present to the future as the time of resurrection and life (5:28-29; 6:39-40). How might these inconsistencies have come about? Scholars have made various suggestions concerning the possibility that the Gospel came into being in stages, with several authors contributing to it. One scenario posits the creation of a written Gospel (perhaps from an earlier shorter version focusing on Jesus' signs or from oral traditions about Jesus). This written Gospel was subsequently added to and revised by another writer. There is a reference in 21:24 which perhaps indicates that another writer has added to the Gospel: "This is the disciple who is testifying to these things and has written them, and we know that his testimony is true."

Scholars have looked to several cultural-religious traditions and/or events to provide the catalyst for the distinctive presentation of Jesus in this Gospel. Earlier scholarship, particularly that of Rudolf Bultmann, argued for influences from Gnostic and Mandean groups and ideas. Especially important, Bultmann thought, was a tradition concerning a descending and ascending revealer figure. However, the major problem with this theory is that the sources to which Bultmann appealed are much later than the first century, when the Gospel was written.[1]

More recently, some scholars have foregrounded the scene in John 4, in which Jesus converses with a Samaritan woman. Scholars such as Raymond Brown have interpreted this scene to depict the influence of Samaritan believers who introduced ideas about a revealer figure that shaped understandings of Jesus.[2] The major problem with this theory is explaining why this scene in chapter 4 should be singled out as the most influential ahead of all the other scenes in chapters 1–12, such as Galileans under fig trees (1:43-51) or physically impaired Jerusalemites at pools (5:1-18).

1. Rudolf Bultmann, *The Gospel of John* (Philadelphia: Westminster, 1971).
2. Raymond Brown, *The Community of the Beloved Disciple* (New York: Paulist Press, 1979).

A third suggestion has centered on the influence of Jewish apocalyptic traditions involving revealer figures such as Moses (1:17) and Isaiah (12:37-41). These revealer figures were understood in various traditions to ascend into the heavens for a brief tour and then descend with revelations from God. John's Gospel, so the argument goes, contests these traditions by elevating Jesus as God's definitive revealer. The claims about Jesus are made by reversing this pattern. He starts in the heavens with God "in the beginning," as the Word, and descends to be among humans before returning to God by ascension. The significance of the reversed pattern is that Jesus' revelation is shown to be the most reliable. He did not pop up into the heavens for a brief look around, like Moses or Isaiah. He was there with God from the beginning. He knows that which he reveals.

10.2 Afterlives of Biblical Figures

Many biblical figures have a considerable "afterlife" long after they have died. Over a number of centuries, traditions about these figures develop and construct them in different ways so that they become relevant for and address the issues of changing contemporary situations. For example, Moses has been presented as the inventor of civilizing arts like writing, philosophy, religion, and politics. His journey up Mt. Sinai has been understood to involve more than receiving the Ten Commandments. It was said that God showed him paradise (2 Baruch 4.5–6; 4 Ezra 14.3–6). He has also been depicted as a priest, prophet, and king. As king, he is understood to ascend into heaven, where he receives secret knowledge about the past and future, especially the end of the age (Philo, *Life of Moses* 1.158; also 2 Baruch 59.3–12). This exalted treatment of Moses serves to guarantee the law that he taught and the requirement of obedience to it in the light of the end of the age. Similarly, traditions have developed about Isaiah. In one text, the Martyrdom and Ascension of Isaiah 7–11, he is taken on a journey through seven heavens.

A further suggestion focuses on an event around the year 40 in which the Roman emperor Gaius Caligula attempted to install a statue of himself as Zeus in the Jerusalem temple. This was a momentous event for Jewish folks, both in Judea and in the Diaspora, as they negotiated this grave, temple-violating assertion of Roman imperial power. Interestingly, accounts in the writings of the Alexandrian Jew Philo and the Jewish historian Josephus indicate significant points of contact between this episode and aspects of John's presentation of Jesus, including an emphasis on a clash of sovereignties between God and the emperor, claims of making oneself God, and the importance of the notion of agency. Perhaps negotiation of this incident left its mark on developing traditions about Jesus, who had been crucified by Rome but raised by God.[3]

The most commonly accepted explanation for the distinctive shape of John's Gospel appeals to a hypothetical dispute with a synagogue community. This fight over belief in Jesus, so the argument goes, resulted in the Johannine community being expelled from the synagogue. The Gospel was written supposedly to make sense of this painful and alienating experience and to map the way ahead for a group now separated from the synagogue.[4] This scenario has been popular, but it faces some major challenges.[5] One of the most important is its arbitrary selection of chapter 9 to posit an antithetical relation between Jesus-believers with a synagogue as the catalyst for the Gospel narrative. Chapter 11, by contrast, posits very different interactions between Jesus-followers and their neighbors, marked by care and compassion (11:31–33). Privileging and generalizing chapter 9 is arbitrary. Another challenge is that this scenario has been based in part on reports, in later talmudic literature, of the use of a "benediction against heretics" to exclude from synagogue worship Jews who held unorthodox beliefs—for example, in a human being "one" with God. The objection is that these reports are too late to tell us anything about the second half of the first century.

These five approaches attempt to identify traditions or events that might have functioned as the catalyst that shaped the distinctive presentation of Jesus in the Gospel. Of the five approaches, scholars have most commonly appealed to some combination of the second (Samaritan), third (apocalyptic), and fifth (synagogue separation)

3. See Warren Carter, *John and Empire: Initial Explorations* (New York: T&T Clark, 2008), 343–84.
4. J. Louis Martyn, *History and Theology in the Fourth Gospel*, 3rd ed. (Louisville: Westminster John Knox, 2003); Brown, *Community of the Beloved Disciple.*
5. Adele Reinhartz, *Befriending the Beloved Disciple: A Jewish Reading of the Gospel of John* (New York: Continuum, 2001); Carter, *John and Empire*, 7–11, 22–45.

options, even though there are problems with the adequacy of each one, as I have suggested.

In this chapter, I focus on a sixth option. This option proposes that the Gospel author/s drew on wisdom traditions, a form of spirituality found in the Hebrew Bible that wrestles with the issue of the mystery of God's ways among humans, and of how humans might know God and God's purposes and presence. I suggest that the Gospel uses this wisdom paradigm, focused on the revelation of God, to present its central confession, that Jesus is Wisdom, the revealer of God.

I begin by describing some features of this wisdom spirituality or paradigm. Then I note some of the ways in which the Gospel presents Jesus in these terms in both the Prologue and the rest of the Gospel. I finish by suggesting why employing this paradigm might have been so important for John's telling of the story of Jesus.

A Wisdom Paradigm: What Is It?

The wisdom tradition developed through biblical and other Jewish writings.[6] Initially, wisdom refers to the order or principle of creation that was understood to conform to and reflect the will and nature of God. The first twenty-three verses of Psalm 104, for example, celebrate God's work of creation, notably establishing and sustaining a vast, varied, and intricate world of order and beauty. Addressing God, verse 24 admires this order and harmonious variety: "how manifold are your works." The verse then goes on to claim that it was "in wisdom" that God "made them all." The term "wisdom" here sums up the claims of the rest of the Psalm, denoting the source of all this creative work and order, the means of accomplishing it, and its sustaining force. If the order, variety, and harmony of creation are designated "wisdom," and if creation reveals something of God's will and nature, then the term "wisdom" is especially linked with the revelation of God in creation.

The link between wisdom and the revealing of God is elaborated and expanded in Proverbs 1–9. Wisdom becomes more than a principle of

6. Throughout this section, I follow the fine work of Sharon Ringe, *Wisdom's Friends: Community and Christology in the Fourth Gospel* (Louisville: Westminster John Knox, 1999), 29–45.

order in creation (3:19-20) and now appears as a personified female figure, Lady Wisdom, who reveals how people might live in awe or fear of God according to God's purposes in households and society. The personified female figure of Wisdom presents Wisdom as desirable yet elusive, as needing to be actively sought after or received but difficult to find or accept.[7]

The first personification of Wisdom appears in Prov. 1:20-33. Here Wisdom is presented as being among people in daily life, actively summoning them to receive her "reproof . . . thoughts . . . words" (1:23).

> Wisdom cries out in the street;
> in the squares she raises her voice.
> At the busiest corner she cries out;
> at the entrance of the city gates she speaks. (Prov. 1:20-21)

But people are not responsive. They reject her, and ignore her teaching (1:24-25). Wisdom, like an angry, rejected prophet, threatens them with imminent calamity as a consequence of ignoring her (1:26-27). In their distress, people will cry out to her, but, she declares, she will not be found (1:28). Only "those who listen to me will be secure" (1:33).

In Proverbs's second major section presenting personified Wisdom (3:13-20), finding her is presented as better than acquiring "silver . . . gold . . . jewels" (3:14-15). The benefits or blessings of receiving wisdom are subsequently elaborated as "long life . . . riches . . . and honor." Her ways are marked by "pleasantness and peace" (3:16-17). People are exhorted to "get wisdom" (4:5-9).

The third and most lengthy section presenting personified Wisdom occurs in Proverbs 8 and divides into five sections. The opening three verses introduce Wisdom crying out to people in public places. Verses 4-11 set forth her call to people to receive her instruction. The third section narrates benefits from receiving her teaching: opposing evil and perverted speech, offering good advice, authorizing rulers who govern rightly, and gaining riches and honor (8:12-21). She functions

7. The figure of Lady Wisdom is contrasted with Lady Folly or Foolishness (2:16-19; 5:3-14; 6:23-35; 7:1-27; 9:13-18), who represents a way of life opposed to God's purposes. Often she is depicted as misleading young men sexually. To follow her leads to death.

among people, it seems, as one who is independent of God, yet an agent acting on behalf of God. The fourth section presents Wisdom's place in creation, working together with God in shaping creation.[8]

Verses 30-31 are especially important for defining Wisdom's roles:

> then I was beside him, like a master worker;
> and I was daily his delight,
> rejoicing before him always,
> rejoicing in his inhabited world
> and delighting in the human race.

The double use of the term "delight" holds the key. Wisdom is daily God's *delight* in being with God, and she also *delights* in humankind. Wisdom's delight in people means Wisdom comes among human society to represent divine presence and purposes to people and to enable people to encounter God and God's ways. Wisdom thus functions as a key link between God and human beings. Human rejection of Wisdom is a rejection of God, but those who seek and desire Wisdom and receive Wisdom's teaching are drawn into God's presence and purposes. "For whoever finds me finds life and obtains favor from the Lord" (8:35).

The fourth passage again presents Wisdom among human beings, but now as a hostess for a feast to which people are invited (9:1-6).

> Come, eat of my bread
> and drink of the wine I have mixed.
> Lay aside immaturity, and live,
> and walk in the way of insight. (9:5-6)

Wisdom reveals "life" lived in relation to God, knowledge of God's ways, and encounter with God's presence.

Wisdom beyond the Hebrew Bible

Traditions concerning Wisdom continued to develop in Jewish

8. Proverbs 8:22 raises a difficult questions about the origin of Wisdom, whether it existed before creation or was part of creation. Verse 22 poses a difficult translation issue. Commonly the verb is translated "created" ("The Lord created me"), though the term can also be rendered "discovered" or "acquired."

literature known to us in collections called the Apocrypha and the Old Testament Pseudepigrapha. We will briefly survey several of the main texts.

Sirach 24: Personified Wisdom declares her origin from God (24:3), her cosmic reach, her influence among all peoples and nations, her being sent to and dwelling as God's agent in Israel and Jerusalem, and the identification of her teachings with the law of the covenant (24:23; also 15:1). In this development, which localizes Wisdom in Israel and identifies Wisdom with the books of Moses, something of the mystery of seeking and finding elusive Wisdom is decreased. Wisdom's international presence in creation has become localized in a particular people and in a particular tradition. Wisdom is now understood to abound as God's gift in Moses' teaching. To embrace this teaching means a life of wisdom marked by God's will and presence.

> Whoever obeys me will not be put to shame,
> and those who work with me will not sin. (Sir. 24:22)

Baruch 3:9–4:4: Wisdom continues to be presented in a localized manner as God's gift to Israel and is especially made known in the Torah, or teaching, of Moses (4:1). But Israel has not lived accordingly and so has been defeated in battle and exiled from the land to foreign countries. To those who accept her, Wisdom offers peace, strength, understanding, and life. The passage also recognizes the paradox that Wisdom is elusive and mysterious (3:15-37) but is known in the Torah or the books of Moses (4:1-4).

Wisdom of Solomon: The book's opening fifteen verses set out the argument of the first part of this two-part work (chs. 1–9). The verses repeatedly exhort readers to seek God and provide assurances that Wisdom is found by such seekers who are committed to live according to God's purposes and are rewarded with immortality. By contrast, Wisdom is not found among the unrighteous, who know death. Death is contrary to God's intent for all created things to continue to exist (1:12-15).[9] The second part of the book (chs. 10–19) provides evidence

9. Noteworthy in this first part of Wisdom of Solomon is the catalog of twenty-one attributes

from Israel's history that Wisdom does indeed deliver the godly, both righteous individuals and the elect nation. The section initially traces incidents from the lives of Adam to Joseph in which Wisdom protected and delivered the godly (10:1-14). It then takes up the exodus and wilderness periods, in which Wisdom delivered Israel from death to life while punishing the ungodly (e.g., sinful Egypt and Canaan), who live alluring lives of sensual pleasure and idolatry.

1 Enoch 42:1-2: This text, originating from around the middle of the first century CE, several decades before John's Gospel was written, highlights Wisdom's rejection by humans. As a consequence, Wisdom withdraws from among people.

> Then Wisdom went out to dwell with the children of the people,
> but she found no dwelling place.
> (So) Wisdom returned to her place
> And she settled permanently among the angels.

First Enoch generally sees widespread evil among people, especially exploitative practices enacted by ruling elites. People have not lived faithfully to God's purposes. Wisdom's attempts to find a reception among people are unsuccessful, so Wisdom withdraws from among humans to the heavens.[10]

From these various texts, we can construct a Wisdom paradigm that presents Wisdom as a paradoxical figure.

- Wisdom is a principle of order in creation, yet also a personified figure active in public places.
- Wisdom is a gift and agent of God, able to be distinguished from God yet not separated from God.
- Wisdom personifies divine power, presence, and purposes among

of Wisdom in 7:22b-23. Also noteworthy are the various synonyms used for Wisdom including "word" and "holy spirit." So in 9:1-2a, God's creative work is performed by God's word and by Wisdom ("Lord of mercy, who have made all things by your word, and by your wisdom have formed humankind"). And in 9:17, "Wisdom" and "holy spirit" are synonyms as divine gifts: "Who has learned your counsel, unless you have given wisdom and sent your holy spirit from on high?"

10. I omit discussion of Wisdom as a subordinate figure in the writings of the Alexandrian Jewish figure Philo.

people, yet she does not threaten or compromise the affirmation that God is one (monotheism, Deut. 6:4).

- Wisdom is immanent in creation yet distinct from it.
- Wisdom is a heavenly figure but active on earth.
- Wisdom is universally available and present, but particularly at home in Israel and in the Torah.
- Wisdom reveals God, seeking out people to receive her, yet she is mysterious, elusive, and hidden, more often rejected.

Central to this paradigm is the conviction that Wisdom is God in self-manifestation, a revelation of God, God insofar as God can be known by people.

I am suggesting that John's Gospel utilizes this wisdom paradigm to present Jesus as the revealer of God.

John's Prologue and Jesus as Wisdom (1:1-18)

The first evidence for the Gospel's use of this wisdom paradigm appears in the Gospel's opening eighteen verses. The Prologue celebrates the coming of the Word, Jesus, among human beings with a mission to reveal God, to "enlighten everyone" (1:9) and to make God known (1:18). This emphasis on revelation immediately alerts us to the possibility of the use of the wisdom paradigm. In fact, the Prologue utilizes at least twelve features of this wisdom paradigm in its presentation of Jesus.[11]

1. Both Wisdom and Jesus the Word exist before creation:
   John 1:1: "In the beginning was the Word."
   Prov. 8:22: "The Lord created me at the beginning of his work."
   Sir. 1:4: "Wisdom was created before all other things."
   Sir. 24:9: "Before the ages, in the beginning, he created me."
2. Both Wisdom and Jesus the Word begin "with God":

11. In this section, I follow the analysis in Charles Talbert, *Reading John: A Literary and Theological Commentary on the Fourth Gospel and the Johannine Epistles* (New York: Crossroad, 1992), 66–79.

John 1:1b: "And the Word was with God."
Prov. 8:30: "then I was beside him, like a master worker."
Wisd of Sol. 9:4: "Give me the wisdom that sits by your throne."

3. Both Wisdom and Jesus the Word are involved in the act of creation:
   John 1:3: "All things were made through him."
   Prov. 8:24-30: "When there were no depths I was brought forth . . . then I was beside him, like a master worker."
   Prov. 3:19: "The Lord by wisdom founded the earth."
   Wisd. of Sol. 7:22: "wisdom, the fashioner of all things."
   Wisd. of Sol. 9:1-2: "by your wisdom have formed humankind."
4. Both Wisdom and Jesus the Word make life available:
   John 1:4a: "In him was life."
   Prov. 8:35: "For whoever finds me finds life."
   Bar. 4:1: "All who hold her fast will live, and those who forsake her will die."
5. Both Wisdom and Jesus the Word provide light for people:
   John 1:4: "the life was the light of all people";
   Wisd. of Sol. 7:26: "For she is a reflection of eternal light."
   Bar. 4:2: "Walk toward the shining of her light."
6. Neither Wisdom nor Jesus the Word can be overcome by darkness/evil:
   John 1:5: "The light shines in the darkness, and the darkness did not overcome it."
   Wisd. of Sol. 7:30: "against wisdom evil does not prevail."
7. Both Wisdom and Jesus the Word come among people to reveal God:
   John 1:9-10: "The true light, which enlightens everyone, was coming into the world. He was in the world."
   Wisd. of Sol. 6:16: "She goes about seeking those worthy of her, and she graciously appears to them in their paths, and meets them in every thought."
   Sir. 24:7: "Among all these I sought a resting place."

1 En. 42.2a: "Then Wisdom went out to dwell with the children of the people."

8. Both Wisdom and Jesus the Word experience rejection by people:
   John 1:10-11: "He was in the world . . . yet the world did not know him. He came to what was his own, and his own people did not accept him."
   1 En. 42.2: "She found no dwelling place. (So) Wisdom returned to her place."
   Bar. 3:20-21: "But they have not learned the way to knowledge, nor understood her paths, nor laid hold of her."
9. Both Wisdom and Jesus the Word enable receptive people to encounter God:
   John 1:12-13: "But to all who received him, who believed in his name, he gave power to become children of God, who were born, not of blood or of the will of the flesh or of the will of humans, but of God."
   Wisd. of Sol. 7:27: "In every generation she passes into holy souls and makes them friends of God."
   Wisd. of Sol. 9:18: "People were taught what pleases you, and were saved by wisdom."
10. Both Wisdom and Jesus the Word lived among humans:
    John 1:14a: "The Word became flesh and dwelt among us."
    Bar. 3:37: "Afterward she appeared on earth and lived with humankind."
    Sir. 24:11-12: "Thus in the beloved city he gave me a resting place, and in Jerusalem was my domain. I took root in an honored people, in the portion of the Lord, his heritage."
11. Both Wisdom and Jesus the Word are described as "unique":
    John 1:14: "We have seen his glory, the glory as of a father's only son" (also 1:18).
    Wisd. of Sol. 7:22, 25: "There is in her a spirit that is . . . unique."
12. Both Wisdom and Jesus the Word know God and reveal God:
    John 1:18: "It is God the only Son . . . who has made him known."
    Wisd. of Sol. 8:4: "For she is an initiate in the knowledge of God."

> Wisd. of Sol. 9:9-10: "She understands what is pleasing in your sight and what is right according to your commandments. Send her forth from the holy heavens . . . that I may learn what is pleasing to you."

These significant similarities introduce Jesus as Wisdom. The Gospel's opening eighteen verses provide this framework for the presentation of Jesus in the rest of the Gospel. Throughout, Jesus personifies Wisdom's role to reveal God and make God's presence and purposes known among people.

Before examining the rest of the Gospel and noting the pervasiveness of these twelve features in the presentation of Jesus, an interesting question needs to be addressed. Given these significant similarities between Jesus and Wisdom, why does John's Gospel not begin by identifying Jesus explicitly as Wisdom? Why does it, instead, call Jesus the Word?

At least three factors account for identifying Jesus as the Word. First, "word" is a synonym for Wisdom. So in Wisd. of Sol. 9:1, "wisdom" and "word" are synonyms for God's creative activity:

> O God of my ancestors and Lord of mercy,
> who have made all things by your *word*,
> and by your *wisdom* have formed humankind.

The Jewish writer Philo links the Wisdom of God with the Word of God: "This issues forth out of the Eden of the wisdom of God, and that is the word of God" (*Allegorical Interpretation* 1.65). A similar link appears in Sir. 24:3, when Wisdom describes her origin from the mouth of God: "I came forth from the mouth of the Most High."

Second, gender accounts for the use of the term "Word" rather than "Wisdom." The wisdom tradition consistently presents Wisdom as a female figure. The noun "Word" is masculine in Greek (*logos*), more appropriate for the male figure Jesus, even as it belongs to and evokes the wider wisdom paradigm.

And third, the term "Word" is associated with communication. Words communicate, or more appropriately for the Wisdom paradigm, words reveal. From the beginning of the biblical tradition, words are efficacious in expressing God's will and purposes in creation ("And God said," e.g., Gen. 1:3, 6, 9). Words enact God's presence. The use of the term "Word" emphasizes the revealing work that Jesus as Wisdom will carry out in his actions and in his words.

Jesus as Wisdom in His Public Ministry

The presentation of Jesus as Wisdom in 1:1-18 provides the framework for the presentation of Jesus as Wisdom in the rest of the Gospel. I'll explore three dimensions in relation to the twelve features identified above.

As Wisdom, Jesus Mediates Divine Presence and Life (Nos. 4–7)

Jesus' relationship "with God" (nos. 1 and 2 above) provides the foundation for his activity of revealing God's presence and life among people. The things he saw and heard in being "with God" from the beginning are revealed in his word and actions:

> Jesus said to them, "Very truly, I tell you, the Son can do nothing on his own, but only what he sees the Father doing; for whatever the Father does, the Son does likewise. The Father loves the Son and shows him all that he himself is doing." (John 5:19-20; see also 26, 30, 36; 3:11-13; 6:46)

God and Jesus inter-dwell each other (14:10-11). To know Jesus is therefore to know God (14:7). To see Jesus is to see God (14:9). To hear Jesus' words is to hear God's words (14:10). To see Jesus' works is to see the works of God (14:11). To receive Jesus is to receive God (13:20). To reject Jesus is to reject God (15:23-24). To honor Jesus is to honor God (5:23).

Central to Jesus' revealing work is to make available "life." He announces himself as "life" (11:25; 14:6), and declares both that he "gives life" just as God does (5:21) and that he has come among humans that they "may have life, and have it abundantly" (10:10). This life is "eternal," and encountering it means passing "from death to life."

> Very truly, I tell you, anyone who hears my word and believes him who sent me has eternal life, and does not come under judgment, but has passed from death to life. (John 5:24)

What is this "eternal life" that Jesus reveals?

The term "life" has multiple dimensions in the Gospel. It denotes physical wholeness as Jesus heals the official's son in Capernaum, who "was at the point of death," but now lives (4:46-54, esp. 50-53). Similarly, Jesus restores somatic wholeness to a paralyzed man who walks (5:5-9), a blind man who sees (9:1-7), and a dead man, Lazarus, who lives (11:38-44). Several times, these life-giving actions are linked with light shining in darkness (9:5; 11:9-11).

In addition to restoring health, Jesus provides abundant food and drink—first at a wedding in Cana (2:1-11), then in feeding a crowd of five thousand (6:1-15), and finally in ensuring a large catch of fish (21:4-11). "Life," then, also denotes abundant fertility.

Along with these physical and somatic displays is the Gospel's emphasis on bodily resurrection. Chapters 20–21 narrate Jesus' resurrection from his death by crucifixion at the hands of an alliance of Jerusalem leaders and the Roman governor. As Wisdom, Jesus cannot be overcome by evil (no. 6 above). Jesus also declares that somatic resurrection awaits believers (5:28-29; 6:39-40, 54; 11:44). The notion of resurrection emerged in the second century BCE in a context of injustice and martyrdom. It affirms that death and evil cannot stand in the way of God's life-giving and justice-doing work (see 2 Maccabees 7). Resurrection, then, is the ultimate victory over death and evil. This victory is evident with Jesus' resurrection. The ruling powers, an alliance of Jerusalem leaders and the Roman governor who oppose Jesus as God's agent by putting him to death, are not able to keep him dead.

Physical healing, abundance and fertility, and somatic resurrection are significant dimensions of the "eternal life" Jesus as Wisdom reveals and imparts. The translation of the adjective *aiōnios* with "eternal" is problematic. While we often understand it to mean "without end" or "timeless," literally the Greek word means "of the age" or "agely" life. That is, it represents a way of thinking called "eschatology," which sees the goal of God's purposes to be the establishment of a new age or time. In this age, God's life-giving and just purposes are established and God's presence known (17:5). The "life" of this new age that Jesus reveals is marked by, among other things, the absence of death and evil, the oppression and injustice of Rome's empire, physical wholeness, fertility, and the presence of God.

Interplay of Acceptance and Rejection of Jesus Wisdom (Nos. 7–10)

As Wisdom, Jesus' activity among people of revealing God causes a divide among people. People either receive and believe Jesus (1:12), or they do not know or accept him (1:10-11). Those who believe in Jesus as the Son or agent of God have eternal life, while those who disobey or reject Jesus do not see life but "endure God's wrath" (3:36). Those who believe are born from God as children of God (1:12; 3:1-10), while those who reject him are designated as children of the devil (8:43-47). The former are from above like Jesus; the latter, from below (8:23). The former are not of the world; the latter belong to the rejecting world (8:23b; 1:10). Those who believe hear Jesus' words; they have passed from death to life and already experience in part the abundant life of the new age (5:24; 6:40), while those who do not believe "are condemned already" (3:18). Those who receive eternal life walk or live in the light, while those who reject Jesus live in darkness (12:35-36) because they love and perform evil deeds (3:19-21). Those who believe in Jesus "remain" or "abide" with Jesus and form a community marked by love for one another (13:34-35), bearing fruit from doing his commandments and teaching (15:1-17). This community of believers is identified as Jesus' friends (15:15). Those who do not abide with Jesus and his believers hate the community of believers/friends and are thrown away and burned (15:6, 18-24). The Gospel's dualistic formulations embody the division that Jesus as Wisdom causes.

The ultimate rejection of Jesus centers on his crucifixion. It is a complex event that the Gospel presents with rich ironies. On one level,

Jesus' crucifixion results from his increasing conflict with the Jerusalem-based alliance of leaders, especially the chief priests and Pharisees. They reject Jesus' claims to be God's agent, oppose his activity, and fear Roman retaliation if they lose control of the people to Jesus (11:46-53). In alliance with the Roman governor, they put Jesus to death. Yet, ironically, he does not resist them. It is not so much their victory as his, since Jesus gives himself to die in accord with God's will (10:18; 18:4-8; 19:10-11). And, further irony, his death also seems to be the devil's work, yet it involves Jesus' disciples (13:2; 18:4).

The ironies continue in the presentation of his crucifixion. What is a scene of apparent defeat and death is also a coronation that proclaims Jesus' identity as king or agent of God's purposes (19:14, 19-22). What ought to be a shameful end is a means of glorification, an opportunity to display the presence and power of God among humans in his resurrection and ascension (chs. 20–21). He is "lifted up" in crucifixion, resurrection, and ascension to return to God (3:14; 8:28; 12:23). His enemies cannot successfully oppose the agent and purposes of God.

Jesus/Wisdom's Saving Presence among the People (Nos. 9–12)

The Gospel uses four key motifs from wisdom traditions to present Jesus' public ministry: encounters in public places, a pattern of descent and ascent, his identity as a teacher of Wisdom's ways, and his self-presentation as an agent of God. I consider each in turn.

Encounters in Public Places

Wisdom is active among humans, at street corners and in marketplaces, calling people to encounter God. So too is Jesus. He calls Nathaniel to follow him under a fig tree in Galilee (1:48). He attends a wedding at Cana, talks with a Samaritan woman at a well (4:5-7), heals an official's son in the town of Capernaum (4:46), heals a paralyzed man by a pool in Jerusalem (5:2), feeds a crowd on a mountain near the Sea of Tiberias in Galilee (6:1-3), and goes to Jerusalem for the Festival of Booths, where he teaches (ch. 7). In chapters 11–12, he goes to the village of Bethany to be with Mary, Martha, and Lazarus. Like Wisdom, Jesus conducts his activity in public among people.

Pattern of Ascent and Descent

Like Wisdom, Jesus' identity is defined by his origin from God and his destiny in returning to God. So 13:3 declares, "Jesus, knowing that . . . he had come from God and was going to God. . . ." The Gospel employs this pattern of descent and ascent throughout. Jesus comes "from above" (3:31-36), from heaven (6:41-51). God is commonly the one who "sent" Jesus: "For I have come down from heaven, not to do my own will, but the will of him who sent me. And this is the will of him who sent me . . ." (John 6:38-39). Jesus' origin from God is the source of and the authorization for his revelation: "I know him, because I am from him, and he sent me" (7:29). Jesus is sent to do God's will to reveal eternal life and to save the world (3:16-17).

The descending-ascending pattern is associated with Jesus as Son of Man (3:11-15). This term can refer to a human being (Ezek. 2:1; 3:1; NRSV translates "O mortal") as well as to a heavenly figure to whom in Daniel 7 God entrusts "everlasting dominion" and "kingship" over all peoples. In describing Jesus as the son of Man who descends from heaven and then ascends to heaven, the Gospel also combines wisdom traditions with traditions about Moses. Just as God commanded Moses to put a serpent on a pole so that those who were bitten by a snake could look at it and be healed (Numbers 21), so the crucified Jesus, descending and ascending, gives life and reveals his identity as God's agent (8:28):

> No one has ascended into heaven except the one who descended from heaven, the Son of Man. And just as Moses lifted up the serpent in the wilderness, so must the Son of Man be lifted up, that whoever believes in him may have eternal life. (John 3:13-15)

Being "lifted up" is the means by which Jesus returns to God. There, he prepares a place for his believers, whose destiny is also with God (14:2-3). He also sends the Spirit, another form of Wisdom, to be with his followers in his absence (14:26; 16:7; 20:22). And from there he promises to return.

Teaching Wisdom's Ways

As Wisdom, Jesus is designated a teacher (1:38; 8:4; 13:13-14), and the verb "teaching" commonly describes his activity (6:59; 7:14-17; 8:20; 18:20). He teaches or reveals God's presence and ways so that his followers can order their lives. Jesus is the way (14:6), teaching a way of love (13:4; 15:12-17) and of justice enacted in resurrection (5:24-25). In the lengthy monologues and conversations of chapters 3–17, he reveals key matters concerning his origin from above/God (ch. 3, Nicodemus), his identity as Savior of the world (ch. 4, the Samaritan woman), his authority and mission (ch. 5), his echoes of Moses as "bread from heaven" (ch. 6), his divisive impact (ch. 7), his manifestation of God's presence or light (ch. 8), his identity (ch. 9), his roles as good shepherd and revealer of eternal and resurrection life (chs. 10–12) and as teacher of his followers (chs. 13–17). As with Wisdom, his teaching is received by some (chs. 13–17) and rejected by others, especially the Jerusalem-based elite (5:18; 6:52-59; 7:32-36).

His style of teaching employs techniques typical of wisdom traditions. Extended metaphors such as that of the bread of life/from heaven (6:22-59), the shepherd (10:1-21), and the vine (15:1-17) mark his teaching. Wordplays, riddles, and misunderstandings abound. For example, Jesus tells Nicodemus that to enter God's reign, he must be born "from above" (3:3) by receiving God's action and presence that Jesus reveals. Jesus' declaration employs a riddle because the Greek word *anōthen* has a double meaning. It can be translated "again" or "anew," as well as "from above." Nicodemus misunderstands Jesus' meaning and responds by asking how it is possible for a man to enter his mother's womb again (3:4). The question is ridiculous and shows Nicodemus to not have a clue about Jesus' revelation of God's action. He is defeated by the wordplay and riddle.

Double meanings figure in the exchange with the woman at the well, but in contrast to the benighted Nicodemus, they lead not to confusion but to increased understanding. So Jesus' initial request for a drink becomes the occasion for his revelation that he gives the water of eternal life (4:14). The woman is not befuddled but immediately asks for this water (4:15) and subsequently discerns Jesus' identity as the Messiah (4:25-26). Jesus' teaching reveals those who accept and reject his teaching.

Jesus' Self-Presentation

References in John	**Jesus in John**	**Wisdom References**	**Meaning**
6:35, 51	I am the bread of life	Sir. 24:21 Prov. 9:5	Revealing instruction
8:12; 9:5	I am the light of the world	Wisd. of Sol. 7:26; 18:4	Revealing God's presence
10:7, 9	I am the gate	Prov. 8:34-35 ("door")	Revealing God's protection
10:11, 14	I am the good shepherd	No reference.	
11:25; 14:6	I am the resurrection and life	Prov. 3:18; 8:35	Revealing life of the age with God
14:6	I am the way	Prov. 3:17; 8:32 Sir. 6:26	Revealing the way to encounter with God and appropriate living
14:6	I am the truth	Prov. 8:7 Wisd. of Sol. 6:22	Revealing God's saving faithfulness
15:1, 5	I am the vine	Sir. 24:17, 19	Revealing relationship with God as the source of life

A further feature involves John's Jesus presenting himself as Wisdom. The Gospel employs some wisdom-derived descriptors as complements in clauses introduced by "I am." The descriptors name an aspect of Wisdom's identity and apply them to Jesus' identity and role in revealing God, enabling encounter with God, and/or providing instruction about the appropriate way of life.[12]

By employing descriptors of Wisdom, Jesus performs these roles and functions of Wisdom.

Using the Wisdom Paradigm to Present Jesus

Why does John's Gospel employ this wisdom paradigm in its distinctive presentation of Jesus? John's Gospel was written toward the end of the first century, after Roman troops had destroyed Jerusalem and the temple in the year 70 CE. This was a momentous event for first-century Judaism and raised profound theological questions about the presence and purposes of God, and how one might live in God's favor. It also raised important questions about what faithful living looked like in this new world.

In this context, there was considerable interest in revelations of God's presence and purposes. Surviving texts attest accounts of the visions and heavenly journeys of various revealer figures such as Enoch, Abraham, Levi, Baruch, Adam, Isaiah, and Moses. Commonly, such figures were understood to ascend into the heavens, glimpse some heavenly mysteries, and descend with a revelation.

As we have seen, John's Gospel reinterprets wisdom traditions from the Hebrew Bible and other Jewish texts in relation to Jesus to present him as one who reveals God's presence and purposes. But Jesus is not presented as one more revealer among many, as one more revealer in a supermarket of numerous options. Rather, the Gospel presents him as *the* revealer of God.

John's Gospel does this by using wisdom traditions to show Jesus' origins in the beginning "with God." As Wisdom, he does not begin on earth, ascend to heaven, and then descend to people on earth as these other revealer figures do. Rather, he begins "with God" in the heavens, descends among people to reveal what he has seen and heard "with God," and then returns to God. He does not briefly glimpse something in the heavens on a quick ascent but abides there from the beginning with God before descending to be among people. Using the wisdom

12. "I am" sayings also occur in the Gospel without a complement or descriptor. Evoking Exod. 3:14 and passages like Isa. 43:25; 45:18; 48:12, the construction is one of divine revelation.

paradigm to identify Jesus as Wisdom, John's Gospel reverses the ascent-descent pattern and prolongs Jesus' heavenly encounter with God. These features, especially the reversed descending-ascending pattern, allow the Gospel to present Jesus as *the* definitive revealer of God and of eternal life lived in relation to God (17:3). As Wisdom, Jesus is God (1:1) in the sense that he reveals God; he is God in God's knowability, visibility, and audibility.

Questions for Review and Reflection

1. What is the central question with which this chapter is concerned?
2. The opening pages mention five approaches that have been suggested to account for John's distinctiveness. What are the five approaches, and what are their weaknesses?
3. The chapter puts forward another option. What is it, and what is its central focus?
4. What are the main features of a "wisdom paradigm" in the biblical tradition? What are the key texts?
5. What are the relevant texts for that paradigm beyond the Hebrew Bible?
6. In summary, what are the seven paradoxes of a wisdom paradigm?
7. What evidence does the Prologue (1:1-18) provide for the Gospel's use of this wisdom paradigm?
8. How does the presentation of Jesus' public ministry draw on this wisdom paradigm?
9. Why does John's Gospel employ a wisdom paradigm in its presentation of Jesus?
10. The chapter has illustrated both the contribution of the Gospel writer to the presentation of Jesus and the fluidity of traditions about Jesus when the Gospels were written. How does this awareness affect your reading of the Gospel according to John?
11. We have now read and thought about the four Gospels. Does one of the four Gospels resonate more with you than the other three? If so, what in particular takes your attention?

11

Conclusion

In the opening two chapters, I discussed the genre of the Gospels and possible models of the way traditions about Jesus were transmitted in the time between Jesus' crucifixion and the writing of the first Gospel. Then I considered each of the four Gospels in turn, outlining the particular shaping of the gospel story in each Gospel and then in a following chapter discussing an aspect of how that particular Gospel makes meaning in relation to its context.

These previous chapters have demonstrated that each of the four New Testament Gospel writers reworked oral and written traditions about Jesus to formulate their respective versions of the story. They expressed their distinctive understandings to address the particular circumstances of their audiences. I suggested Mark's Gospel addressed folks living in difficult circumstances such as those experienced in urban imperial Rome. Matthew's Gospel addressed folks defining their identity and way of life in competition with synagogue communities in the troubled and challenging post-70 circumstances. Luke's Gospel offered assurance and security to followers of Jesus who had received some instruction but who experienced uncertainty and insecurity about God's workings, or "kingdom." John's Gospel employed wisdom traditions to present Jesus as the definitive revealer of God's presence and purposes to provide a way ahead in the post-70 world in the quest for divine knowledge.

In this concluding chapter, I briefly take up two matters, one concerning how these four Gospels came into the New Testament canon, and the second concerning the relationships between the Gospels and the historical Jesus.

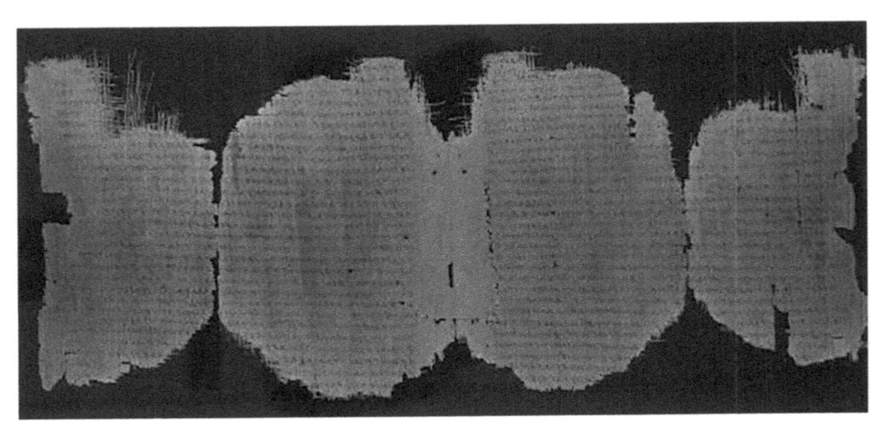

11.1 Folios 13-14, with part of the Gospel according to Luke, from Chester Beatty Papyrus I (3rd century CE), the oldest known manuscript of the Gospels, ca. 250; Chester Beatty Library, Dublin; Commons.wiimedia.org.

Gospels and the Canon

Two dynamics are at work in the Gospel-writing process. On one hand, these four Gospel writers do not regard traditions about Jesus as fixed. They treat them as flexible and malleable. As they demonstrate in their Gospels, they expand, abbreviate, omit, and combine traditions to form new accounts of the story for new situations.

Yet on the other hand, the act of writing is an act of fixing the ever-moving traditions. It is an attempt to stabilize the traditions and to limit their expansion. It inscribes them at a particular moment in a particular form for specific circumstances.

The consequence of these two dynamics—fluid traditions and

attempts to fix them in writing—was, interestingly, a proliferation of written Gospels! Writing did not succeed in fixing or stabilizing the traditions about Jesus, at least not in a way acceptable to all. In fact, accounts of Jesus' actions and teachings continued to be written. As we noted at the outset of this book, by one scholar's count, we know of thirty-four written Gospels in existence by the end of the second century CE.[1] Copies of some of these exist today as complete writings, some exist only in fragments or in citations, and some are known only by name. But what is especially important for us to observe is that only four of them ended up in the New Testament canon when it was "finalized" late in the fourth century.

Two key questions emerge: Out of all the Gospels in existence, why should there be four Gospels in the canon? Why *these* four Gospels?[2] We don't know everything about the formation of the canon, but we can observe several important dynamics.

One thing is clear. By the end of the second century, four Gospels—those known as Matthew, Mark, Luke, and John—seem to have been fairly widely regarded as authoritative among Christian groups. The writing of Irenaeus, the bishop of Lyons in southern France, dating from near the end of the second century, attests their acceptance even as he makes several arguments for privileging these four Gospels. First, he notes that even the "heretics" whom he opposes as enemies of conventional or right-thinking Christians utilize these four Gospels for their errant teaching: "So firm is the ground upon which these Gospels rest, that the very heretics themselves bear witness to them" (*Against Heresies* 3.11.7).[3] That is, Irenaeus argues that these four Gospels are widely recognized by proponents and opponents of Irenaeus's orthodoxy alike as authoritative.

Then Irenaeus adds a strange, second argument. He argues that

1. Charles Hedrick, "The Thirty-Four Gospels: Diversity and Division among the Earliest Christians," *Bible Review* 18 (2002): 20–31, 46–47; summary 28–29.
2. For an outline of the process of "closing" the canon, Warren Carter, *Seven Events That Shaped the New Testament World* (Grand Rapids: Baker Academic, 2013), 133–54.
3. Citations and references of Irenaeus are to Alexander Roberts and James Donaldson, eds., *The Ante Nicene Fathers: Translation of the Writings of the Fathers Down to 325 a.d.* (1885–1887; repr., Peabody, MA: Hendrickson, 1996).

having these four Gospels as authoritative is "natural." He bases this argument in the observation that there are four points on the compass and that the wind blows from the north, south, east, and west! From this observation he—strangely—claims it is fitting that a worldwide church has four Gospels as pillars.

> It is not possible that the Gospels can be either more or fewer in number than they are. For, since there are four zones of the world in which we live, and four principal winds, while the Church is scattered throughout all the world, and the "pillar and ground" of the Church is the Gospel and the spirit of life; it is fitting that she should have four pillars. (*Against Heresies* 3.11.8)

As though this "natural" argument is not strange enough, Irenaeus then offers a third "natural" or "obvious" reason for regarding these four Gospels as authoritative. He appeals to the four living creatures in Rev. 4:6-7—creatures like a lion, an ox, a human, an eagle (representatives of wild and domesticated animals, humans and birds)—not only to justify the number four but also to find correspondences between these figures and aspects of Jesus' significance outlined in each of these four Gospels.

> For the cherubim, too, were four-faced, and their faces were images of the dispensation of the Son of God. For, [as the Scripture] says, "The first living creature was like a lion," symbolizing His effectual working, His leadership, and royal power; the second [living creature] was like a calf, signifying [His] sacrificial and sacerdotal order; but "the third had, as it were, the face as of a man"—an evident description of His advent as a human being; "the fourth was like a flying eagle," pointing out the gift of the Spirit hovering with His wings over the Church. And therefore the Gospels are in accord with these things.

Irenaeus claims that four authoritative Gospels are "natural" because of the four points of the compass. Further, it is not just a matter of numbers. As Irenaeus's example using the four living creatures shows, it is also a matter of acceptable content. The proliferating written Gospels and oral collections of material presented their own interpretations of Jesus, and Irenaeus, it seems, is worried about the acceptability of some of these interpretations. His favored four

Gospels—Matthew, Mark, Luke, and John—present images of Jesus that he considers consistent with the four living creatures. He thereby offers a means of evaluating the images of Jesus advocated by different Gospels. Irenaeus attempts to solve the problem of the ever-increasing number and variety of presentations of Jesus in oral traditions and written Gospels by recognizing and advocating for four authoritative Gospels.

But of course the matter is not as obvious or as natural as Irenaeus wants to suggest. Having four authoritative Gospels because there are four compass points is no more obvious or natural, for example, than arguing that since an octopus has eight limbs or a centipede has one hundred legs, so too the church should have eight or one hundred Gospels![4]

The "closing" of the canon in 397 CE at the Council of Carthage, some two hundred years after Irenaeus's writing, confirmed Irenaeus's solution to the problem of too many and too diverse presentations of Jesus. It canonized these four favored Gospels. But it is clear that even in Irenaeus's time not everyone agreed with his "solution" that these four Gospels were "naturally" to be recognized as authoritative. Other "solutions" were proposed. They challenged every aspect of Irenaeus's advocacy: the authority of these four writers, the privileging of these four Gospels, the very notion of four Gospels, and the existence of diverse accounts.[5]

We will survey several of these challenges so as to highlight that Irenaeus's solution favoring these four Gospels was anything but "natural."

Challenges to Irenaeus's Four Authoritative Figures

While Irenaeus claims the Gospels associated with Matthew, Mark,

4. Despite their name deriving from two Latin words meaning "one hundred feet," I know that centipedes do not actually have one hundred legs. Nevertheless, this popular perception facilitates my point.

5. The following discussion is shaped by the helpful discussion of Francis Watson, "The Fourfold Gospel," in *The Cambridge Companion to the Gospels*, ed. Stephen C. Barton (Cambridge: Cambridge University Press, 2006), 34–52.

Luke, and John are widely recognized as authoritative, the authority of these four figures was not universally recognized. Producers of other Gospels challenged the preeminence of these four figures and claimed other figures as authorities for their Gospels. The Gospel of Thomas, for example, begins: "These are the secret sayings which the living Jesus spoke and which Didymos Judas Thomas wrote down."[6] The opening of the Gospel highlights Thomas's authority and attributes to Thomas privileged and exclusive knowledge that he received from Jesus. He records "secret sayings" that Jesus exclusively conveyed to Thomas. Subsequently in the Gospel, Jesus has an exchange with his disciples that seems to diminish the reliability and standing of Matthew and Peter (the traditional source of Mark's Gospel) while elevating that of Thomas.

> Jesus said to his disciples, "Compare me to someone and tell me whom I am like." Simon Peter said to him, "You are like a righteous angel." Matthew said to him, "You are like a wise philosopher." Thomas said to him, "Master, my mouth is wholly incapable of saying whom you are like." . . . [Jesus seems to like Thomas's answer the best]. . . . And he [Jesus] took him [Thomas] and withdrew and told him three things. When Thomas returned to his companions, they asked him, "What did Jesus say to you?" Thomas said to them, "If I tell you one of these things which he told me, you will pick up stones and throw them at me. (saying 13)

This scene resembles the "who do you say I am?" scene in the Synoptics (Mark 8:27-29; Matt. 16:13-15). But here, Matthew and Peter are demoted in significance with inadequate responses to Jesus, while Thomas is elevated. He is Jesus' favorite, receives special teaching from Jesus, and withholds it from Matthew and Peter who, it is suggested, will not be able to accept it. Thomas expresses it in his Gospel. The Gospel of Thomas thus presents Jesus giving special sanction to its own content. This framing positions Thomas and his Gospel as a rival to Irenaeus's four.

A similar thing takes place in the Gospel of Mary.[7] Here it is Mary

6. "The Coptic Gospel of Thomas," in *Lost Scriptures: Books That Did Not Make It into the New Testament*, ed. Bart Ehrman (New York: Oxford University Press, 2003), 20.
7. "Gospel of Mary," in Ehrman, *Lost Scriptures*, 35–37.

who is elevated as the source of special knowledge about Jesus. In the Gospel, Jesus instructs the disciples and then departs. The disciples are grieved, fearing a hostile reception from gentiles to their imminent preaching mission. Mary steps forward to refocus and reassure them. Peter then says to Mary, "Sister, we know that the Savior loved you more than the rest of women. Tell us the words of the Savior which you remember—which you know (but) we do not, nor have we heard them." Mary agrees to pass on to them the teachings she received from the Lord in a vision, but which have been hidden from the male disciples. But just what *most* of these teachings might be remains unknown because the next three pages are missing from the manuscript! After the gap, as she finishes up her teaching, several of the male disciples respond negatively to her and discredit her teaching. Andrew doubts that her teaching comes from Jesus. "I at least do not believe that the Savior said this. For certainly these teachings are strange ideas." Peter similarly doubts that the Savior "really spoke with a woman without our knowledge (and) not openly? . . . Did he prefer her to us?" Mary protests that Peter thinks she made up the teaching and lied "about the Savior." Levi comes to her defense against Peter, declaring, "If the Savior made her worthy, who are you indeed to reject her? . . . This is why he loved her more than us." Levi then exhorts the apostles to get on with the task of preaching as they have been commanded to do.

The Gospel of Mary shows both the commending and discrediting of Mary's teaching. Mary is presented as having a leading role among the apostles. She has a special relationship with Jesus marked by love. Jesus has entrusted her with special teaching that Peter and the other disciples did not receive. Her Gospel passes along this teaching. Levi testifies to her special standing with Jesus and the value of her teaching. Yet her teaching is also discredited and opposed. Much of her teaching remains unknown because pages from the Gospel are missing. The missing pages and the preserved incomplete form of her Gospel silence her. Andrew doubts that her teaching came from Jesus, and he calls it "strange." The authoritative figure Peter also challenges the notion that Mary had a special relationship with Jesus and that Mary really received this teaching from Jesus. The preservation of an incomplete Gospel both commends and discredits Mary.

The fact that Gospels such as these associated with Thomas and Mary survived suggests some support for these alternative authorities. The discrediting of apostles such as Matthew and Peter and advocacy of other figures such as Thomas and Mary suggest competition with the authoritative figures promoted by Irenaeus in relation to his four dominant Gospels. History shows, however, that these challenges could not displace Irenaeus's favored four.

Replacing Three, Elevating One

Another challenge to the four authoritative Gospels commended by Irenaeus derives from the second-century figure Marcion. Marcion rejected four Gospels and elevated one Gospel, that of an edited version of Luke. Marcion was concerned with the content of the four Gospels, particularly their presentations of God and the use of Jewish traditions. For Marcion, the God of the Christian message had to be differentiated from the God who created the world, the God presented in the Jewish Scriptures. He saw this corruption as being present in the four Gospels commended by Irenaeus, with three of them infected beyond redemption. Marcion saw Luke's Gospel, though, as rescuable, and he set about doing so by making various omissions. Irenaeus disparagingly describes Marcion's work as "the most daring blasphemy against Him who is proclaimed as God by the law and the prophets" and labels his editing of Luke's Gospel as a "mutilation."

Marcion thus replaces Irenaeus's four authoritative Gospels with a version of Luke's Gospel edited according to Marcion's theological agenda.

11.1 Marcion's Gospel According to Irenaeus
He mutilates the Gospel which is according to Luke, removing all that is written respecting the generation [birth] of the Lord, and setting aside a great deal of the teaching of the Lord, in which the Lord is recorded as most dearly confessing that the Maker of this universe is His Father. He likewise persuaded his disciples that he himself was more worthy of credit than are those apostles who have handed down the Gospel to us, furnishing them not with the Gospel, but merely a fragment of it. In like manner, too, he dismembered the Epistles of Paul, removing all that is said by the apostle respecting that God who made the world, to the effect that He is the Father of our Lord Jesus Christ, and also those passages from the prophetical writings which the apostle quotes, in order to teach us that they announced beforehand the coming of the Lord. (*Against Heresies* 1.27.2)

Rejecting Four by Harmonizing Them into One

Another challenge to Irenaeus's four authoritative Gospels came from Tatian and his *Diatessaron*. Tatian regarded the very existence of multiple and different accounts of Jesus' activity as problematic. So he sought to remove the differences by harmonizing Irenaeus's four authoritative Gospels into one Gospel. In places, he seems to succeed in combining sections from different Gospels with invisible seams. The *Diatessaron*'s opening reads very smoothly in combining Mark 1:1 ("The beginning of the Gospel of Jesus Christ, Son of God") with the opening five verses of John's Gospel ("In the beginning was the Word . . ."). At this point, Tatian inserts the first chapter of Luke's birth story, which ends with John's birth and growth, followed by the account of Jesus' birth from Matt. 1:18-19. The successive placement, though, of much of Luke 2 and then Matthew 2 is not seamless, and there are obvious problems. Luke 2 has Joseph, Mary, and Jesus return to Nazareth, while the following Matthean account has the wise men visit them still in Bethlehem!

Tatian's attempt to resolve the problem of difference among the Gospels by harmonizing four accounts into one was very popular in some areas such as Syria. But it did not solve the problem itself. Tatian's account reinscribed differences from his four source Gospels. And of course, ultimately, the formation of the canon rejected his option in favor of the four different authoritative accounts recognized by Irenaeus.

11.2 Crypt of the Church of St. Irenaeus, Lyon, France. The bishop's tomb was desecrated by Protestants in 1562, but the crypt has been restored. Photo: Xavier Caré; Commons.wikimedia.org.

Supplementing the Gospels

While some contested the authority of the four figures associated with the Gospels recognized by Irenaeus, Marcion thought there was too much material and Tatian thought there was too much diversity, and advocates of another option thought there was not enough information. So as often happens in religious traditions, texts emerged that filled in perceived gaps in the four Gospels that Irenaeus regarded as authoritative.

For example, the Proto-Gospel of James expands the accounts of Jesus' birth that appear in Matthew 1–2 and Luke 1–2.[8] The account especially focuses on the figure of Mary, supplying her with an elaborate backstory. It identifies her parents as Joachim and Anna. It describes her own conception as miraculous. Her upbringing centered on the temple, including being a seamstress for its curtain. She has a

8. "The Proto-Gospel of James," in Ehrman, *Lost Scriptures*, 63–72.

strangely arranged "marriage" as a twelve-year-old to the aged Joseph, who already has sons but whose age means he poses no threat to her virginity. Her conception of Jesus is miraculous as well as socially scandalous. She gives birth as a virgin in a cave near Bethlehem. After the birth of Jesus, a midwife inspects Mary to confirm that she is still a virgin. Toward the end, scenes involve the magi, Herod searching for John the Baptizer, and the murder of his father Zechariah.

Another example of supplementing the four Gospels elaborates Jesus' childhood. Among the four favored Gospels, only Luke's Gospel says anything about the child Jesus in narrating one incident in the temple (Luke 2:41-51). Taking its cue from this account, the Infancy Gospel of Thomas fills in the gap, providing numerous stories of the child Jesus performing miraculous actions.[9] He exhibits miraculous power over nature and the Sabbath, including providing abundant harvest from a single grain of wheat for poor folks. He exposes the ignorance of his teachers and shames them. He interacts with other children in his village, sometimes harming them, sometimes healing them. In his father's workshop, he corrects his woodworking mistakes. The Gospel ends with the story of Jesus in the temple teaching "the elders and teachers of the people."

Other Gospels expanded on other aspects of or "gaps" in the four favored Gospels. The Gospel of Thomas, mentioned above, offers more teachings attributed to Jesus, some of which are similar to teachings in the Synoptics, some of which are quite different. Another omission in the four Gospels is any description of the resurrection itself. The Gospel of Peter turns Matthew's guards at the tomb into witnesses of the resurrection effected by two gigantic angels, whose heads reach into the heavens and who lead an even bigger figure, Jesus, out of the tomb. This cosmic-sized Jesus is followed by his cross. The cross talks, confirming that Jesus had been preaching to the dead.

The closing of the canon by including the four Gospels of Matthew, Mark, Luke, and John confirmed Irenaeus's solution two centuries later. It thereby rejected these various attempts to replace, harmonize,

9. "The Infancy Gospel of Thomas," in Ehrman, *Lost Scriptures*, 57–62.

unify, or supplement them. The canonical decision to include four Gospels expressed an intersection of a variety of factors.

- Catholicity or widespread use: the inclusion of these four Gospels recognized their wide use and their long-standing authority among many ecclesial communities.
- Variety: the inclusion of these four Gospels in the canon recognized some variety of perspective in the presentation of Jesus. It did not share Tatian's fear of difference nor Marcion's desire for unity.
- Limits: But accompanying the recognition of variety in understandings was a recognition of limits to acceptable variety. Irenaeus's promotion of four of the more than thirty Gospels in existence was sustained over the next two centuries. Most of these written Gospels did not receive the same recognition or acceptance. Irenaeus's arguments about these Gospels' widespread use and acceptable content proved more persuasive than appeals to the naturalness of the number four.
- Valuing of diverse theological insights: Yet the problem of difference that Tatian and Marcion sought to address by reducing four Gospels to some form of unity did not go away. Instead of seeing difference as a problem, Irenaeus and his successors saw it as a strength in understanding that it was a means of expressing a depth of rich theological insights. This solution elevated diverse theological insights over uniformity of historical accuracy and detail. It enabled these four Gospels to continue to address diverse pastoral ecclesial situations across the ages.

The Quest for the Historical Jesus

But not everyone has been satisfied with the elevation of theological insights over historical accuracy. Especially since the Enlightenment of the seventeenth and eighteenth centuries, a number of scholars have pursued a quest for the historical Jesus. This quest has sought the figure behind these Gospels that have privileged Jesus' theological and pastoral significance. This quest has resulted not only in numerous constructions of Jesus but also in quite distinctively different portraits.[10]

The quest for the historical Jesus has often been controversial. Some have not understood the nature of the quest. At its heart, this quest is historical, not theological. It seeks to answer these questions: What can be known historically about Jesus of Nazareth, crucified around 30 CE? What can be known about what he did and said?

But therein lies its central challenge. The major sources for information about Jesus are the Gospels. While there are a couple of references to Jesus in sources outside the Jesus-movement, the Gospels remain the primary sources. And as we have seen in the preceding chapters, the Gospels were written some fifty or so years after Jesus' death and they are not neutral about him. They are theologically shaped narratives presenting different understandings of Jesus and addressing a pastoral-theological word to particular communities. Can such texts be used as historical sources for the life of Jesus, and if so, how?

A related issue concerns what was happening in Christian communities between 30 CE and the time of the writing of the Gospels in the period from the 70s to the 90s. As we have observed in chapter 2 above, traditions about Jesus circulated orally during this period among communities of followers of Jesus. What was the nature of the transmission process of traditions about Jesus? Was it one of creative (re)interpretation or one of careful preservation and memorization, one of maintaining continuity in the portrait of Jesus or creating significant discontinuity between the pre-30 Jesus and the Jesus of the Gospels? What was the impact of the communities' experiences of worship, the study of Scripture, mission, instruction of believers, and conflict with other groups on traditions about Jesus? What was the role of storytellers and performers of these traditions? How much

10. For discussion, Catherine Murphy, *The Historical Jesus for Dummies* (Hoboken NJ: Wiley, 2008); James Charlesworth, *The Historical Jesus: An Essential Guide* (Nashville: Abingdon, 2008).

continuity or discontinuity existed between the time and presentation of Jesus pre-30 and the Jesus proclaimed in the gospels who has come to be referred to as "the Christ of faith?" These questions are hard to answer, and there has certainly been disagreement among those who have tried to address them.

Another area of debate has centered on how the quest should be conducted. What are the rules of evidence or criteria for pursuing the quest? Various criteria have been suggested, and there has been much debate. What is at stake in the debate about criteria is evident in a controversial criterion called *dissimilarity*. At one stage of the quest, this criterion was dominant and it had a significant impact. It sought to identify what was unique to Jesus' teachings by foregrounding dissimilarities with his context. It sought to isolate material in the Gospels that had no parallel in, or was not influenced by, other Jewish traditions or by church teachings or practices. This criterion isolated Jesus from other possible influences. It constructed Jesus as a figure who was not influenced by his culture and had no subsequent influence on any of his followers. Not surprisingly, it identified very little material in the Gospels as authentic to the historical Jesus.

As a consequence, other criteria have come to the fore, and they have produced a much greater body of material. One criterion and starting point has been to identify *redactional alterations* in the Gospels. Attention to the placement of, additions to, omissions from, and distinctive words in source materials such as Q has provided access to earlier versions of the tradition and closer access to the historical Jesus. For example, Matthew's scene of Jesus' baptism by John has Jesus instruct John to baptize him in order to "fulfill all righteousness" (Matt. 3:15). Did Jesus give John this instruction? Attention to the three words shows them to be important theological terms commonly used in Matthew's Gospel but not in the other Gospels. This suggests Matthean redaction in the form of an addition to the tradition. Moreover, the instruction is missing from the accounts in Mark 1:9 and Luke 3:21. These observations suggest that these words are most probably Matthew's redaction, added to explain, perhaps, why Jesus was baptized.

What about the act of Jesus' baptism itself? Interestingly, the criterion of dissimilarity indicates its historical probability. No New Testament writing appeals to Jesus' baptism as a justification for the church's practice of baptism. No New Testament writing argues that believers should be baptized because Jesus was baptized. That is, according to the criterion of dissimilarity, the absence of a link between Jesus' baptism and the church practice of baptism suggests that references to Jesus' baptism are authentic. Another use of the criterion of dissimilarity points to the same conclusion. John baptized "for the forgiveness of sin." Jesus' submission to baptism implied his need for forgiveness, quite *dissimilar* to subsequent church teaching that Jesus was sinless.

Another criterion used in the quest is that of *multiple attestation.* This criterion posits that a saying or an action attested in two or more independent sources or traditions probably derives from Jesus. So in the case of Jesus' baptism, this event is attested in Mark's Gospel (Mark 1:9) and in John's Gospel (John 1:31-33, probably). Two distinct independent traditions provide multiple attestation.

A fourth criterion takes seriously Jesus' context of *first-century Judaism and his Galilean-Judean environment.* This criterion seeks to set Jesus in what we know of this historical context. Efforts to understand Jesus' intentions or goals in this context and why he was crucified have been especially important. This approach has, accordingly, been attentive to cultural movements and theological emphases such as eschatological orientations, or wisdom traditions, or the political, social, and economic realities of life under Roman imperial rule. In this context, for example, Jesus' baptism by John is shown to be historically probable given a context of the use of water and rituals of cleansing among other first-century Judeans and Galileans.

But while this emphasis on a first-century Jewish context has been a very important factor in the quest for the historical Jesus, it has also posed a challenge. Scholars have increasingly learned that first-century Judaism was not monolithic and comprised multiple cultural traditions and practices. Jesus can be understood to belong to any number of various cultural strands. The result is multiple and diverse pictures of Jesus.

A fifth criterion prominent in recent discussions is the criterion of *embarrassment.* This criterion takes note of instances in the Gospels that are not flattering to leading characters, concluding that it would be unlikely for such scenes to be created and added. So, for example, Jesus seems to promise the full establishment of God's reign in the lifetime of those who are listening, something that clearly did not happen (Mark 9:1). And there are unflattering presentations of Jesus' disciples, including the scenes involving Peter's denial of Jesus (Mark 14:66-72). Given the importance of Peter subsequently as a church leader, it is unlikely that such unflattering scenes would be created.

A sixth criterion, that of *distinctive form*, has focused attention on ways of talking associated with Jesus. This criterion takes seriously a context in which oral performance is dominant (see chapter 2). It highlights Jesus' role as a teacher of wisdom who employs forms of speaking such as parables and proverb-like sayings called aphorisms. These comprise short, provocative, often shocking sayings ("let the dead bury the dead") that are often critical of the status quo and its conventional wisdom and everyday expectations ("blessed are the poor"). These sayings also include exaggeration, paradox, and humor. Their effect is to provoke a new way of seeing everyday life and God's workings in it.

And seventh, the criterion of *coherence* has been used to expand the database of sayings and/or actions established by other criteria. That is, a saying or action that coheres or agrees with, or is consistent with, actions or sayings established by other criteria is deemed probably to be authentic to the historical Jesus.

While these criteria have been among those commonly used in the quest for the historical Jesus, they have not resulted in anything like a uniform picture of Jesus. While some see significant continuity between the Gospels and the historical Jesus, others see significant discontinuity.[11] This diversity of reconstructions results from various problematic factors.[12]

One factor involves decisions scholars make as to which criteria to employ and which to disregard. Another involves which criteria to prioritize. For example, if one begins with the criterion of dissimilarity, one is sure to identify very little historical material. Moreover, the criteria have been unable to identify the precise words Jesus might have uttered and at most can only identify that Jesus might have said something like this. Nor can they identify the context or contexts in which Jesus might have said something. Growing appreciation of the dynamics of oral performances has highlighted the difficulty of any quest for an original utterance and originating context. Since context is crucial for establishing meaning, the absence of such originating settings does not allow us to interpret sayings precisely in relation to Jesus' activity. A further matter concerns focus. Much work on the historical Jesus has been attentive to his words. A more recent development has given increasing attention to his actions and their significance.[13] There is also a question of sources. Some scholars have used not only the four canonical Gospels but also some of the other Gospels. Some have argued, for example, that Gospels like the Gospel of Thomas contain sayings authentic to Jesus. Others have employed social-science models to provide interpretive contexts in which to make sense of Jesus' words and actions. For example, one approach has used peasant studies to reconstruct possible dynamics of the first-century world. Others have appealed to the lifestyle and roles of sages or wisdom teachers, or to popular prophets of various kinds, or to dimensions of Roman imperial Judea.[14]

Given these challenges, the quest for the historical Jesus is difficult.

11. For example, the Jesus Seminar concluded that Jesus might have spoken only about 18 percent of what is attributed to him in the Gospels. Robert Funk, Roy Hoover, and the Jesus Seminar, *The Five Gospels: The Search for the Authentic Words of Jesus; What Did Jesus Really Say?* (New York: Macmillan, 1993).

12. The following paragraphs draw in part from Stephen Fowl, "The Gospels and 'the Historical Jesus,'" in Barton, *Cambridge Companion to the Gospels*, 76–96 (with bibliography).

13. E. P. Sanders, *Jesus and Judaism* (Philadelphia: Fortress, 1986).

14. For example, Richard A Horsley, *Jesus and the Politics of Roman Palestine* (Columbia: University of South Carolina Press, 2014).

No doubt scholars will continue to pursue it, but they will need to develop more refined methods. And no doubt they will construct more diverse portraits of Jesus.

What's at Stake?

The remaining question concerns the significance of this quest for the historical Jesus. Does this historical inquiry have implications for believers? What is the relation between history and faith? Does it matter, for example, that Mark, Matthew, Luke, and John disagree in places on what Jesus did and said, sometimes in minor ways, sometimes in major ways? Answers to this question line out along a spectrum.

At one end of the spectrum are those who think that much is at stake in the quest. Often this assessment takes the form that if the Gospels are not accurate and reliable in historical matters, then their theological truth might be undermined. This approach often sets genuine historical inquiry aside, assuming that whatever the Gospels say is both historically and theologically reliable and that there is no disparity between the two. This approach, which cannot separate historical inquiry from theological insight, leads, however, to some real difficulties in trying to reconcile the disparate accounts in the four Gospels.

At the other end of the spectrum are those who argue that the quest is either not possible or is not important for Christian faith. The argument that it is not possible rests on evaluations of the Gospels as theological texts, not historical sources, and the ineffectiveness of the criteria discussed above for reconstructing the historical Jesus. The argument that the quest is not important maintains that Christians have not elevated historical knowing to be the most important form of knowing. The Gospels do not require that their hearers undertake historical research. Rather, they invite hearers to faith, to commit themselves to the one whom the Gospels announce to be present among them.

In between these points are those who think the quest can achieve some historical information using the criteria and/or frameworks outlined above. The relationship of such knowledge to theological claims, however, is assessed in various ways. Some have no interest in this relationship at all and are concerned only with establishing historical data. Others see historical work in various relationships to theological claims. Historical research could, perhaps, threaten theological claims because the proclamation includes historical data. If, for example, historical research could establish that Jesus did not die on a Roman cross or that he did not associate with marginal figures and outsiders, it would threaten fundamental aspects of the theological proclamation. But would it have a similar destabilizing effect if a much more minor detail or saying was shown not to be historically authentic? Or perhaps the historical quest is theologically necessary because the proclamation affirms the world of human beings as a sphere in which God is encountered? Or perhaps it alerts us to not creating Jesus in our own image by reminding us of our temporal and cultural distance from him and his world? And of course, the quest for the historical Jesus illustrates how faith and the Gospel proclamation have come into being. Most religious traditions seek information about their founding figures, and it is no different with Jesus. The Gospels show us, then, how some of his first followers understood his significance.

Conclusion

In this chapter, we have considered two questions that emerged from our discussions in the previous chapters of the four canonical Gospels. First, we considered the establishment of these four Gospels as authoritative interpretations of the significance of Jesus among Christian groups and in the context of numerous other Gospels and approaches. Second, we took up the complex question of the possible relationships among the four Gospels and the quest for the historical Jesus.

Both of these questions concern ways in which Gospel readers have made meaning of Jesus in particular situations. Such a task is not confined to the past. It is the ongoing task of every generation of

Gospel readers to continue to make meaning as they engage the Gospel accounts in new and changing circumstances.

11.3 The Gospel writers are depicted paired with their symbols (a man, an eagle, an ox, a lion, the figures from Rev. 4:6-7) in this illustration from the Aachen Gospels (ca. 820); Aachen, Germany, Cathedral Treasury; Commons.wikimedia.org.

Questions for Review and Reflection

1. When the canon was "closed" in 397 at the Council of Carthage, it recognized these four Gospels as authoritative. Summarize the importance of Irenaeus's comments about the status of the four Gospels of Matthew, Mark, Luke, and John at the end of the second century. What problem was he trying to address?

2. Everyone, of course, was not happy with Irenaeus's proposal. What challenge did each of these situations present?
    a. Gospels written in the names of other authoritative figures?
    b. Marcion's revisions?
    c. Tatian's *Diatessaron?*
    d. Supplementing the four Gospels?
3. What values did the confirmation of the four Gospels in the canon recognize?
4. What is the quest for the historical Jesus?
5. What are its main challenges?
6. How has the quest been conducted? The chapter identifies eight criteria.
7. Why has a uniform picture of Jesus not resulted?
8. What is at stake for Christian believers, if anything, in the quest for the historical Jesus?

Glossary

Apocalyptic: This adjective literally means to "take something out of hiding," hence a "revelation" or a disclosure. The revelation may comprise, for example, something related to the end of the world (called "apocalyptic eschatology"), to God's purposes, to the layout and mysteries of the heavens. Revelations can be made by significant figures in dreams, ascents into the heavens, or journeys through the heavens.

Apothegm: This term refers to short, pointed sayings attributed to Jesus that express a significant truth. A *chreia* is another name for this literary form, though some distinguish the two by insisting that the latter arises from a specific situation.

Criticism: Biblical criticism does not mean an attack on or criticism of the Bible. Rather, it refers to the task of making meaning of the biblical text by using different methods. Methods such as "form criticism" or "redaction criticism" (see below) provide a particular focus or set of questions that provide insight into various dimensions of the text.

Eschatology: The term refers to the completion of God's purposes. Often the explanation is given that it indicates "end things" in the sense that God's purposes end the reign of sin and death in human life (judgment, heaven, resurrection, etc.) and (re)create a new world. While this is true, a better sense of the term moves beyond this "end" to its "goal" or "purpose," namely, the establishment of God's good and life-giving purposes. These are the "final things."

Feminist criticism: This form of criticism (see above) particularly attends to roles of women in the biblical texts, and to retrieving the roles and histories of women in the early Christian movement assumed by but written out of the biblical stories. More recent studies have broadened their focus to gender studies, which include constructions of masculinity in biblical texts.

Form criticism: This form of criticism (see above) examines how traditions about Jesus were transmitted in the time between Jesus' crucifixion and the writing of the first Gospel, namely, through activities in particular community life settings such as preaching or worship that shaped individual units of tradition.

Gospel: This term can designate both an announcement of various kinds of good news—proclamations of imperial power and of God's rule—as well as a literary genre or writing that tells tales about Jesus.

Imperial-critical approach: This approach foregrounds the interactions between the Gospels and the Roman Empire. It understands the New Testament texts to emerge in contexts of domination and subjugation as texts that negotiate the imperial world with a wide range of strategies involving accommodation, imitation, reinscription, opposition, and mockery to name but some.

Intertextuality: At its center, this controversial term refers to the interaction(s) among various texts. But there is considerable debate about these interactions. For example, do authors or readers create intertextualities? Do authors control the interactions by signifying (and limiting) the texts that interact by quoting a text or evoking it with shared language? And in these interactions, does the original context of the text play any major part, or is it subsumed to its new context? Or do readers/hearers create intertextuality in deciding whether to put only the quoted verse in play? Or can the audience/hearer bring the larger passage into play in making meaning? Or more creatively, can a reader/hearer bring any texts into play including nontextual "texts" or media like images or festivals?

Intratextuality: This term refers to making meaning by connecting various elements that occur within the same text.

L: This abbreviation designates material found only in Luke's Gospel such as the parables of the good Samaritan (10:29-37) and the prodigal son (15:11-32). There is no agreement as to whether this was a coherent collection or various independent traditions, or how much of it the Gospel author created.

M: This abbreviation designates material found only in Matthew's Gospel. There is no agreement as to whether this was a coherent collection or various independent traditions, or how much of it the Gospel author created.

Narrative criticism: This approach focuses on the final form of the Gospels rather than the traditions that constitute the Gospels. Narrative criticism uses literary categories such as plot, character, setting, and point of view to make meaning of the Gospel tales.

Oral performance: Stories about Jesus were passed on initially in oral not written form. Storytellers performed stories for audiences. Hearing a Gospel creates a different dynamic for making meaning than does reading it.

Parable: This is one of the distinctive literary forms employed by Jesus in the Gospels. As a literary form, it is primarily a form of comparison. The word means "to throw or set alongside." Commonly, Gospel parables set the kingdom of God alongside a short narrative that draws on everyday scenarios and structures from the imperial world such as master and slaves, farming, weddings, and households. The juxtapositions can be surprising, even shocking, which engages the hearers' attention in making meaning of the comparison. Sometimes there are numerous points of connection between the story and the world beyond it producing an allegory of God's actions.

Parousia: This Greek word mean "presence" or "coming." It refers in the New Testament to the "second coming" of Jesus, his return at the end of the age, to establish God's reign in its fullness.

Passion narrative: This term refers to the account of Jesus' betrayal, arrest, condemnation, suffering, death, and burial. Some scholars include the resurrection accounts. The passion narratives are not only an account of Jesus' death, but offer interpretations of the meaning of this event. The narratives raise important questions about Roman power, anti-Jewish perspectives, and the significance of Jesus' death.

Pericope: This word has nothing to do with periscopes on submarines, though the moment you type it, various text-processing programs will turn it into the latter. Rather, the word means "cut around." It refers to segments of texts in the Gospels.

Q: This abbreviation for the German *Quelle* refers to a hypothetical "sayings source" that comprises the "double tradition" of material comprising mostly sayings of Jesus common to Matthew and Luke but not in Mark. Two main arguments support the hypothesis. There are significant degrees of verbal agreements in the material common to Matthew and Luke but not in Mark, prompting the hypothesis of a common source. And second, the order of this material is often the same in both Gospels, again suggesting a common (written? oral?) source. Scholars debate whether the collection was written or oral, whether it existed in one form or several editions, the extent of this collection, and its date and place of origin.

Redaction criticism: This approach to studying the Gospels focuses on the editorial or redactional techniques (additions, combinations, omissions, key terms, etc.) employed by the Gospel writers in shaping the sources from which the Gospel is written. Readers interpret these redactional alterations as signifying the particular theological and pastoral concerns of the writer, as well as reflecting the circumstances or "setting in life" (*Sitz im Leben*) of the community of followers of Jesus to whom the Gospel was addressed.

Synoptics: This term refers to the Synoptic Gospels, Matthew, Mark, and Luke. The word comes from two Greek words meaning "seeing together." The central concept is that these three Gospels "look alike," quite different from the Gospel of John.

Synoptic problem: This problem involves attempts to explain both the significant degree of similarity in the words and order of material in these Gospels, and the significant differences among them. The most commonly accepted explanation posits that Mark was the earliest Gospel, which both Matthew and Luke used, and to which they added material from a source they both shared called Q, and from their own sources of special material, M for Matthew and L for Luke. In addition, both Matthew and Luke did not merely copy this material but edited or redacted it to express their own insights for the particular situations of their readers.

Vaticinium ex eventu: This Latin phrase means "a prophecy from an outcome or event." It refers to a literary technique whereby passages in the Gospels appear to predict an event, when in fact that event had already occurred at the time of writing. So predictions about the fall of Jerusalem placed on Jesus' lips in the Gospels are examples of this technique (Mark 13:2-4; Luke 19:41-44).

Index

Lightning Source UK Ltd.
Milton Keynes UK
UKHW02f0818280618
324913UK00018BA/533/P